The Battle
of the
Reichswald

The Battle of the Reichswald

Rhineland
February 1945

Tim Saunders

Pen & Sword
MILITARY

First published in Great Britain in 2023 and republished in this format in 2026
by
PEN & SWORD MILITARY
an imprint of Pen & Sword Books Ltd
Yorkshire – Philadelphia

Copyright © Tim Saunders, 2023, 2026

ISBN 978-1-39901-687-2

The right of Tim Saunders to be identified as the author of this work has been asserted by him in accordance with the Copyright, Designs and Patents Act 1988.

A CIP catalogue record for this book is available from the British Library.

All rights reserved. No part of this book may be reproduced, transmitted, downloaded, decompiled or reverse engineered in any form or by any means, electronic or mechanical including photocopying, recording or by any information storage and retrieval system, without permission from the Publisher in writing. NO AI TRAINING: Without in any way limiting the Author's and Publisher's exclusive rights under copyright, any use of this publication to 'train' generative artificial intelligence (AI) technologies to generate text is expressly prohibited. The Author and Publisher reserve all rights to license uses of this work for generative AI training and development of machine learning language models.

Typeset by Concept, Huddersfield, West Yorkshire, HD4 5JL.
Printed and bound in England by CPI Group (UK) Ltd, Croydon, CR0 4YY.

The Publisher's authorised representative in the EU for product safety is Authorised Rep Compliance Ltd, Ground Floor, 71 Lower Baggot Street, Dublin D02 P593, Ireland – www.arccompliance.com

For a complete list of Pen & Sword titles please contact
PEN & SWORD BOOKS LTD
47 Church Street, Barnsley, South Yorkshire, S70 2AS, England
E-mail: enquiries@pen-and-sword.co.uk
Website: www.pen-and-sword.co.uk
or
PEN & SWORD BOOKS
1950 Lawrence Rd, Havertown, PA 19083, USA
E-mail: uspen-and-sword@casematepublishers.com
Website: www.penandswordbooks.com

Contents

Acknowledgements vi
Introduction vii
Glossary of Terms ix
1. Winter 1944–45 1
2. The Defenders of the Reich 27
3. The Opening Fires 45
4. Attack on the Forward Position 59
5. Advance through the Reichswald, 9 February 1945 95
6. The Reichswald and the Maas Plain, 10 February 129
7. The Gennep Bridgehead and the Hekkens Crossroads, 11 February . . 147
8. The Niers Bridgehead, 12–13 February 163
9. The Welsh Division – Attack and Counter-Attack 179
Appendices
   I. Order of Battle: Phase 1 Grouping 199
   II. German and British Ranks 203
Notes 205
Index 209

Acknowledgements

An author has always had to be grateful to those whose works have trod overlapping paths before, but for today's historian there is a much larger cast to thank. This is especially so as this book was written at a time when archives and libraries across the UK were closed as a result of the COVID pandemic or had severely restricted access in the aftermath of 'lockdowns'. Chief among those who have given me unfettered access to their personal libraries are my friend and co-conspirator Richard Hone and the library of the Land Warfare Centre, whose collection of divisional regimental histories has been invaluable. In a similar vein, the staff of The Rifles' museums have been of great assistance in copying the war diaries of the Wessex Division that I had missed or were not available from the National Archives.

At a time when travel has been severely curtailed, help from fellow members of the International Guild of Battlefield Guides, particularly from the Netherlands contingent, has as always been much appreciated. They and sundry military history blog writers, with their detailed knowledge of the Reichswald, have helped refresh my memory of the ground, which is so important in accurately placing events. Thank you one and all.

I must also pay tribute to Canadian historians, whose work has provided me with a new appreciation and understanding of the qualities of General Crerar, his headquarters staff and the way they went about their business. Dealing with allies is seldom easy and authors in Canada have shown that in the case of VERITABLE, Crerar's patience and listening to the suggestions of General Horrocks and his subordinate commanders did much to make XXX Corps at home in First Canadian Army. The result was that throughout the battle Horrocks and his divisional staffs rarely found themselves looking back over their shoulders.

Once again, I have to thank the Pen and Sword team for all that they have done to nurse this project into print.

Tim Saunders
Warminster, 2023

Introduction

The project to fill the void in the historiography of the first phase of Operation VERITABLE in February 1945 was originally intended to be a single volume but during writing it grew to a size and complexity such that it needed splitting into two. This volume covers the fighting in the Reichswald forest by the Welsh and Highland Divisions and the struggle to open a southern axis south for the breakout into the Rhineland. The second volume will focus on the 15th Scottish Division's attack through the Siegfried Line north of the Reichswald to seize Kleve, and the initial faltering breakout by 43rd Wessex Division.

Both volumes examine XXX Corps' fighting during a battle that was originally conceived as a fast and fluid strike into the Rhineland but a thaw at the end of January condemned British and Canadian formations to fighting in appalling ground and weather conditions. The battle to break into the Reichswald, the fight through the forest and flanking country, became a dogged struggle. A struggle in which mud, blown-down trees and floods, as much as the German soldier, his trenches and mines, were the enemy. All of which provided levels of 'friction' that even Clausewitz would have deemed impossible.

As the Welsh and Highland divisions fought through and around the 'Reichswald Plug', to force the 'Gateway to the Rhineland' for exploitation by fresh mobile divisions, German reinforcements arrived to contain the offensive. With slow Allied progress, General Schlemm received the reinforcements from *Fallschirmjäger* divisions and the armour of XLVII Panzer Corps that he had been arguing for since he took command.

In the long winter of 1944–45, the Reichswald stands out in the letters, diaries and memoirs of those who fought there as being a grim struggle. An officer of 5th Seaforth Highlanders described the Reichswald and provides a vivid impression of what it was like to fight in the forest:

> The Reichswald was planted on strictly Teutonic lines, with the trees evenly spaced and dressed smartly by the left. The trunks of the more mature ones were trimmed for the first few feet, so that when we moved off the ride we found ourselves among endless pillars with a solid ceiling of branches overhead. In other places, a patch of young trees thickly planted made movement except on the ride impossible; and in others again the monotonous pines gave way to more open stretches of free-planted oak and beech. The ride itself was so boggy in parts that the only vehicles which could get through were tanks.

A photograph taken at General Crerar's First Canadian Army headquarters prior to Operation VERITABLE. From left to right, Major General Vokes (4th Canadian Armoured Division), General Crerar, Field Marshal Montgomery, Lieutenant General Horrocks (XXX British Corps), Lieutenant General Simonds (II Canadian Corps), Major Spry (3rd Canadian Infantry Division), and Major General Mathews (2nd Canadian Division).

It is almost impossible to describe the atmosphere of the Reichswald. One might say that it was an evil place, that it stank of danger, that it was one long natural ambush, and yet that gives little clue to the impression it made upon us. Still, putting oneself in the boots of a man in the leading platoon, something of the quality of the place may be appreciated. Such a man walked slowly forward through the trees near the edge of the ride knowing all the time that a German with a machine-gun could be hidden within fifty yards of him. Behind him were the tanks, roaring like tractors in an empty church. He felt sure the Germans must hear the tanks. He felt sure the Germans must know they could not move off the ride and that he, the man, must be close to them. Somewhere in the next half-mile the Boche would be waiting. All he could do was move quietly forward over the carpet of pine-needles, keep his head, and watch for the flicker of a cheek dropping to the stock of a Spandau.[1]

Although there were further hard battles in the Rhineland, crossing the Rhine and during the advance deep into Germany, many of those who wrote their formation and unit histories felt that the Reichswald 'was their worst experience since Normandy'. Invariably they go on to say that it was in the first phase of Operation VERITABLE that they 'broke the back of German resistance'.

Glossary of Terms

Abbreviations abound in war diaries and accounts. The main ones are listed here but, in an army, where combat training had priority over staff work, many non-standard and local variations were used. The following list will help.

2iC	Second in Command
A1 Echelon	Immediate replenishment of combat supplies
A2 Echelon	Further back planned replenishment of combat supplies
AA	Anti-aircraft
ADC	Aide de Camp
Adjt	Adjutant Unit commanding officer's staff officer
Admin	Administration
Adv	Advance
AGRA	Army Group Royal Artillery, a corps' artillery 'division', consisting of heavy, medium and field regiments plus anti-aircraft guns
AFV	Armoured Fighting Vehicle
Amn	Ammunition
AOP	Air Observation Post
AP	Armour Piercing
APDS	Armour Piercing Discarding Sabot (anti-tank ammunition)
APIS	Air Photo Interpretation Section
Arty	Artillery
Assy Area	Assembly Area, where troops regroup (e.g. tanks, infantry and gunners) for an operation prior to moving to the FUP
A/Tk	(+ variants) Anti-tank
AVRE	Armoured Vehicle Royal Engineer
Axis	The central direction of advance
BC	Battery Commander
B Echelon	The entry point of combat supplies into a unit's logistic infrastructure
BCR	Battle Casualty Replacement
Bde	Brigade (British) equivalent to a US or German regiment
Bn	Battalion
Br	Bridge
Bty	Battery

Cas	Casualties
Casevac	Casualty evacuation
CCP	Casualty Clearing Post
CCS	Casualty Clearing Station
C in C	Commander in Chief
Civ	Civilian
CL	Centre Line or axis of advance
CO	Commanding Officer*
Co-ax	Coaxial machinegun mounted in tanks alongside the main armament
Conc	Concentrate, also Conc Area, where units assigned to an operation gather before moving forward to the assy area
Comd	Command
Coord	Coordinate
Coy	Company
CP	Command Post
Cpl	Corporal
CPO	Command Post Officer (artillery)
CS	Close Support
CSM	Company Sergeant Major
D Day	The day on which an operation begins
DD	Tank Duplex Drive amphibious tank (Sherman)
Dem	Demolition
Dets	Detachments
DF	Defensive fire, Pre-planned artillery, mortar or medium machinegun target areas on likely enemy approaches, etc.
Div	Division
DP	Distribution Point (logistic)
DR	Dispatch rider also 'Don R' or 'Don Romeo'
DZ	Drop Zone
Ech	Echelon, normally referring to fighting echelon and logistic echelons of a unit
En	Enemy
Enfilade	Fire from a flank
Fd Regt	Field Regiment RA
FOB	Forward officer Bombardment – naval gunfire
FOO	Forward Observation Officer (artillery)
FUP	Forming Up Place
Fwd	Forward
Gd	Guard typically advanced, flan or rear guard

*Today the distinction between CO and OC is well-defined, with the former commanding a unit such as a battalion and the latter a sub-unit such as a company, but in many British Second World War memoirs and documents they are transposed or used inconsistently.

GOC	General Officer Commanding
Gr	Grenadier
H Hour	The hour (time) at which an operation starts
HE	High Explosive
HQ	Headquarters
Inf	Infantry
Int	Intelligence
I Sec	Intelligence Section
JNCO	Junior Non-Commissioned Officer
KIA	Killed in action
KO	Knocked out
LAA	Light Anti-Aircraft
LAD	Light Aid Detachment
LCA	Landing Craft Assault
LCpl	Lance Corporal
LCT	Landing Craft Tank
Ldr	Leader
Line	Field telephone wire
LZ	Landing Zone
MG	Machine gun
MIA	Missing in action
MMG	Medium machine gun
MSR	Main Supply Route
O Group	Orders group, assembly of subordinate commanders for the issue of orders
OC	Officer Commanding
OP	Observation post
Op Sec	Operational Security
P Hour	Time of a parachute drop
PIAT	Projector Infantry Anti-Tank
Pl	Platoon
Posn	Position
Pt	Point
Pte	Private (rank)
Pz	Panzer
RAP	Regimental Aid Post
Rd	Road
Regt *or* Rgt	Regiment
RHA	Royal Horse Artillery
RHU	Reinforcement Holding Unit
RMO	Regimental Medical Officer
RPM	Rounds per minute
RSM	Regimental Sergeant Major

RSO	Regimental Signals Officer
RV	Rendezvous point
SA	Small Arms
SB	Stretcher-bearer
Sec *or* Sect	Section
Shellrep	Report of enemy shelling, used to locate enemy batteries
Sgt *or* Sjt	Sergeant *or* Serjeant
Sitrep	Situation Report
SL	Start Line
Smk	Smoke
SNCO	Senior Non-Commissioned Officer
SP	Self-propelled
Sub-unit	Company, squadron or battery sized unit
Sups	Supplies
Sqn	Squadron
Tac	Tactical, usually used in context of a tactical headquarters
Target	All guns within range when a '*xxxxx* target' was called (Mike = regiment; Uncle = division; Victor = corps; and York = army)
TCP	Traffic control point
Tgt	Target
Tk	Tank
Tp	Troop
Tpt	Transport
Unit	An infantry battalion or a British artillery or armoured regiment
Wef	With effect
WIA	Wounded in action
X Rds	Crossroads
yd *or* yds	Yards

Chapter One

Winter 1944–45

The failure of Operation MARKET GARDEN at Arnhem was not the end of British attempts to finish the war in Europe by Christmas 1944; the country was running out of manpower and was in an increasingly parlous financial state. Denied MARKET GARDEN's bridgehead across the Rhine and direct access to the North German Plain, as soon as 1st Airborne Division was withdrawn across the Rhine, planning for an alternative route into the Reich started. Field Marshal Montgomery fell on an opportunity that had already been identified by his staff but dismissed as an option; to attack eastwards through the Reichswald. The obvious difficulties of a narrow frontage and just two decent roads mitigated against this as an option of first choice. However, avoiding the strength of the main defences of the West Wall or 'Siegfried Line', clearing the west bank of the Rhine and enveloping the Ruhr without having to make a second assault river crossing of the Mass did have its attractions. Operation GATWICK, with its planned D Day of 10 October, was first delayed and then cancelled by General Eisenhower, in favour of a resumption of his broad front strategy aimed at closing up to the Rhine from Switzerland northwards. At this point in the campaign, combat supplies were still being trucked forward all the way from Normandy and the resulting slim allocations of resources could only be issued to armies in their turn. Consequently, the breathing space for the German recovery afforded by the Allied logistic crisis of September 1944 lengthened into the autumn.

Following their remarkable operational recovery on the western borders of the Reich, the Germans proved to be far from beaten as Allied optimists believed following the Wehrmacht's defeat in Normandy and the subsequent pursuit across northern France. Throughout the autumn they fought hard in a series of bitter battles in which the majority of the Allied armies were held west of the River Maas and the Rhineland. As winter set in, only the First Canadian and Seventh US armies were actually on the banks of the Rhine but in both cases only at its northern and southern extremities. Elsewhere, there were only modest incursions into Germany and only a few small breaches of the Siegfried Line.

Eisenhower had no firm plan beyond reaching the Rhine on his broad front. Consequently, there was a resumption of army commanders lobbying the Supreme Commander, as they had following the Allied triumph in Normandy. All of them presented their plan for final victory over Germany, with of course their army playing the leading role! For example, Patton advocated a thrust by the Third US Army across the Rhine via Metz, while Montgomery, as his only viable though increasingly difficult option, again proposed an attack during

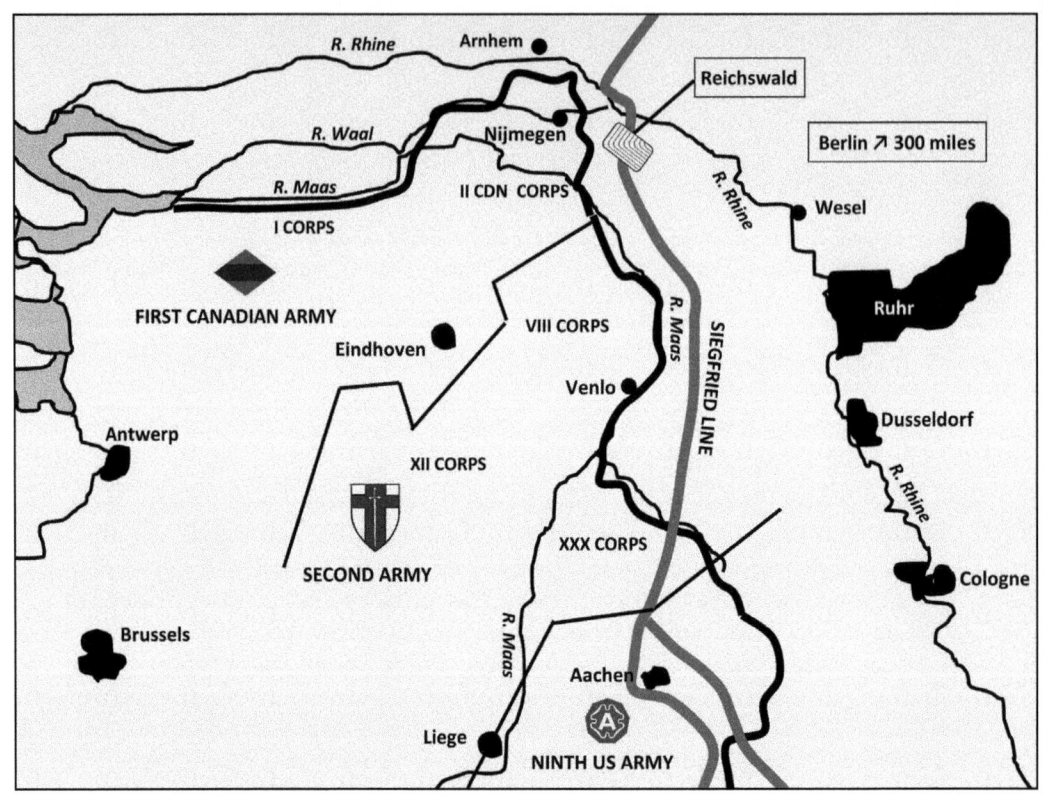

The 21st Army Group situation in the winter of 1944–45.

November through the Reichswald.[1] Patton, however, failed, suffering heavy casualties in one of his few set-piece battles and Eisenhower rejected all the other proposals for reasons such as them lacking a strategic objective, being politically unacceptable or simply logistically unsustainable.[2] The result was rampant jealousy among the generals, born of overweening personal ambition, which in turn led to levels of suspicion, discord and division between the Allies that even Hitler noted and hoped to exploit.

Denied a continuation of Operation MARKET GARDEN while the Germans were arguably still off balance, Montgomery's 21st Army Group's main effort became the opening of the Scheldt Estuary and the port of Antwerp for large tonnages of combat supplies. This was undertaken by First Canadian Army, which was strung out along the Channel coast dealing with the various ports and their 'fortress' garrisons that had been left behind to deny them to the Allies. Meanwhile, from Nijmegen eastwards, General Dempsey's Second British Army, in a series of relatively modest-scale operations, fought to clear the western bank of the Maas and the stoutly held enemy pockets.

With his latest option to attack through the Reichswald turned down, Montgomery wrote somewhat disingenuously to General Crerar, who now had responsibility for the area south of Nijmegen, on 28 November:

> There is no intention of launching this operation now, and I have never expressed a wish to do so. All I want you to do is to examine it and put the

planners on to thinking it out. It will NOT be launched till spring, i.e. March or later.³

General Eisenhower was, however, determined not to give the Germans another opportunity to recover and strengthen their defences. He instructed his armies to maintain pressure on the enemy at every opportunity and announced his intention to resume the offensive in January. At a conference he held with his army group commanders at Maastricht on 7 December, the Supreme Commander stated that he favoured the northern route into the Rhineland. At this stage, however, the northern thrust was only one of the competing options Eisenhower was considering.

The matter of inter-Allied relations had again come to a head during the Maastricht conference, where Montgomery once more overplayed his hand. He demanded sole command of forty of the seventy-five Allied divisions with which to mount a single, concentrated thrust to Berlin that he had espoused for so long. Eisenhower, of course, refused, again reverting to his preferred broad front strategy. He did, however, place General Simpson's Ninth US Army under 21st Army Group's command for the northern thrust. The field marshal therefore had to settle for fighting the Allied armies into a position where, he the master of the set-piece battle, could deliver Eisenhower's 'assured crossing of the Rhine'.

The problem was that the obvious route via Venlo into the Rhine was heavily defended and to reach the Ruhr an assault crossing of the both the rivers Maas and Rhine would be required. However, the Reichswald, the 'plug' between the Maas and the Rhine, if forced quickly and cleanly, offered the field marshal an attractive option to deliver the northern attack into the Rhineland. Thus, following Eisenhower's direction, a little over a week after dismissing the Reichswald as an early option, Montgomery rang General Crerar to discuss proposals for an attack through the Reichswald Plug!

Within days, 21st Army Group issued a concept for the offensive north of the Ruhr via the Reichswald to generals Crerar, Dempsey and Simpson. In his directive of 16 December, Montgomery outlined the framework of 21st Army Group's operations for the Battle for the Rhineland and the Rhine Crossing:

> The future layout that we want to achieve is to face up to the Rhine from Orsoy [10 miles south of Wesel on the Rhine] northwards on a front of two armies, Second Army being on the right and Canadian Army on the left. American formations are then to be included in 21 Army Group and, with the co-operation of strong airborne forces, the Rhine will be crossed.
>
> Before we can begin to develop successfully large-scale operations across the Rhine, we must clear the enemy completely from the west of the river and must join up with the American Ninth Army coming up from the south; we must in fact be in undisputed possession of all territory west of the Rhine from inclusive the general line Orsoy-Venlo northwards.

The Battle of the Reichswald

Two of Montgomery's armies were to mount attacks into the Rhineland. The First Canadian Army would launch an attack from the north through the Reichswald Plug, in an operation now code-named VERITABLE, while several days later the Ninth US Army would launch Operation GRENADE to the south across the River Roer. Meanwhile, General Dempsey's Second Army, having cleared the west bank of the Maas and been squeezed out of the line by the advance of the Canadian and US armies, would make preparations to mount a subsequent assault crossing of the Rhine astride Wesel. However, for a variety of reasons that will become apparent, Simpson lacked sufficient divisions and resources with which to secure his envisaged starting positions right up to the point of the launching of VERITABLE and GRENADE.

General Harry Crerar, commander of First Canadian Army.

Eisenhower (centre) and his northern commanders Montgomery, left, and Bradley, right. Back rank, left to right, generals Crerar, Simpson and Dempsey.

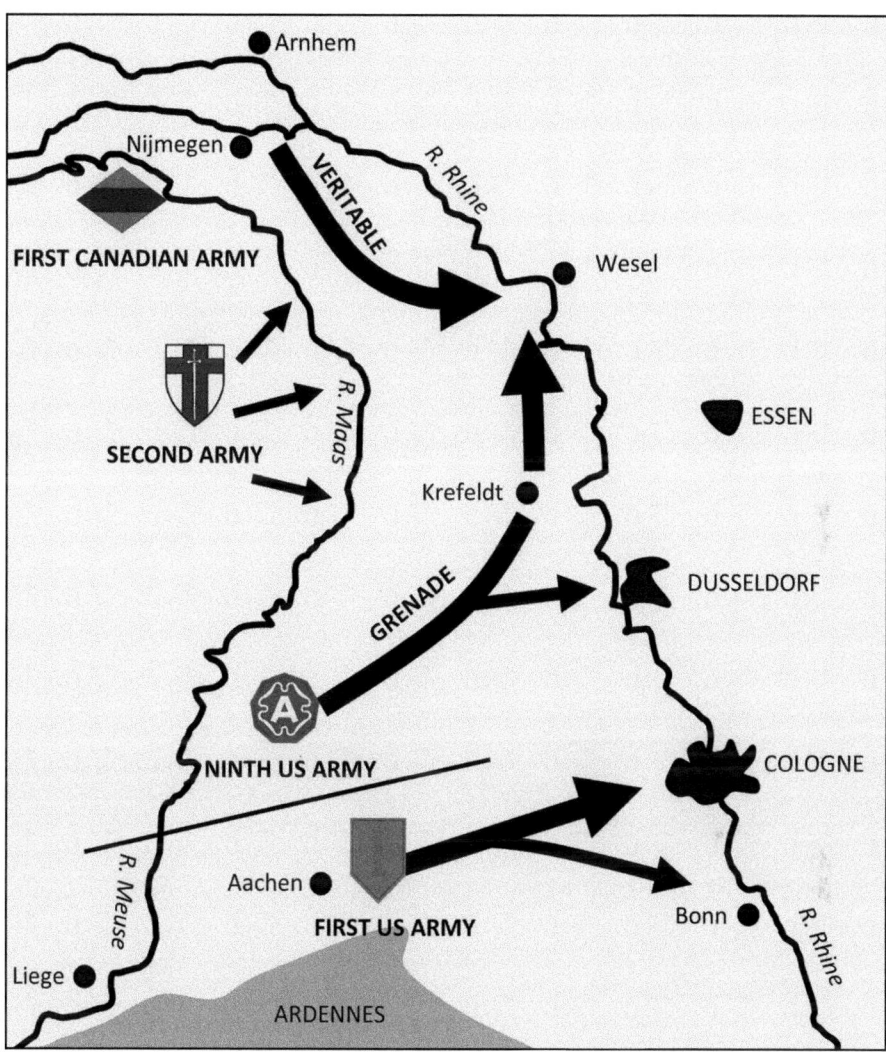

Field Marshal Montgomery's concept of operations for the Rhineland in 1945.

The German Strategic Position

The Western Allies' victory in Normandy was more than matched by the Red Army's spectacular successes on the Eastern Front during the summer of 1944, the result of which was that Hitler's forces were faced with the defence of the Reich itself on two fronts. The Germans, however, made good use of the Allied logistic crisis of September and the autumn to continue their strategic recovery, stabilising and then strengthening their defences. To replace some of their heavy losses of 1944, not only were men combed out from redundant posts in the Luftwaffe and Kriegsmarine, but the age of conscription was increased to between 16 and 60. Older men, those unsuitable for military service and the disabled were directed to the factories, thus freeing up fit, younger men for the army. The economy had been only belatedly placed on a complete total war footing and, despite the Allied bombing offensive, production of weapons and ammunition peaked.

The Allied strategic bombing offensive of 1943 into 1944 had manifestly failed to strangle German war production and had not produced the hoped for collapse of Germany. During late 1944 there was a change of target priority from cities and production to attacking oil supplies and refineries, which very quickly created severe problems for German manufacturing. The availability of petrol, oils and lubricants was reduced from 1 million to just 350,000 tons, with the supply of aviation fuel being particularly marked.

The integrated radar and night fighter system known as the Kammhuber Line had throughout 1942 and 1943 evolved to remain effective despite successive changes in tactics by the Allied bomber commands. The lack of fuel by the end of 1944, however, meant that the Luftwaffe could only launch fifty night fighter sorties per night, which greatly reduced the hitherto very high toll on Allied aircraft and airmen, and in turn increased the effectiveness of their bombing of oil targets. This also had an effect on production of high explosives and synthetic rubber, which slumped.

To the annoyance of the bomber barons, following the tactical success of attacks on the French road and rail system that choked off supplies to the fighting in Normandy, the next priority for attack was the German transport network and military traffic. As a result, by the time of Operation VERITABLE and the opening of the Battle of the Rhineland, German roads, railways and canals were working at a fraction of their former capacity. This not only created difficulties of redeploying troops but also slowed the arrival of raw materials at factories, causing a further dramatic drop in arms production. In short, the air effort, despite the appearance of enemy jet fighters, was according to General Eisenhower having 'a definite influence upon the ground battle'.

Montgomery, in common with other senior Allied commanders believing the Germans lacked any offensive capability, wrote in his directive issued on 16 December:

> The enemy is at present fighting a defensive campaign on all fronts ... at all costs he has to prevent the war from entering a mobile phase; he does not have the transport or the petrol that would be necessary for mobile operations ...

Coincidentally, the Germans launched an offensive on the same day Montgomery issued his directive to the army commanders specifying January for the resumption of the attack on Germany. Rather than the Germans sitting out the winter as expected, the Allies were rocked by Hitler's surprise offensive in the Ardennes. Launched under cover of poor weather before dawn on 16 December 1944, the attack by twenty-eight divisions caught the First US Army ill-prepared for what

Allied bombers targeted German production and communications by day and by night.

developed into one of the biggest battles of the North West European Campaign; the Battle of the Bulge.

It was quickly apparent though that with two panzer armies thrusting west, VIII US Corps in danger of collapse and with XXX Corps being called south to provide a backstop on the River Meuse, operations in the Rhineland needed to be postponed until the fighting in the Ardennes was resolved.

On 12 January 1945, the Soviets launched their winter offensive with almost 200 divisions of the Red Army, outnumbering the Germans five to one. Believing that by targeting Antwerp with V1 and V2 weapons, along with the shock effect of the Battle of the Bulge, the Allies would be prevented from resuming the offensive in the west, Hitler ordered the redeployment of formations to mount a desperate attempt to shore up the collapsing Eastern Front. Nonetheless, in less than a month the Red Army had advanced nearly 200 miles from the Vistula to the Oder and was within 40 miles of Berlin.

The Reichswald Plug

First Canadian Army had been studying the Reichswald as an option since taking over the front from XXX Corps in early November. The ground that the Canadians referred to as the 'Reichswald Plug' was the 10 miles of low terrain between the Maas and the Rhine, but of that distance in the centre the Reichswald forest occupied 5 miles of slightly higher ground. A low ridge inside the western and northern extremities of the wood culminated in the broad, open Materborn feature overlooking the city of Kleve. If the Germans were allowed to redeploy their reserves to this vital ground, the operation was bound to become both slow and costly.

The Reichswald itself was a commercial forest divided up into parcels of woodland of pines and deciduous trees by forest rides and tracks. It varied from newly felled open areas through dense patches of saplings to areas of mature trees that offered modest fields of fire. Movement by most vehicles would be confined to the forest tracks that divided the Reichswald into blocks typically 200 by 500 yards in dimension. The heavy Churchill tanks, where the trees were not too substantial or thickly planted, could plough through the forest but this invariably risked a close-quarter encounter with a *panzerfaust* armed infantryman if not protected by their own infantry. Some of the main forest tracks were surfaced with a layer of crushed stone, but they were not designed for sustained heavy armoured movement and in the event both they and the forest rides dissolved into deep mud.

The ground between the rivers and in the centre, the 'Reichswald Plug'.

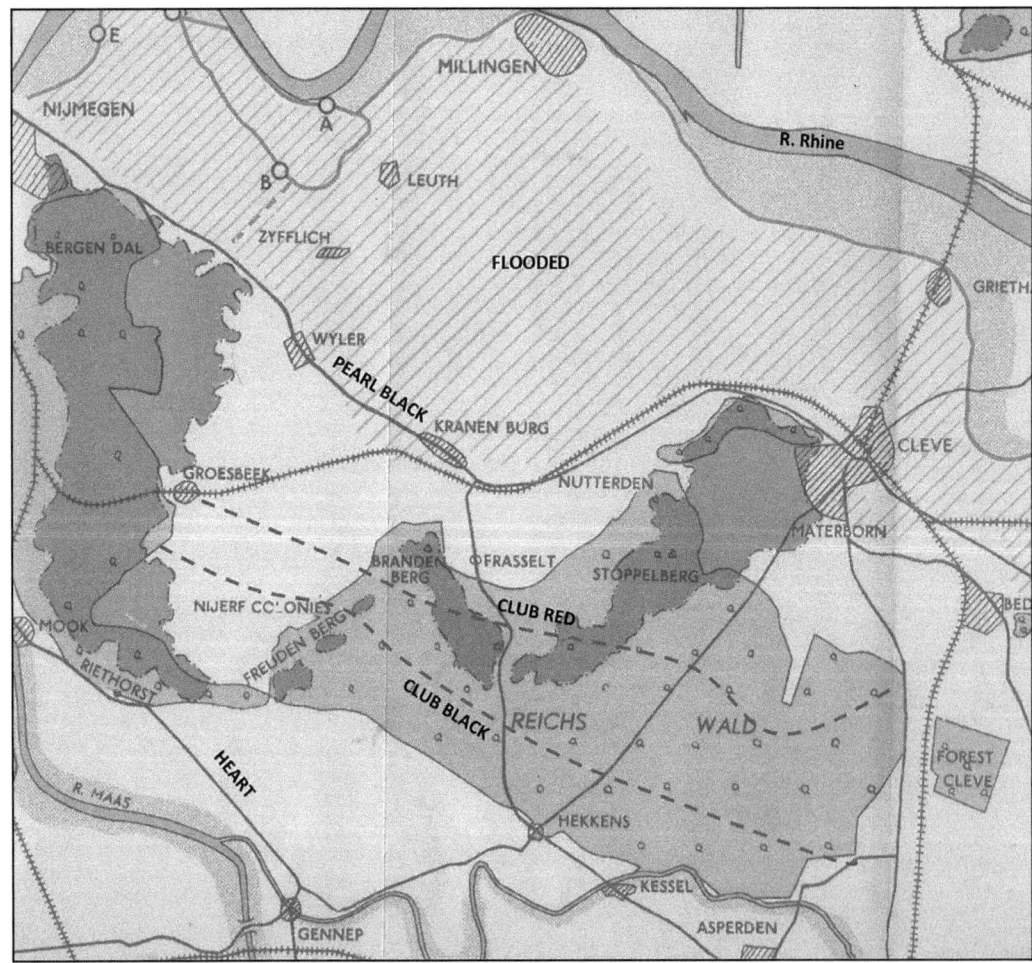

An extract of the 1:25,000 scale map showing the division of the Reichswald into blocks and the lighter-coloured, more open areas.

The Reichswald was flanked by narrow strips of open ground, along which the only vaguely decent roads ran. Of these corridors, the one to the north, along which ran the Nijmegen–Kleve Road, at just a mile wide, offered the best going. With its access to Kleve and the Materborn feature, this was initially to be General Crerar's main effort. It was, however, also by far the most obvious approach, as operations to the south of the Reichswald on the Maas floodplain would involve crossing the swollen River Niers as well.

To the left and right of these manoeuvre corridors the ground dropped away to the open river floodplains. The Germans had already breached the Rhine dykes and flooded much of the Betwe or 'Island' between Nijmegen and Arnhem. It was rightly assumed they would do the same again north of the Reichswald when the water levels in the Rhine rose with melt water. This would render the plain impassable except via the embanked roads or by amphibious vehicles. Looking further east, the ground beyond the Reichswald widened out to 20 miles between the Rhine and the Maas but much of it was still floodplain and, in the centre, lay some defensible broken ground, plus the cities of Kleve, Goch and Uedem, as well as other large towns.

Planning VERITABLE

Crerar's overall VERITABLE plan was in three phases:

Phase 1. The clearing of the Reichswald and the securing of the line Gennep–Asperden–Kleve.

Phase 2. The breaching of the enemy's second defensive system east and south-east of the Reichswald, the capture of the localities Weeze–Uedem–Kalkar–Emmerich and the securing of the communications between them.

Phase 3. The 'break-through' of the 'Hochwald lay-back' defence lines and the advance to secure the general line Geldern–Xanten.

Having reached this line it was expected that the Canadians and the Ninth US Army in Operation GRENADE would meet west of Wesel, having completed the clearance of the Rhineland from the south.

General Crerar had assumed that Simonds' II Canadian Corps would lead the first phase of the assault but Montgomery so engineered matters that XXX Corps would inevitably conduct this first phase. This was, of course, an affront to the Canadians, but 3rd Canadian Division was to play a significant role in the Reichswald battle by clearing the floodplain and the enemy's strong forward defences on the northern flank.

General Horrocks' XXX Corps took over responsibility for the initial assault of the enemy's forward defences on the Groesbeek Heights, along with fighting

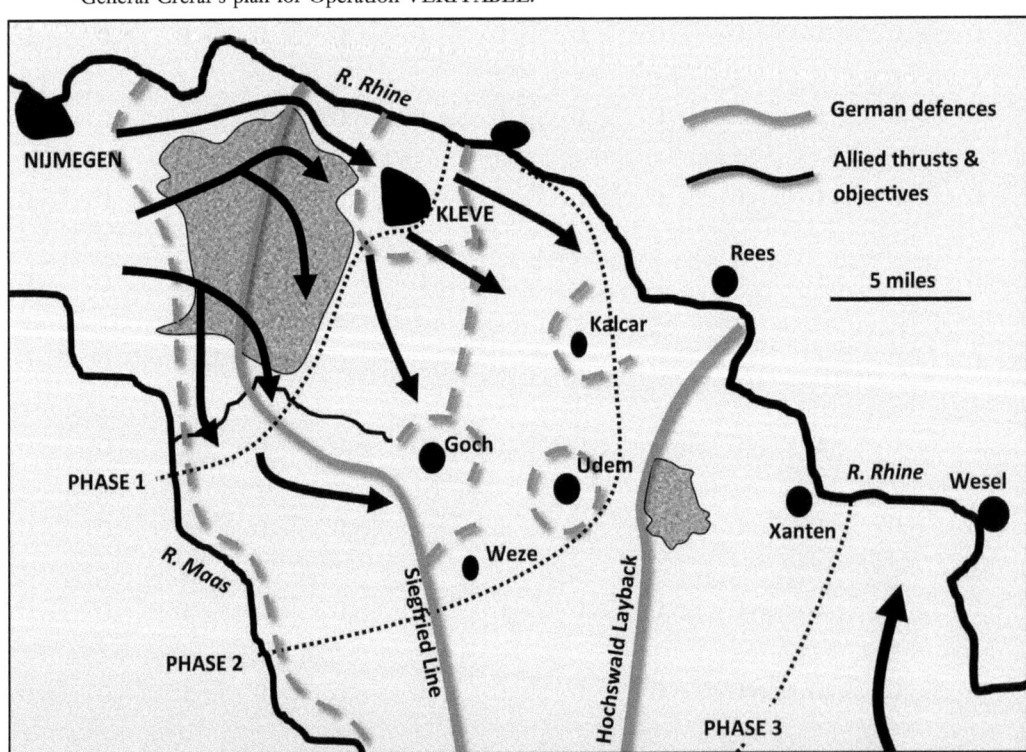

General Crerar's plan for Operation VERITABLE.

General Sir Brian Horrocks, commander of XXX Corps.

through the Reichswald. In subsequent phases, as the ground opened up, Crerar would order II Canadian Corps to join the battle on the left flank adjacent to the Rhine. The whole operation to clear the Rhineland was optimistically expected to take around four days to complete if the winter freeze persisted.

For deception purposes, under the cover story of Dutch political pressure to liberate the rest of their country, further north, I British Corps':

> ... chief role was to 'implement and maintain' a cover plan indicating a prospective attack across the Waal and the Lek [Lower Rhine] directed on Utrecht, designed to liberate the northern Netherlands. It was hoped that the movement of British units from Second Army into the Canadian Army area might be interpreted by the enemy as related to this project.[4]

Despite the employment of the whole panoply of deception measures, the Germans were not deceived by I Corps, clearly seeing that a crossing of the Rhine between Emmerich and Wesel would cut off the northern Netherlands anyway, without a significant fight. They believed that the threat lay with the Second Army and the US Armies further south, and that any attack further north would be a feint.

As far as VERITABLE's detail was concerned, General Crerar directed that two plans be prepared based on the state of the ground and briefed his orders group as late as 4 February that:

> If everything broke in our favour, weather, ground, air support, enemy dispositions and reactions – I would not be surprised if armour of 30 Corps reached the Geldern-Xanten line in a few days. On the other hand, if conditions are against us, I see three 'set-piece' operations, one for each Phase, and the battle may well last three weeks …

If the firm going persisted, as soon as the initial breakthrough had been made, armoured formations would be released 'to disrupt and disorganise enemy resistance in the rear in the quickest possible time'. If, however, the ground conditions were wet, then a plan for a more methodical and inevitably slower attack would be adopted. It was, nonetheless, stressed that: 'Should the enemy's resistance crumble, no opportunity was to be lost of exploiting favourable situations irrespective of which plan was in force.' In the event, the weather changed from January's dry, deep cold and crisp conditions, with good firm going, to a wet February when a rapid thaw set in on 30–31 January. The formerly frozen, snow-covered ground quickly became sodden. Consequently, the second more methodical plan was put into operation.[5] Even so, in the changed conditions it is remarkable that commanders were determined the operation would go ahead.

The thaw also found, for example, the Churchills of 34 Armoured Brigade fully winterised with their tanks whitewashed and 700 tons of 'ice bar tracks' employed to prevent the build-up of ice on track shoes that in the Ardennes had in the worst cases became so thick that turrets were lifted from their mountings. In the Reichswald, instead of ice the Churchills faced thick mud that, along with branches, had the same lifting effect despite 'mud ploughs' and other stripper devices.

XXX Corps' Plan

> Intention. 30 Corps will destroy the enemy between the River Maas and the River Rhine and breakthrough in a southerly direction between these two rivers. [XXX Corps Op Instruction No. 47]

VERITABLE was to be the first battle in which General Horrocks fought under the command of General Crerar. He wrote in his memoirs that:

> During the build-up period I had little to do, except to go around visiting troops. I had so far not come in contact with the Canadians, so I set out to try and get to know them better. I also saw quite a lot of their Commander, General Crerar, who, in my opinion, has always been much underrated,

Churchill tanks in the Groesbeek area prior to the battle.

largely because he was the exact opposite to Montgomery. He hated publicity but was full of common sense and always prepared to listen to the views of his subordinate commanders.

In explaining his plan for VERITABLE, General Horrocks wrote: 'We had to smash through this bottleneck before breaking out into the German plain beyond'; in other words, a frontal attack of the narrow frontage of the Reichswald Plug. His other concern resulted from his MARKET GARDEN problems on Hell's Highway:

> I badly wanted the metaled roads [sic], which ran through it because I knew from experience how difficult it was to maintain a force, with all its manifold requirements, by a single road. So, I determined to use the maximum force possible from the outset and to attack with five divisions.

To sustain the advance, four routes forward through the battle area were planned: the two metalled roads flanking the forest and two of the stone-topped tracks that ran through it. The northerly hardtop road between Nijmegen and Kleve was designated 'PEARL BLACK' and secondary routes through the forest called 'CLUB RED' and CLUB BLACK' were to use country roads and forest tracks. The Corps' secondary supply route, 'HEART', was the metalled road from Mook south of the woods, which crossed the River Niers at Kessel and led on to Goch.

The British divisions grouped with XXX Corps for the initial assault were 15th Scottish, 53rd Welsh and 51st Highland, and the allocated Canadian formations were a brigade from the 2nd Division and the 3rd Infantry Division. The

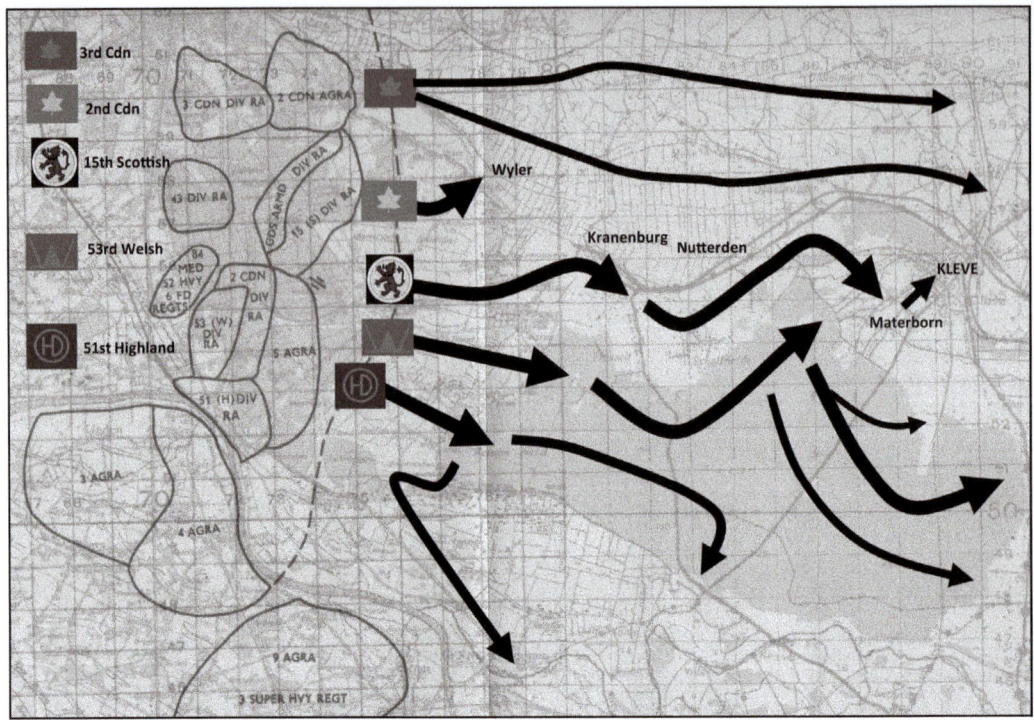

An outline of the XXX Corps' plan for VERITABLE's first phase and gun areas.

Guards Armoured and 43rd Wessex Divisions were prepared for exploitation beyond the Reichswald, and two further British divisions were held as Montgomery's reserve. Support was provided by the three armoured brigades and sundry units of assault armour from 79th Armoured Division.

On the left flank the Canadians were to open the Nijmegen–Kleve Road (Route PEARL BLACK) at Wyler and clear the Rhine floodplain. The 15th Scottish and 6 Guards Armoured Brigade, holding the Corps' main effort, were to fight through the forward German defences into that narrow corridor of higher ground between the floodplain and the forest, breaking the Siegfried Line beyond Kranenburg. Once through these defences they were to dash and seize both the Materborn feature and Kleve. The 43rd Wessex Division and the tanks of 8th Armoured Brigade were to conduct a passage of lines and breakout into the Rhineland in the direction of Goch.

The two British divisions due to attack through the Reichswald itself, on the right of XXX Corps, were the 53rd Welsh and the 51st Highland, supported by 34th Armoured Brigade. They too were to break into the enemy's forward defences and fight through the forest to the Siegfried Line. Having overcome these defences, the Welsh Division was to advance to the north-eastern tip of the forest before wheeling south east to clear the bulk of the Reichswald. Meanwhile, the Highland Division would swing south out of the forest onto the Maas floodplain, where they were to clear enemy defences and secure crossings of the River Niers. Once bridges and routes forward on this flank were open, the Guards Armoured Division would be released into the Rhineland.

The infantry divisions were both pre-war Territorial Army formations but even though they had had a very different war so far, the distinction between regular army war-raised and territorial divisions had narrowed considerably.

The original 51st Highland Division had fought in the 1940 campaign but, unable to be evacuated, it had surrendered at St-Valery-sur-Somme. Reformed, the division fought with distinction in the deserts of North Africa and in Sicily, and numbered among the 40,000 veterans that Montgomery brought back to spearhead the invasion with combat experience. As was the case with some other veteran formations, the Highland Division did not initially perform well in Normandy. Montgomery noted that they had failed in all their operations, and they became known as one of the 'non-fighting divisions'. While this is true to an extent, with their reintroduction to battle and the steady stream of casualties, particularly among officers and NCOs, suffered holding ground east of the Orne it is understandable. Major General Bullen-Smith was sacked and replaced by Thomas Rennie, who as a Scot began the long process of restoring the fortunes of the division. By the time of VERITABLE, having fought in the Ardennes, the 51st Highland Division was back at the top of its game but in common with some other infantry formations the British manpower crisis meant battalions were under strength, most having three rather than four rifle companies.

The 53rd Welsh Division was a first line Territorial Army division brought up to the established strength of 18,000 with conscripts, and in spring 1940 it was located in Northern Ireland thanks to an expectation of a German landing in the south. This gave the division ample scope for training and in November 1941 it was brought back to the mainland, where it continued to take part in ever larger-scale exercises. In March 1942 the division joined XII Corps in the south-east corner of England in the anti-invasion role, where it became one of the experimental New Mobile or 'mixed' divisions, losing an infantry brigade to 11th Armoured Division and gaining the Churchills of 31 Tank Brigade. This experiment was short lived, and the tanks were duly replaced by the infantry of 71 Brigade, bringing two English battalions and a Scottish battalion into the division to join 1st Manchesters (MG). Despite four of the ten infantry battalions being English, the division, with its headquarters and most of its supporting arms being long-

XXX Corps' sign.

The 51st's Divisional sign.

The 53rd's Division sign.

standing territorials, retained its Welsh identity. As 1943 ended and plans and orders of battle firmed up, the 53rd, as a part of XII Corps, would cross to Normandy during the build-up phase at the end of June 1944.

These two divisions would cross the Operation VERITABLE start line at H Hour and fight their way into the Reichswald supported by the Churchills of 34 Armoured Brigade. Despite having had their title changed from 'Tank' to 'Armoured', the brigade's primary role remained unchanged: two of its three regiments equipped with the more heavily armoured Churchill infantry tanks were to provide close support to infantry divisions in the attack.

The shoulder flash of 34 Armoured Brigade.

As was now customary, early in an operation's planning process officers from 79th Armoured Division became involved to advise on the most effective way to use the division's assault armour – as well as ensuring that it was not misused. Those units attached to Brigadier Duncan's 30 Armoured Brigade consisted of flail tanks, the crocodiles of 141 (The Buffs) Regiment Royal Armoured Corps (RAC) and the Fife and Forfar Yeomanry, plus the Armoured Vehicle Royal Engineers (AVREs) of 6th and 42nd assault regiments RE.

The badge found on vehicles of 79th Armoured Division.

Regarding artillery allocation, Horrocks noted: 'The artillery support was very carefully worked out and was on the most massive scale I ever remember.' He had under his command no fewer than five British and Canadian Army Groups Royal Artillery (AGRA), which were in effect artillery divisions. These were in addition to the seventy-two 25-pounders that every infantry division held, bringing the artillery total to 1,050 guns, including a regiment of super heavies and the 1st Canadian Rocket Battery.

Fire support in the form of the Rocket unit's 'Land Mattress' was fired by a battery of twelve projectors, each having thirty-two launch tubes, with every launcher being the equivalent of a salvo by an entire field artillery regiment. The rockets were fired on a ripple system to avoid collisions in the air and each salvo impacted in an area of approximately 400 sq yards. A total of 4,608 rockets were available to be fired in fifteen strikes during the initial phase of the operation. The assault divisions submitted bids for this fire and thirteen targets were earmarked for engagement between 0500 and 1400 hours on 8 February. As the warhead's effect was more blast than splinter, the targets were engaged, as far as safety limits allowed, immediately before the infantry arrived in the target area. It was, however, found that by engaging the target with 25-pounders, which had a shorter

Launchers of 1st Canadian Rocket Battery being prepared for action.

danger area, after the rockets, even better results were obtained as the enemy was still stunned when the attacking infantry arrived.

Logistics

In contrast to the increasingly parlous German logistic situation, the opening of the Schelte and Antwerp's port facilities had by mid-December transformed those of the Allies. The tonnages of combat supplies available to be assembled for Montgomery's next well-resourced 'colossal crack' was vast, but an equally large engineering effort was required to facilitate their delivery to the front.

In advance of the move forward of supplies, fifty companies of British and Canadian engineers and twenty-nine companies of pioneers had to repair and maintain hundreds of miles of roads, most of which were not designed to sustain heavy military traffic. Some seventy bridges had to be built to take the weight of trucks and transporters, as well as the elimination of choke points, typically at bends and houses in villages. An additional five Bailey bridges, including a railway bridge, were built across the Maas, the latter bridge being the record-breaking Ravenstein 'high-level' pontoon bridge, which was 1,280ft long, and known as the QUEBEC Bridge.

Supplies were initially dumped in the Canadian Army's rear area and the build-up went on throughout the Battle of the Bulge. With the Supreme Commander's indications that VERITABLE would take place by 25 January, they were soon flowing into the forward area at a rate of 7,500 tons per day.

A convoy of Canadian vehicles being led through a badly damaged village.

By far the largest commodity in weight and volume to be moved forward to feed the 1,050 guns was artillery ammunition. For instance, each 25-pounder was allocated 1,677 rounds of ammunition, which was variously dumped at gun positions, held on first- and second-line unit transport or at corps and army dumps. To keep a 25-pounder battery in action, each gun required eight 3-ton truck loads, each of 200 rounds, to be brought forward to gun positions.

With XXX Corps numbering 200,000 men and with II Canadian Corps poised to join the battle, the First Canadian Army had accumulated 2,319,222 rations in its maintenance areas. These supplies and much more besides required 25,000 vehicles to bring the tonnage forward prior to and during the battle, which in turn would consume 1,300,000 gallons of fuel.

Royal Army Service Corps soldiers stacking ration boxes.

Due to both security and a lack of space in the Nijmegen area, 15th Scottish Division's ordnance field park unusually supplied all three of the British phase one assault divisions.

Operational Security and Observation

Montgomery insisted that every measure be taken to preserve VERITABLE's surprise. Released from operations further south, the formations regrouping with XXX Corps moved into concentration areas up to 60 miles from the start line on the Groesbeek Heights from mid-January onwards. They moved forward by stages at night, only reaching their final assembly areas at the last moment. General Horrocks explained:

> By day the normal amount of transport for the two Canadian divisions already in the area used the roads freely and no change was made, so that

the Germans would not become suspicious, but from dusk until dawn the roads were packed with transport, moving nose to tail, and before it became light, almost like magic the units would disappear into their concealment areas.

Of equal importance to movement was the control of radio communication, which had to be maintained at the same level as had existed before movement started. All moves were executed under radio silence and were controlled by 1,900 military policemen. In the forward area, however, 'more important than anything else was the control of reconnaissance'. Horrocks continued:

> ... literally thousands of officers and NCOs had to be given a chance to study the ground over which they were to attack. The Germans, who had become used to seeing very little movement on the wooded hills held by the Canadians in front of them, would suddenly have seen these same hills almost covered by figures wearing a different-coloured khaki battledress (the Canadian battledress was darker than ours), studying maps, using field glasses, and so on. There is an old Army saying, 'Time spent in reconnaissance is seldom wasted', and this unusual amount of movement could only mean one thing – an impending attack. We therefore had to impose the most rigorous control on any movement in the area occupied by the 2nd Canadian Division, and a reconnaissance report centre was established in the Dutch barracks at Grave, where everyone wishing to view the battlefield had to report. The staff at this centre would then control the number of people entering any particular area, by a system of passes, allowing them access to a certain view-point, for a definite period. They were then fitted out in a suit of the darker Canadian battledress. A series of sentries were posted at intervals, to whom the passes had to be shown.

Inevitably the burden of hosting visitors fell on the in-place 2nd Canadian Division's artillery units. The war diary of 4th Canadian Field Regiment for 5 February recorded that regimental headquarters 'really needed a revolving door to accommodate the horde of representatives from the advance parties of the formations coming to join us for the impending shenanigans'.

One of 4th Field's observation posts was the Groesbeek Windmill, which had continued to play an important part in the fighting on the heights since it was first used by 82nd US Airborne Division during MARKET GARDEN. Canadian gunner officer Captain Blackburn was puzzled that it was still standing:

> Why the Germans left that windmill intact will always be a mystery, for obviously it was the best observation post in the countryside. Certainly, had they known what was going on there during the last weeks of January and the first week in February, it would not have been left standing. During that period, it was filled with officers from generals down to subalterns each day planning Germany's destruction.

The Groesbeek Windmill still stands today, although the village, now a town, has expanded around it.

Lieutenant Foley, a troop commander in 107 Regiment RAC of 34 Armoured Brigade, was one of the officers who took his Churchill tank commanders forward to an observation post overlooking the Groesbeek Heights:

> It isn't often one can get a grandstand view of a potential battle-field, and when I took Five Troop along to have a look at it they found it hard to believe that the harmless-looking fields and cottages were deserted except for German listening posts covering the mines which were undoubtedly thickly sewn ...
>
> From the front of a large wood to the west of the Reichswald we stared through our binoculars at Germany. The ground between was low-lying and looked boggy. Here and there derelict gliders of the Arnhem battle dotted the landscape and the burned-out remains of vehicles told of the battles which had already been fought over this stretch of land.
>
> The Reichswald looked sombre and uninviting, the black trunks of the big trees seeming as solid as if carved from granite.
>
> 'There it is,' said Ian quietly. 'That's the objective for the first day. The Germans think the forest is an anti-tank obstacle; maybe it is, too. But you

never know till you try. Personally, I think we should be able to operate in there, providing we pick our trees carefully.'

'We've got to reach it first,' said Tony Cunningham. 'Is that the anti-tank ditch, that white thing zig-zagging across by the group of red houses?'[6]

'That's it,' said Ian. 'But the funnies are going to get us over that.'

107 Regiment RAC had its origins as a Territorial Army battalion of the King's Own Regiment and had retained its badge rather than the mailed fist of the Royal Armoured Corps.

General Hobart's assault armour was to clear the way through the German forward defences. Flail tanks would deal with the mines and Armoured Vehicle Royal Engineers would lay small box girder bridges across the anti-tank ditches and take on defences with their petard demolition guns.

Despite all the comings and goings of recce parties, a measure of the effectiveness of Horrocks' Opsec measures was that at the end of January German operational situation maps recorded XXX Corps as 'Whereabouts unknown'.

XXX Corps' Concentration

The 53rd Welsh Division spent two weeks in the Eindhoven area resting, taking in replacements and training with the Churchills that they were to fight with in the coming battle. Infantry battalion drivers were also sent for instruction on the newly issued small amphibious vehicle, the Weasel.

The move of four additional divisions and armoured brigades, plus reserve formations and artillery into the First Canadian Army's rear area, via the choke points on the River Maas at Grave and Mook, required a continuing engineer effort to keep the roads open now the thaw had set in. Road surfaces broke up under the relentless night-time traffic and the tanks that drove forward on their tracks wore deep ruts and created flooded dips as they carved their way around corners.

The historian of 34 Armoured Brigade recalled the move and assembly with the 51st Highland and 53rd Welsh divisions on the low ground below the Groesbeek Heights:

> The move of 53 miles to concentrate SOUTH of NIJMEGEN was made on our tracks under cover of darkness and in one jump. Once arrived there security demanded no movement of personnel in daylight. Such congested conditions had not been experienced since the NORMANDY bridgehead days, where whole Regiments often sat down in one field. But the great difference now was it was intensely cold and frozen up, so that the tank crews found no hardship in unlimited sleep under cover and regular food at intervals, and were content to wait, knowing that something big was cooking for them just over the GROESBEEK hills in front only 3 miles away.

Infantry aboard a Churchill Mk III an the early version of the 6-pounder gun without a muzzle break.

Eisenhower's Decision

With the nasty surprise of the Ardennes counteroffensive still foremost in his mind, despite the impact of the air offensive against Germany, the Supreme Commander maintained his policy of closing up to the Rhine in order to reduce the possibility of the Germans launching another disruptive counter-offensive. Eisenhower explained:

> In the situation facing us in January, the German enjoyed the great advantage of the Siegfried defences in the area northward from the Saar, inclusive. As long as we allowed him to remain in those elaborate fortifications his ability was enhanced to hold great portions of his long line with relatively weak forces, while he concentrated for spoiling attacks at selected points. This meant that a large proportion of the Allied Force would be immobilized in a protective role, with only that portion on the offensive that could be maintained north of the Ruhr. In that single zone of advance, we could not logistically sustain more than thirty-five divisions.[7]

General Crerar's plans for Operation VERITABLE were presented to Montgomery when he returned north from the Bulge on 16 January. A week later, 21st Army Group's plan for VERITABLE and GRENADE, along with Second

Army's operations to clear the remaining German pockets west of the Maas, were approved in principle by General Eisenhower. Target dates for the operation's D Day were tentatively set for 8 and 10 February.

By mid-January, however, with 12th US Army Group still pushing the Fifth and Sixth Panzer Armies out of the Bulge in the Ardennes, the Supreme Commander delayed giving his final authority to Montgomery. He hoped pressure by General Hodge's First US Army would result in a German collapse in the Ardennes and Eifel that would take the army to the Rhine. In legitimately exploiting success, he would also have been on safe political ground with the US media, but Hodges' army was losing momentum and was soon irrevocably halted. It was not until 28 January that Eisenhower finally gave authority for VERITABLE to be launched as planned on 8 February, but that was not the end of the delays.

Anglo–US relations had plumbed new depths following a combination of Montgomery's lack of tact and a degree of wilful US misunderstanding following a 7 January press conference on the Battle of the Bulge. It resulted in the last vestiges of co-operation between Bradley and Montgomery evaporating. Ordered to break off the battle in the Ardennes on 21 January, Bradley was slow to act and

General Omar Bradley, commander of 12th US Army Group.

21 ARMY GROUP

PERSONAL MESSAGE
FROM THE C-IN-C

(To be read out to all Troops)

1. The operations of the Allies on all fronts have now brought the German war to its final stage. There was a time, some years ago, when it did not seem possible that we *could* win this war; the present situation is that we cannot lose it: in fact the terrific successes of our Russian allies on the eastern front have brought victory in sight.

2. In 21 Army Group we stand ready for the last round.
   There are many of us who have fought through the previous rounds; we have won every round on points; we now come to the last and final round, and we want, and will go for, the knock-out blow.

3. The rules of the last round will be that we continue fighting till the final count; there is no time limit. We know our enemy well; we must expect him to fight hard to stave off defeat, possibly in the vain hope that we may crack before he does. But we shall not crack; we shall see this thing through to the end.
   The last round may be long and difficult, and the fighting hard; but we now fight on German soil; we have got our opponent where we want him; and he is going to receive the knock-out blow: a somewhat unusual one, delivered from more than one direction.

4. You remember the poem written by a soldier of the Eighth Army in Africa before going into battle, in one verse of which he described what he considered we were fighting for:

   "Peace for the kids, our brothers freed,
   A kinder world, a cleaner breed."

   Let us see to it that we achieve this object, so well expressed by a fighting man of the British Empire.

5. And so we embark on the final round, in close co-operation with our American allies on our right and with complete confidence in the successful outcome of the onslaught being delivered by our Russian allies on the other side of the ring.
   Somewhat curious rules, you may say. But the whole match has been *most* curious; the Germans began this all-out contest and they must not complain when in the last round they are hit from several directions at the same time.

6. Into the ring, then, let us go. And do not let us relax till the knock-out blow has been delivered

7. Good luck to you all—and God bless you.

B. L. Montgomery
Field-Marshal
C-in-C 21 Army Group.

Holland
February, 1945

Montgomery's message to the troops that were to take part in Operation VERITABLE.

regroup divisions to Simpson's army, arguing that water that could be released from the Roer dams in his area would prevent Simpson's army attacking across the river below the dams. He wanted to keep these divisions for his own projected 12th US Army Group offensive, hoping to continue to hold the Allied main effort, and he had therefore failed to secure the dams for his own benefit. With Bradley having failed to regroup the divisions as directed, on 1 February Eisenhower was forced to issue a direct order to release the divisions to General Simpson.

The combined impact of Bradley and Hodge's actions, particularly the failure to capture the dams until after the Germans had badly damaged the gates, prevented Simpson from crossing the river until 23 February. This condemned First Canadian Army to fighting without the Ninth US Army's pincer for two weeks rather than the planned two days. There is no doubt this delay cost valuable time and thousands of casualties. It also undermined 21st Army Group's intent to envelop and destroy German forces west of the Rhine, allowing them to withdraw across the river in relatively good order and fight another day.

One of the Roer dams photographed by a RAF PRU aircraft in the days before VERITABLE.

Chapter Two

The Defenders of the Reich

Field Marshal von Rundstedt had been brought back as titular Commander-in-Chief West in September 1944 following his sacking in July at the height of the battle for Normandy. However, he had little power other than to guide his army group commanders, but he was a safe pair of hands and the architect of the German battle for the Rhineland, loyally supporting Hitler's decision to fight west of the Rhine. There was, however, little agreement in the German high command as to where the fighting would be or over their capacity to defend the Reich!

Von Rundstedt believed that the Americans would attack further south, in the area of their salient around Aachen, with the British conducting an assault crossing of the Maas near Venlo several days later. This was a view with which General Blaskowitz, who had taken over Army Group H from General Kurt Student during January 1945, concurred, believing the direct route to the strategically vital Ruhr was the most likely Allied option. Responsible for the long front from Walcheren on the North Sea coast south towards Aachen, Blaskowitz deployed the bulk of German reserves, principally XLVII Panzer Corps, were accordingly placed to cover this southern or Venlo flank. In the aftermath of the Battle of the Bulge, General von Lüttwitz could, however, only muster about ninety panzers across his weak corps to support General Schlemm's First *Fallschirmjäger* Army.

Hitler's vision of the West Wall or Siegfried Line was of an impregnable belt of steel and concrete, however von Rundstedt reported unfavourably to Berlin. General Blumentritt recorded that:

> Rundstedt alluded very critically to the West Wall in a report to the German Supreme Command and described it as a mousetrap – this drastic report about the West Wall aroused Hitler's deepest displeasure. He called it positively insulting and gave it as his opinion that the enemy would tremble before these 'fortifications'.

General Straub, commanding LXXXVI Corps, was also critical of the defences in his area, which were 'a farce ... It wasn't a wall, it was an idea'. The Allies may not have 'trembled' but the difficulty in breaching the Siegfried Line most definitely featured in their calculations.

General Schlemm had taken over command of the First *Fallschirmjäger* Army when its erstwhile commander, General Kurt Student, had been promoted to briefly command Army Group H during the autumn. He disagreed both with Hitler's view of the Siegfried Line and the likely direction of the forthcoming

Allied offensive. His own estimates concluded that the Allies were most likely to attack south from the Groesbeek Heights between the rivers Rhine and Maas. He argued that with the Germans still controlling the Roer dams and its potential flood waters, this could not be the Allied main effort and he further argued that the British would not commit themselves to an assault crossing of the Maas when

Field Marshal von Rundstedt, C in C West.

General Blaskowitz, commander of Army Group H.

they could attack from Groesbeek between the two rivers. Despite the work on his defences of the Reichswald, and the suitability of the direct approach to the Rhine from the Maas at Venlo for armour, Schlemm still concluded that the Reichswald represented a 'side door to the Ruhr' and this was where the Allies were most likely to attack. He had 7th *Fallschirmjäger* Division in reserve, parts of which could intervene in the battle within six hours if tasked promptly. A report on Schlemm's post-war questioning reads:

> Schlemm claims that Blaskowitz at Army Group and Rundstedt, the C-in-C West, believed the next big Allied move would be an American offensive launched from Roermond together with a British attack across the river at Venlo. This was opposed to Schlemm's personal view who expected the big blow to come south through the Reichswald as it eventually did. He advanced this view to his seniors but was constantly assured that there was no evidence of large concentrations in the Nijmegen area. The worst that

General Alfred Schlemm.

could be expected there was a holding attack launched by two or three Canadian Divisions, he was told.

The formation responsible for the majority of the layered defence of the Rhineland south of Nijmegen, including the Reichswald, was General Erich Straube's LXXXVI Corps. Straube was competent but slow to make decisions, often becoming bogged down in minor detail to the great frustration of his staff, who nicknamed him the Little Watchmaker. His view was that the floodplains of the Rhine and Maas and the bulk of the Reichswald were entirely unsuitable for large-scale operations, and he therefore believed that any attack through the

General Erich Straube, 'The Little Watchmaker'.

'side door' was likely to be diversionary. Despite Schlemm's requests, with few reserves available to Blaskowitz, the only reinforcements Straube received were a handful of decidedly second-rate battalions.

The Defences

Following their defeat in Normandy and the precipitate retreat east back to Germany in September 1944, plus subsequent fighting during the autumn, the Germans were back on their border manning the West Wall or Siegfried Line. Its northern extremity in the Reichswald had not been completed during pre-war construction and throughout the length of the line much of its weaponry, fixtures and fittings had been removed to be recycled into the Atlantic Wall. Consequently, most of the hastily renovated concrete positions were used as shelters for the surrounding field positions, which had been dug to thicken up the defences to some depth.

On the First *Fallschirmjäger* Army's front, General Schlemm, believing that the Allies would attack via the 'side door' and the weakest Siegfried defences, prepared their defences in depth. Here, the Germans laboured on three main lines of defence, namely, the Forward Line, the Siegfried Line and the Hochwald Layback. In addition, there were intermediate entrenched positions, and the major Rhineland towns were ringed with defences transforming them into strongpoints.[1]

The Forward Line was a strong outpost position with an anti-tank ditch and a complex double trench system that was occupied by six battalions each on a frontage of approximately 1,500 yards, with depth from the outposts to the rear companies of some 2,000 yards. Here a further line was dug inside the western edge of the Reichswald for the reserve companies. Unlike the defences in the open farmland that had been mapped from air photography, detailed intelligence of this position was limited, as photo reconnaissance was of course blinded by the forest's tree cover.

Much of the vast amount of labour involved in digging these defences had been completed by Soviet prisoners of war and forced labour. The principal features they worked on were anti-tank ditches, which were normally 12–15ft wide at the top, narrowing to 6ft at the bottom, and were 8ft deep, containing 1–4ft of water, depending on the height of the water table. To save labour wherever possible, the numerous drainage ditches that already existed were enlarged. One such on 51st Highland Division's front was the Leigraaf Ditch. To the front of the ditch, minefields had been laid and infantry positions prepared that covered the whole obstacle with overlapping and interlocking arcs of fire. Communication trenches had also been dug, allowing the defenders to redeploy rapidly from one side of the obstacle belt to the other as well as laterally.

Somewhat over 2 miles to the rear, the Siegfried Line defences cut through the Reichswald from Tühees on the edge of the Rhine's floodplain, south to Hekkens, then crossed the River Niers and ran south-east inside the German frontier to the east of the Maas. The sector of the line that XXX Corps was to breach, other than the seven identified large bunkers, lacked the formidable network of concrete casemates that Ninth US Army would encounter further to the south, but such concrete as existed was enhanced by a similar layout of field defences as found in the Forward Line.[2] Again, however, tree cover prevented detailed intelligence being developed, but the stretch of line running 1½ miles to the north of the Reichswald, where 15th Scottish Division was to attack, was well photographed and mapped.

The whole of the Reichswald was considered by the Allies to be 'a self-contained centre of resistance', beyond which were the not inconsiderable intermediate defences on the ridge of high ground known as the Materborn feature, which overlooked the city of Kleve. Of the defended towns beyond the Reichswald and Kleve, General Horrocks wrote:

> ... the small Rhineland towns had been turned into fortresses prepared for all round defence. I was told that the houses of all these German frontier

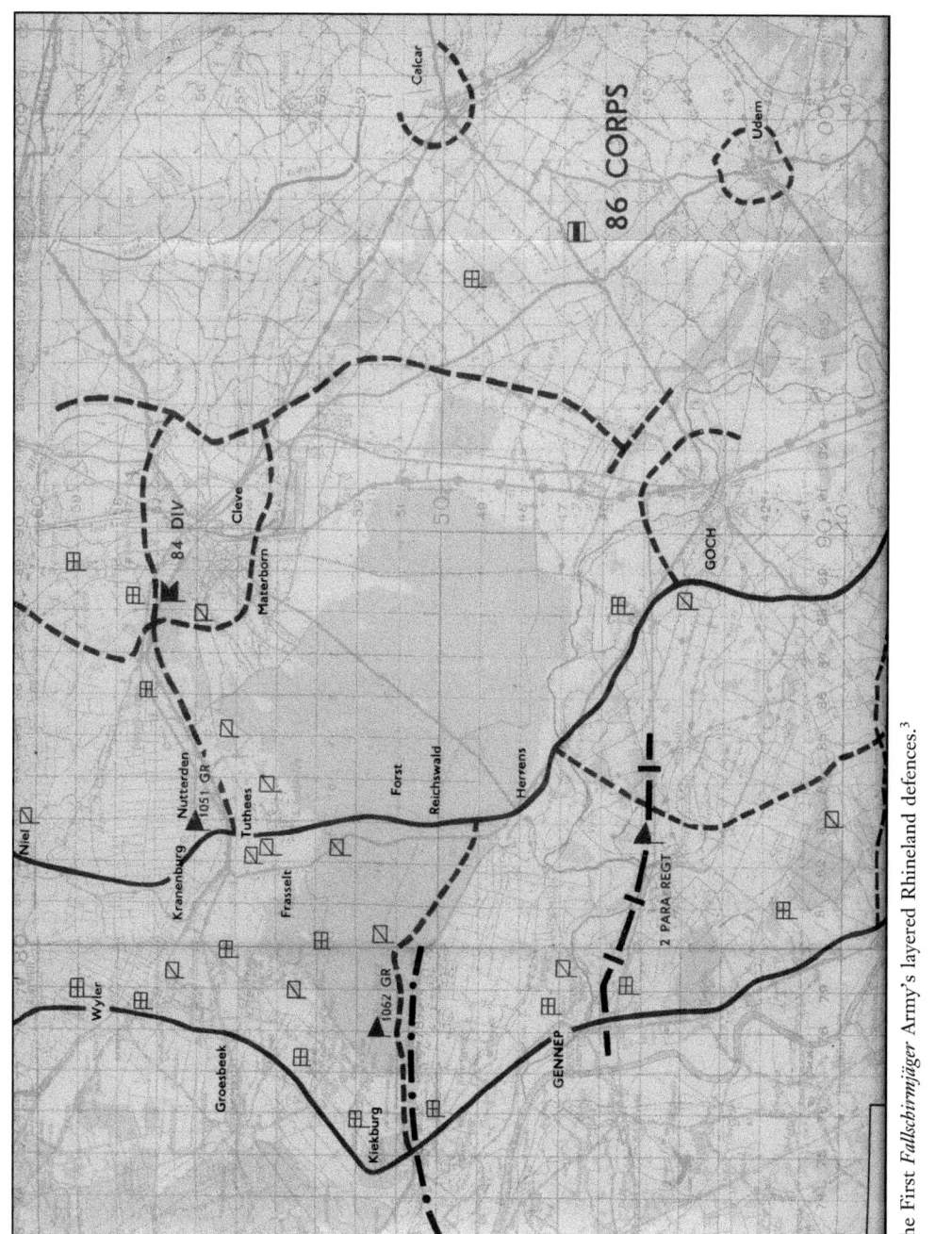

The First *Fallschirmjäger* Army's layered Rhineland defences.[3]

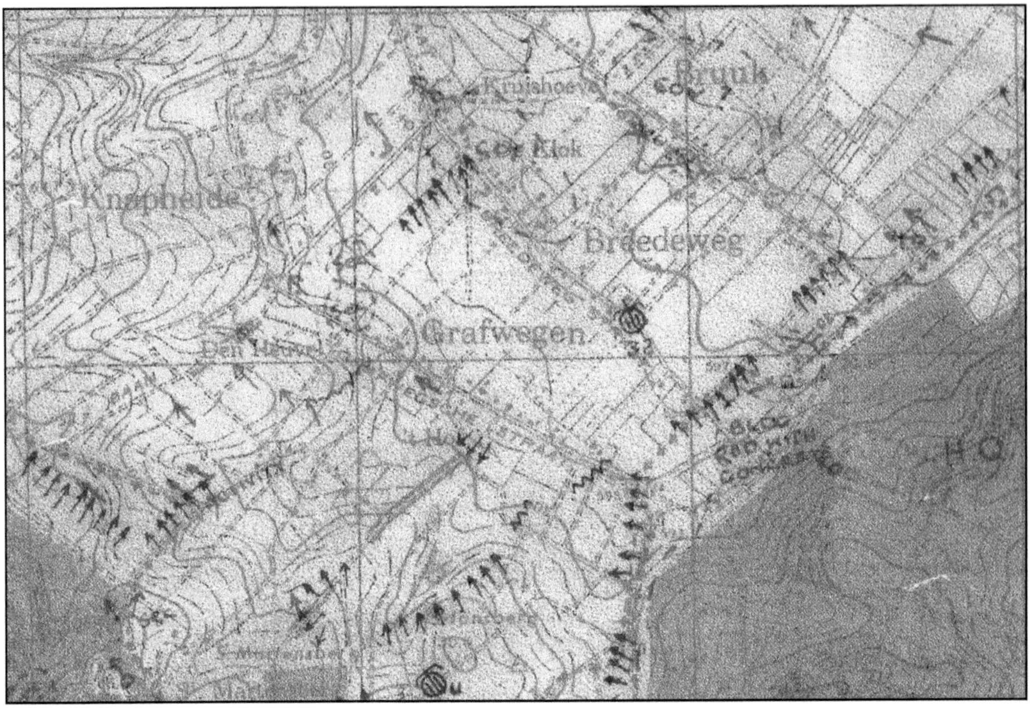

34   *The Battle of the Reichswald*

Extract of the Defences Overprint maps showing the same section of the Forward Line west of the Reichswald on 15 October 1944 (prepared by the 43rd Wessex Division) and the same area in front of 53rd Highland Division on 2 February 1945.[4]

The Defenders of the Reich 35

towns had been specially constructed for battle; with loopholed concrete basements they were capable of all round defence. In war, as in most things, the Germans certainly are thorough ... The chief enemy resistance came from the cellars in the villages.[5]

A further 5 miles south-east lay the defences of the Hochwald 'Layback', which covered the approaches to the Rhine around Xanten.

On the Rhine floodplain there was little in the way of formal defences, as they were simply not needed due to the ground being wet, flat and intersected with drainage ditches and old river channels. During a normal winter the Rhine floods

German civilians digging an anti-tank ditch around Uedem.

were contained by the numerous dykes. The VERITABLE planners were, however, aware that given the return of the Rhine's high-water levels with the thaw, the Germans, by blowing these dykes, would inundate most of the floodplain.

To the south of the Reichswald where 51st Highland Division was to advance, the floodplains of the smaller Maas and Niers rivers were very similar and, as was the case with the Rhine, natural winter floods could extend 1,000 yards astride the Maas and up to 75 yards in the case of the Niers. There were, however, no opportunities for the Germans to create significant inundations, but with numerous ditches and culverts to blow, going on this flank was nonetheless poor.

Defenders of the Reichswald

From 1939 through until the end of 1941 the Germans may have seemed invincible, but Hitler's adventurism in invading Poland had committed Germany to another war for which, by his own estimate, the country was not prepared for. At a naval briefing in July 1939 Hitler told his audience of senior officers that Germany would not be ready to resume the struggle until 1943 or 1944. Despite this the Wehrmacht seemed impressive but there was little depth or resilience in its structures for a long war, and with mounting losses that followed Stalingrad, Tunisia and Kursk in 1943, sustainability reached a critical level. Consequently, by late 1943 Germany was well and truly on the back foot. Add further losses in 1944 on the Eastern Front, Italy and Normandy, and by the autumn of that year the situation for the defence of the Reich, in terms of manpower, equipment and weapons, was critical. The Wehrmacht's capacity to mount a defence was further and fatally undermined by Hitler's Ardennes offensive, thanks to heavy consumption of fuel and ammunition, along with losses of men and armour.

The 84th Infantry Division, deployed in the Reichswald facing XXX Corps' attack, was typical of German formations fighting in the west in early 1945. The division had been formed from the *Erzatzheer* (Reserve Army) during 1943 and deployed to the 15th Army in the Pas-de-Calais during February 1944. When the invasion came, the 84th was at Rouen and, along with most of the rest of the German infantry divisions, it was only released to march to Normandy in July. Then it was a slow business, conducted by night thanks to Allied air interdiction. Arriving on 4 August, the division joined LXXXIV Corps, which was struggling to contain the US breakout. The division fought at Vire and during the Mortain counter-attack before being encircled in the Falaise pocket, from which only one regiment and supporting arms escaped. The 84th's original commander, General Menny, was captured.

Having suffered losses of 5,500 men, the remnants of the division fell back to the Somme and subsequently marched back across northern France to the borders of Germany. While fighting the Guards Armoured and 82nd US Airborne divisions in the Nijmegen area during September 1944, General Heinz Fiebig took command of the shattered division.

At the outbreak of war in 1939, Major Fiebig had led an infantry battalion during the Polish campaign. By August 1944, via various regimental, staff and

84th Infantry Division's badge.

General Heinz Fiebig.

training appointments, as a colonel he rose to divisional command, briefly in Russia and then for a short period he led the 712nd Coastal Division in Belgium. Having taken command of the 84th Infantry Division, Fiebig was responsible for its reconstitution back in Germany to the *Aufstellungswelle* 32 (recruitment wave 32 of late 1944) order of battle. He was promoted to *Generalmajor* in December 1944 and established his headquarters in the eastern suburbs of the city of Kleve some 10 miles behind his division's front line.

General Fiebig was 6ft tall and described as being 'striking and usually debonair'. His post-war British interrogators, however, described him as 'a charming fellow to have at a party; the last man to lead a division in the field'.

Although the 84th Division was not titled a '*Volksgrenadier* division' as many others had been during the autumn, it was reconstituted with a mix of rear-area units; a *Landwehr* fortress battalion, redundant Luftwaffe and Kriegsmarine personnel, along with conscripts. However, it broadly conformed to the same

Welle 32 establishment, but every division differed in detail thanks to shortages and weapons being issued in lieu of those that were unavailable. A variety of *Volkssturm* units were attached from neighbouring towns but again details are scant.

The division initially consisted of two regiments, with a third, the 1062 Grenadier Regiment, joining the division in December; each regiment now being reorganised with two battalions. There was also an independent fusilier battalion,[6] which was mobile to an extent on bicycles, for the recce and 'fire brigade' roles. Attached to the division were two police battalions and two others made up of soldiers that were incapacitated in two ways, there was an ear or *ohern* battalion and a stomach or *magen* battalion. The bayonet strength of the 84th was by January 1945 approximately 4,000 infantrymen plus 1,500 attachments.

The usual divisional troops such as pioneers and artillery had been reduced to weak battalions or companies numbering approximately 4,200. Along with reductions in infantry manpower, this had seen the German infantry division progressively drop in overall manpower from a total of 18,000 men in 1939 to 10,279, and even then few divisions were up to strength.

With regard to weaponry, the reduction in manpower had been to an extent compensated for by the introduction of an automatic assault rifle, the *Sturmgewehr* 44, and additional light machine guns, which provided an overall increase in firepower. Artillery was similarly reduced to seven batteries each of four guns

The *Sturmgewehr* 44, a weapon emblematic of late-war German infantry.

The 120mm mortar and crew. The *Granatwerfer* 42 was an almost exact copy of the Soviet weapon that had been captured in large numbers. Both mortars hurled a 15.6kg bomb 6,050 metres.

across three battalions, but companies of four 120mm mortars each were found in the infantry regiments to compensate.

The highly effective Pax 40 75mm anti-tank gun had by early 1945 been completely replaced in infantry regiments by additional handheld weapon systems including the *Panzerschreck* 43/54 launchers (six per battalion) and a plentiful supply of its shorter-range cousin, the *Panzerfaust*.

The divisional *panzerjäger* battalion now had just a single company of nine towed Pak 40 guns and a company of self-propelled anti-tank-guns (Stug III, Stug IV or Hetzer). As there was no longer a flak battalion, the company of nine 37mm *Flakvierling* now formed the *panzerjäger* battalions' third company.

Post-war British operational analysis demonstrated an increased reliance by the Germans on handheld anti-tank weapons. They calculated armoured losses to

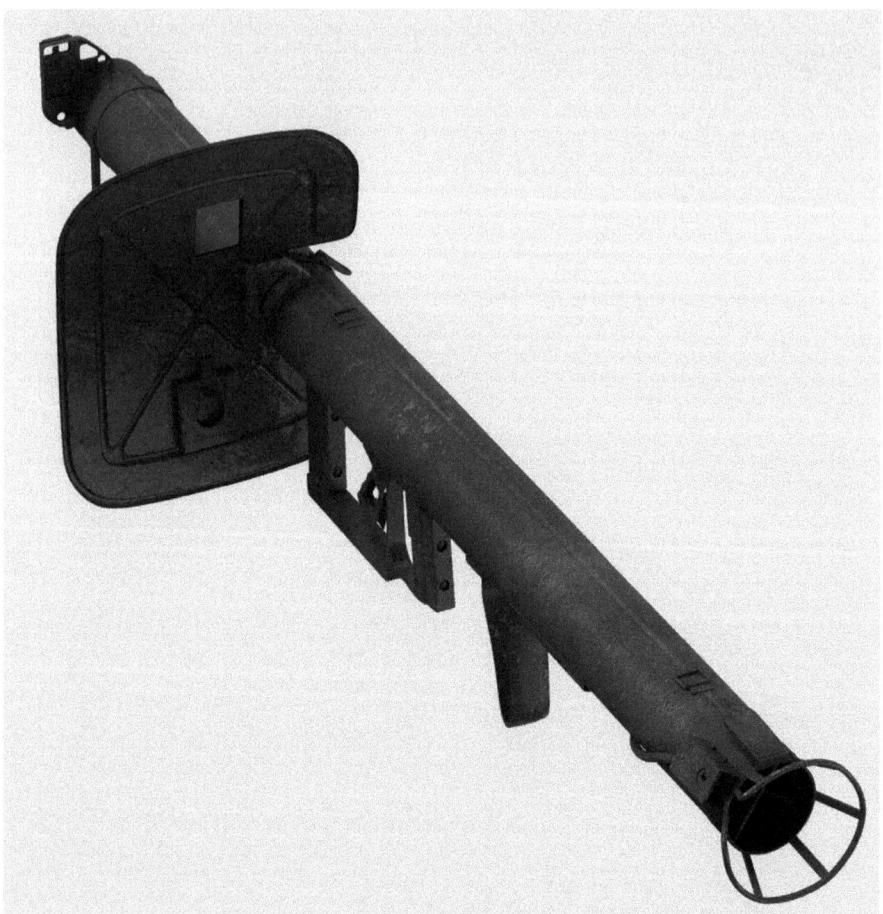

The *Raketen Panzerbühse* 43 anti-tank rocket launcher, better known as the *Panzershreck*.

these weapons in Normandy was just 6 per cent, but later in the North West European Campaign, when the number of 75mm anti-tank guns dwindled, this figure increased to 34 per cent.

It is clear from the number of *panzerjäger* and artillery pieces faced by XXX Corps during the first two days that General Fiebig had under his command some LXXXVI Corps assets. When it was accepted that the Allied attack was not a feint, Schlemm's own units of Army troops, which had already been rushed to the front, were later joined by 655th Schwere *Panzerjäger* Battalion. This unit had a company of the highly effective *Jagdpanthers* and two companies of *Jagdpanzer* IVs[7] to bolster the division's defences. The 655th *panzerjäger* was reported to have a strength of thirty-six vehicles at the time of the Bulge but this had been reduced to twenty operational by late January 1945.

The *Jagdpanther* of 655 *Schwere Panzerjäger* Battalion. This AFV used the same 88mm gun as the Tiger, while the *Jagdpanzer* IV had the same 75mm gun as the Panther.

A *Flakpanzer* IV of 655 *Schwere Panzerjäger* Battalion, known as the *Mobelwagen* (removal van) due to its high sides in traveling configuration. 655 had four of these on strength at the start of the battle, plus another four quad-barreled 20mm *Flakvierling Wirblewind*.

German Intelligence

Thanks to XXX Corps' operational security measures during the move north from the shoulder of the Bulge, plus the Germans' own convictions that the Allied blow would fall further south, they lacked useful warning of the offensive through the Reichswald Plug.

Though not sharing his commander's views on the likelihood of the Reichswald being subjected to the main Allied attack, throughout January General Straub regularly dispatched patrols as deep as 6 miles into Allied territory. Lying up for two to three days observing, these patrols only reported seeing the vehicles of 2nd and 3rd Canadian divisions and soldiers wearing the distinctive green-coloured Canadian battledress. This was nothing to be concerned about but following a rare day of Luftwaffe reconnaissance flights on 6 February (D-2), the Germans spotted indicators of Allied concentration and preparations for an offensive. Camouflaged supply dumps were identified and what had hitherto been reported as dummy artillery positions were occupied by men and guns. The forward dumping programme had begun on 26 January and by 6 February, the number of troops and weapons and the vast dumps of supplies and ammunition were almost impossible to conceal.

Though still not entirely convinced that the impending attack would be little more than a diversionary affair, Blaskowitz was prevailed upon by Schlemm to redeploy a regiment from the Twenty-Fifth Army to bolster LXXXVI Corps in the Reichswald. What this reinforcement of just 2,000 men lacked in numbers it made up for in both the quality of men and weapons. As a part of the original *fallschirmjäger* division, 2 *Fallschirmjäger* Regiment had retained much of its quality and by 3 February it was positioned around the south-west tip of the Reichswald, where it proved to be the toughest of the defenders to overcome. The presence of the *fallschirmjäger* reinforcements was, however, revealed to 51st Highland Division's intelligence staff by three deserters brought in by a Canadian patrol.

Fallschirmjäger, equipped with a variety of helmets and uniforms typical of the late war, evacuate a casualty on the company hand cart.

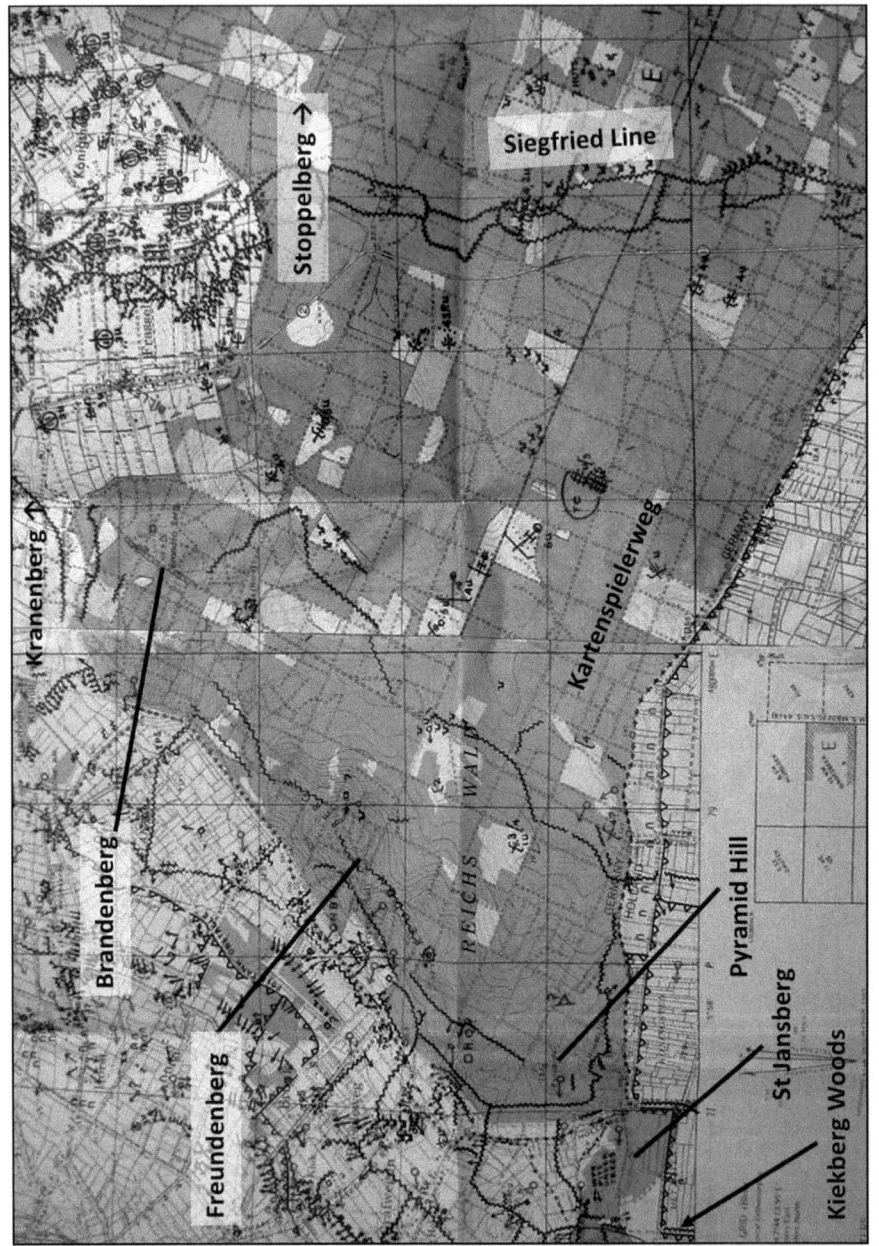

An extract of the Reichswald tactical overprint map.

Chapter Three

The Opening Fires

> The artillery support for Operation VERITABLE was intended to be a battle-winning factor. [BAOR Battlefield Tour, 1947]

When orders were passed down to troop level, Lieutenant Foley and his NCO tank commanders wondered why H Hour on 8 February for the attack was not to be until mid-morning:

> 'What I can't understand,' said Sergeant Robinson, 'is why we're starting at half-past ten in the morning instead of the usual crack of dawn or nightfall.'
>
> I agreed it was a very gentlemanly hour at which to start a battle, and I told the troop to get as much sleep as they could because the way I looked at things we weren't going to get much of it once the fun began.

With no other option than to launch a frontal attack on the Reichswald, General Horrocks needed to blast his way through the German defences. Consequently, the Army and Corps artillery staff argued that they needed time and daylight for accuracy and therefore effectiveness of the artillery fire and air attack.

The 1,050 guns that had been brought in by stages during the long cold winter nights had finally reached their pre-dug positions during 4 February, but remained silent and well camouflaged, with no daylight movement permitted (see map on page 14 for formation gun areas).

Concealed stacks of ammunition were ready on the gun positions but behind them lay a logistic chain stretching back to the Army roadhead and beyond to Antwerp. While the guns were being brought forward, some 500,000 rounds of

(Left) The red on blue shoulder flash of 2nd Canadian Army Group, Royal Artillery. (Right) The cap badge of the Royal Artillery.

assorted ammunition was dumped in the forward area ready for the opening of the battle, much of it concealed along hedgerows:

> Over one thousand guns, not including anti-tank and Bofors guns, were in support of the attack and initially it was primarily an artillery battle. In planning the operation, it had been decided to take full advantage of the great superiority in artillery and have a heavy preliminary bombardment. The Corps Commander accepted the resultant loss of surprise for the initial attack but stressed the need for reducing as much as possible the time taken to complete the pre-H-Hour programme ... It was hoped to saturate the enemy positions to such an extent that local reinforcement, ammunition supply and movement would be really difficult. As the initial attack was being carried out simultaneously by four divisions, each on a narrow front, both its support and the artillery preparation were planned by the CCRA [Corps Commander Royal Artillery] with the active co-operation of divisions at all stages. Any special tasks which divisions wanted to engage were passed to Corps for inclusion in the programme.[1]

Artillery planning on the scale of VERITABLE required extra resources at both Army and corps level. The BAOR historian continued:

> Extra officers and draughtsmen were employed on the RA Corps staff for the production of this plan and a Royal Engineer reproduction section was attached. The planning team was divided into two, one portion doing the plan, the other dealing with the operation orders, moves, assembly and briefing. Another officer was responsible for the ammunition. Barrage and smoke screen traces were issued on 5 February whilst the bombardment traces and task tables followed a day later. The CCRA's final conference was held on 4 February which was rather late. It would have been easier if the deadline for alterations to the fire plan had been a day earlier. An overprint 1: 25,000 map showing the fire plan, code names for groups of targets and target numbers was produced and issued down to company commander level. These maps proved very valuable.

Not since D Day had mapping and tables been so freely circulated down to company commander level.

Forward Observation Officer Lieutenant Blackburn, away from his OP in Groesbeek Molen, visited his battery's gun position on the eve of VERITABLE:

> The command posts are still completing a mountain of work. The details of the fire-plan for many concentrations and a barrage, including overprinted maps and traces, accompanied by all sorts of complicated timing-schedules and scales of fire, were only received by command post staffs at 7:30 P.M., and the strain of deciphering the meaning of it all and working out the fire-plans for the guns has put everybody in a foul mood. They all pose the obvious question: if they could build roads and bridges, and move up

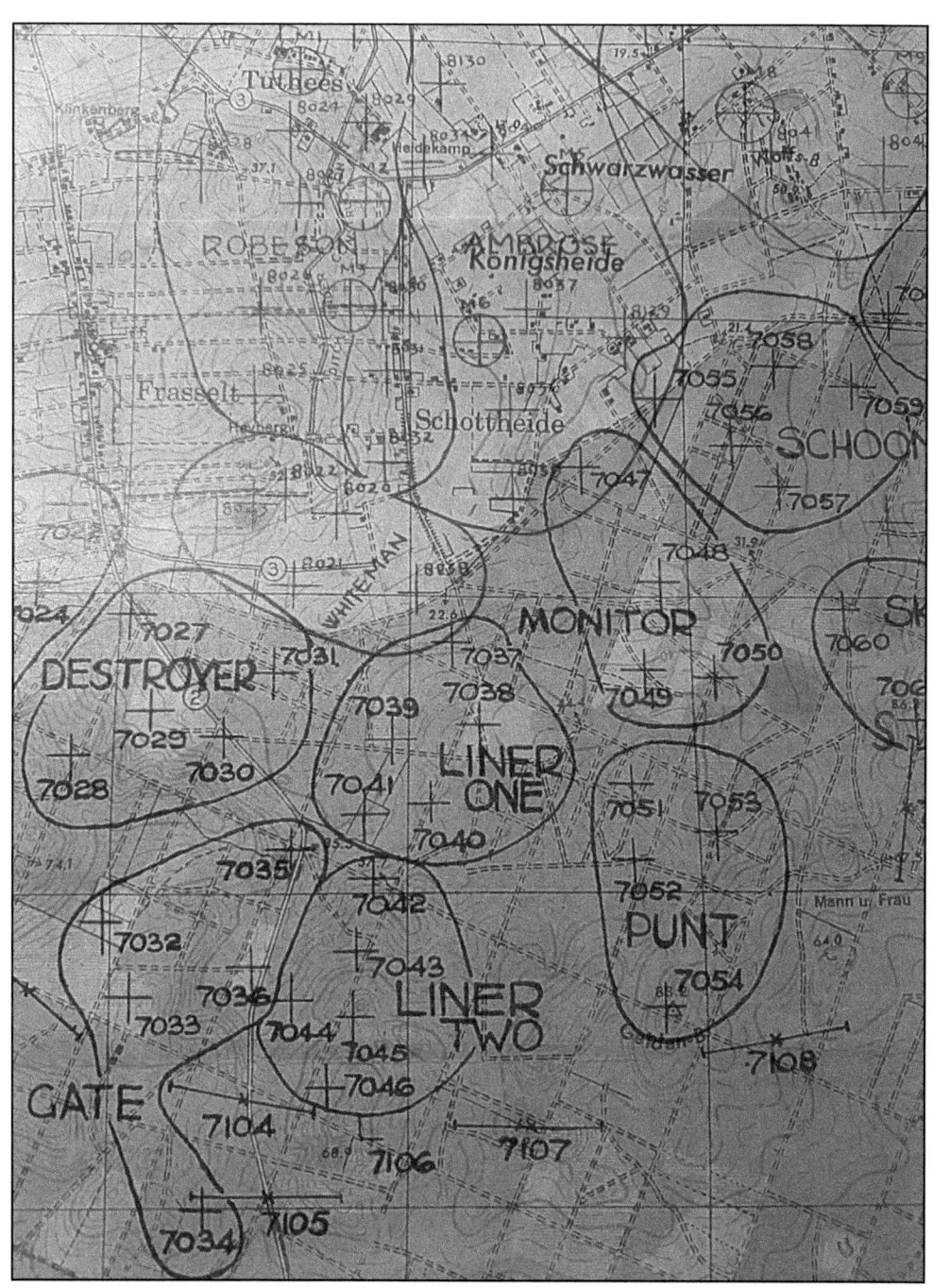

An extract of the 1:25,000 artillery overprint map showing targets for 15th Scottish (top) and 52rd Welsh divisions.

thousands of tons of ammunition in the sixteen days since Monty gave the order for the push, why the hell couldn't the arty brass have completed their plans for the guns sooner?

After a night of little sleep, the gunners' preliminary fires were to begin at 0500 hours, but with artillery commanders estimating that they needed three hours of daylight to complete the fire plan, H Hour would not be until 1030 hours, in order to ensure the fire on both the field and concrete defences was effective.

Included in the preliminary bombardment were PEPPERPOT shoots at specific targets requested by divisions. In these shoots all the Bofors, tanks' main armament, anti-tank guns, mortars and machine guns, which were not required on other tasks, were to engage with indirect fire on the specially selected targets. This deluge fire lasting ten minutes as each PEPPERPOT was fired in turn, was designed to neutralise key points in the enemy's defences and to destroy his morale. The 51st Highland Division's machine gun battalion, 1st/7th Middlesex, for instance fired 7,000,000 .303 rounds from the battalion's seventy-two Vickers guns and thousands of 4.2in mortar rounds in support of PEPPERPOT shoots during the course of the day.

The corps CRA's plan briefed at a conference on 26 January was complex but the outline for the preliminary fire plan lifted from the corps artillery operation order reads:

> Prior to 0500 hours: No fire except normal activity by 2 and 3 Cdn Divs.
> 0500–0730 hours: Artillery Preparation. Bombardment including counter battery, counter mortar and PEPPERPOT.

Bofors anti-aircraft guns with Canadian gunners unpacking rounds and clearing empty cartridge cases during a PEPPERPOT shoot.

0730–0740 hours: Deception smoke screen covering the Corps front.
0740–0750 hours: Silence. Sound ranging and flash spotting detachments detecting active enemy hostile batteries and mortars.
0750–0915 hours: Artillery preparation as above.
0915–1300 hours: Smoke screen north west edge of REICHSWALD.
0920 hours: Intense Counter-battery on the results of information gained earlier. Opening line of barrage (mixed HE and smoke). Rate of fire very slow.
1000–1030 hours: Thickening up of barrage.
H Hour and first lift of the barrage. Smoke screen on 2 Cdn Div left flank.

Control of counter-battery fire was vested in 5 AGRA and the ten-minute check fire or 'silence' was designed to make the Germans believe the attack had started, which it was hoped would prompt the enemy to begin the defensive fire with mortars and artillery. This enabled the detachments of two survey regiments,[2] which were deployed to each division on the Groesbeek Heights, to use sound-ranging equipment and flash spotting to plot German artillery positions. In addition, the emerging technology of mortar-locating radar was to be used. The resulting data from both systems was to be rushed to HQ 5 AGRA and the waiting artillery staff would then plot the location of enemy batteries, including ones that had up to that morning remained masked. At 0920 hours, with the locations of enemy gun positions circulated to the AGRAs' medium batteries, heavy counter-battery fire would be opened for forty minutes. In the event, no fewer than forty-five enemy batteries and nineteen mortar positions were identified or confirmed and this contributed to a much-reduced German response when the advance began. A prisoner of 2nd Battalion, 184 Artillery Regiment, reported that six out of twelve guns had been put out of action by counter-battery fire before the battle started.

Lieutenant Blackburn continued his account of the wait for the opening barrage:

> It's now drizzling rain, cold and miserable – a rotten morning for the gun crews, all of whom have been at their guns for some time now completing the preparation of ammo for the big shoot, taking shells out of their cases, removing safety caps, and stacking them in piles handy to the guns. And as you slosh through mud and stumble up and down over incredibly deep water-filled ruts left by the trucks and quads pulling and winching guns into position around here during the night, you feel for the poor late-arriving British gunners, and most especially for their command post staffs. It must be wicked trying to set up under such wretched conditions for a shoot of such magnitude.
>
> As you pass behind 26th and 14th [battery] positions, and in front of other British field and medium regiments that have been slotted into spaces behind and beside them during the night, you can see very little in the windy, wet darkness, but there are faint sounds of voices calling out orders, and brief,

glowing flickers of subdued light from hooded lamps-electric hovering over dial-sights of guns getting a final check of their 'parallelism' – making sure all are perfectly on line.

Silhouettes of gun muzzles poke up against the night sky where previously there were only scrubby pines. Unseen hordes of gunners, dripping with rain, are now standing to their guns as they carry out last-minute tasks. By the time

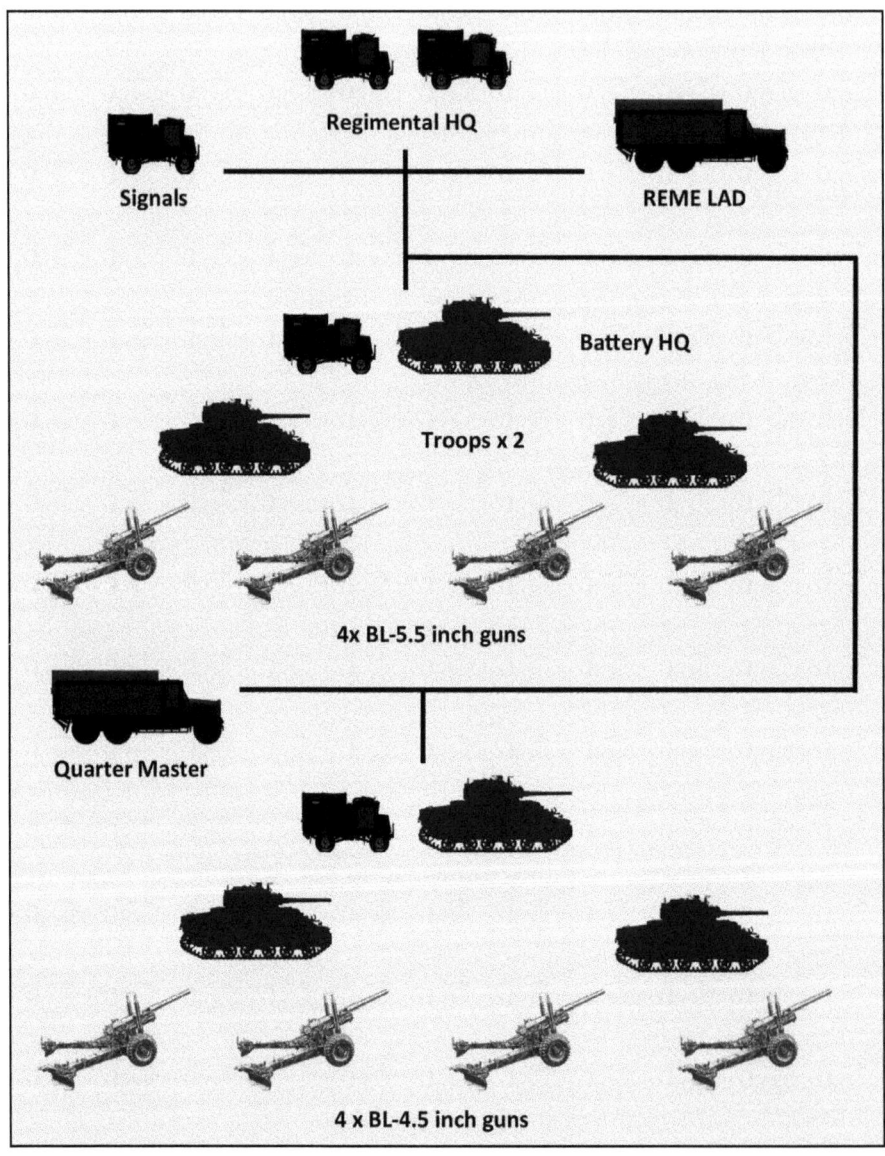

The organisation of RA and RCA medium regiments, including armoured observation post tanks.

you make it to 2nd Battery, ghostly faint voices from Tannoy speakers in gun pits are calling 'Take Post,' an order presently being given on scores of positions. You try to visualize 9,000 gunners arranging themselves in customary gun-drill positions behind their weapons awaiting H-hour, five minutes away.

Until firing gets under way you decide to stay out of the hair of Lieut. Jack Bigg, who is in charge of Baker Troop guns this morning in place of the GPO [gun position officer] Doug MacFarlane, who is up in the Groesbeek windmill, one of twenty [Canadian] forward observers ...[3]

Meanwhile, in an assembly area alongside 51st Highland Division, in the woods to the west of Groesbeek, Lieutenant Foley recalled that 'it was about eleven o'clock that night before I finally rolled into my blankets'. Having satisfied himself that all was 'teed up and ready to go' he mused:

'Oh, well,' I yawned. 'I'll probably sleep until nine-ish, a leisurely wash and shave, some breakfast, and then Heigh Ho for the Start Line.'

It was a nice dream while it lasted. But at five o'clock the following morning I was nearly blasted from my blankets by a deafeningg barrage of noise. The ground shook with the fury of the cannonade and the walls of the sixty-pound tent whipped in and out like sparrows' wings.

We sat up in our blankets, and by means of a mixture of shouting and sign language we agreed that we'd never heard such a noise. Sleep was quite out of the question, so we dressed and went outside the tent. Overhead a solid curtain of Bofors' tracers indicated that even the 40 mm anti-aircraft guns were being used to thicken up the barrage, and the sky behind us was alight with the continual flicker of gunfire.

From the front of our wood, it seemed that the edge of the Reichswald was a solid mass of explosions and it appeared impossible that anything could live in that inferno.

A 25-pounder gun and its ammunition stacked high for the opening barrage.

'It should be a walk-over by half-past ten!' shouted Bob Webster; but we both knew that the Germans had a peculiar aptitude for emerging unscathed from the fiercest bombardment. Still, it was an encouraging thought.

While Lieutenant Foley and his troop were denied their sleep, the British and Canadian gunners laboured on the fire plan. The BAOR historian explained:

> The preliminary bombardment for each phase was to follow the principle of hitting known enemy localities, headquarters and communications as often as possible in the time available. Each locality was to be subjected to an increasing intensity of fire until the morale of the enemy had been shattered. Five bombardments were to be carried out between 0500 hours 8 February and 0100 hours 9 February and each target was to receive a minimum of six tons of shells. 2 Cdn Div, which had been holding the sector for some time, air photographs and defence overprints supplied the information from which targets were selected and grouped. To make control more easy bombardment groups were formed for each target area.

An officer in 2nd Canadian Division's historical section described the scene:

> The weather promised to be fair, and the sight of the airbursts and tracers in the sky, against the yellow light of the rising sun was very impressive. There was continuous roll of heavy gunfire that was punctuated by staccato bursts of MG fire from all sides ...

One of the Vickers machine guns that fired tens of thousands of rounds in the indirect fire role during PEPPERPOTS, as well as thickening up the barrage. The Mk VIIIz .303 ammunition for indirect fire gave the Vickers a useful range of 4,500 yards in the 'bombardment' role, rather than the normal 2,000 yards.

A few birds were still flying across the sky in a bewildered manner, as the artillery took up their theme again, and the tempo accelerated as the full weight of 1,000 guns was brought to bear against the enemy. Beyond the occasional airburst, and the odd round over a wide area, there was little reply from the enemy and, at this stage, the spectator was left with the impression that hostile positions were being simply smothered. The gaunt trunks and torn branches of trees, ruined farm buildings, and the smoke and cordite fumes that swept across the area all contributed to the strange and fascinating panorama of war.[4]

According to prisoners questioned by First Canadian Army, the concentration of fire had a great effect on their morale, crews were unable to man their weapons until the barrage lifted, and 'communications were totally disrupted':

The Germans had the impression of overwhelming force opposed to them, which, in their isolated state, with no communications, it was useless to resist. On the other hand, prisoners generally agreed that casualties from the bombardment were not high, on a rough average only five per cent. Equipment suffered more than personnel. Counter-battery fire seems to have prevented very much enemy shelling during the attack. During the day well over half a million rounds were fired ...

German Reaction

Even though his headquarters was nearly 20 miles from the front near Rees, General Schlemm was awakened by the noise of the bombardment. With the staff of First *Fallschirmjäger* Army rushing to their desks, Schlemm, convinced that the offensive he had expected had begun, drove forward to assess the situation for himself. Everything he heard from General Fiebig at Headquarters 84th Infantry Division in Kleve confirmed his belief, even though one of the Army Group liaison officers voiced the opinion that it could be a deception. Having on his own initiative ordered 7th *Fallschirmjäger* Division to concentrate for a counter-attack at Gennep, Schlemm returned to his headquarters to report by telephone to Army Group H and request the deployment of XLVII Panzer Corps to his command. General Blastowitz, despite the scale of the bombardment and the attack, was not prepared to act, saying that they must 'consider the possibility of a British attack via Venlo' until 'it is clearly established that the bulk of the British forces are in the Kleve area'. Thanks to good Allied operational security, the basis of German concerns was that their intelligence had been unable to locate XXX Corps since they came out of the line in the Ardennes–Liege area, and Blastowitz was also rightly concerned that the Ninth US Army would join the offensive from the south. Consequently, not only did the army group commander reject the request for the deployment of XLVII Panzer Corps, but he also ordered 7th *Fallschirmjäger* Division back to Venlo.

The German conviction that 21st Army Group's main blow would fall in Second Army's sector further south played into the hands of generals Crerar and

Horrocks. If they were able to break into the Reichswald and overcome the Siegfried Line defences in the fight through the forest, before German reinforcements could arrive, VERITABLE would be making a good start.

Air Support

Winter weather permitting, VERITABLE was to be aided by lavish air support by the Second Tactical Air Force. Support was planned by the RAF officers from Headquarters 84 Group in conjunction with Canadian Army and XXX Corps Headquarters. However, due to the unpredictability of February weather and the twenty-four hour limit on forecasting at that time, it was originally proposed that D Day could be delayed by a day to ensure air support. On 1 February, however, SHAEF ordered that VERITABLE was to start on 8 February no matter what flying conditions pertained.

In addition to the heavy bombers, medium aircraft were available from the RAF's No. 2 Group and the USAAF's Ninth Air Force. The plan for their use was:

> *Before D Day.* Road and rail interdiction against railways, bridges and ferries leading to the battle area. In this case care was to be taken not to give any indication of the point of attack. Selected ammunition, petrol and stores dumps were also to be attacked.
>
> *D-1.* Focal points leading to the main battlefield [Kleve, Goch, etc.] to be attacked by heavy bombers with further interdiction on the main North and South routes in the battlefield area.

An RAF Regiment armoured car with a Vickers K gun providing air defence to an airfield in Holland.

Night of D-1/D Day. Villages and towns selected by Intelligence [Uedem, Kalkar, etc.] to be attacked but care to be taken to avoid heavy cratering.

D Day. The main task was the destruction and demoralisation of the enemy in the NUTTERDEN and MATERBORN defences. Isolation of the battlefield was to be achieved by armed reconnaissance and intruders by night. Artillery was to be silenced by attacks by fighter bombers controlled by a Forward Control Post (FCP). Military headquarters and telephone communications were to be attacked but not at the expense of close support.

Night of D Day/D+1. All approaches to the battlefield area to be covered to prevent the arrival of enemy reserve formations. These routes were to be selected as a result of information received from tactical reconnaissance and armed reconnaissance on D Day.

D+1. All roads and railways leading to the battle area and *all* the RHINE crossings to be covered by armed and tactical reconnaissance in order to maintain an effective disruption in the possible arrival of enemy reserves.[5]

In addition to these planned sorties, a Forward Control Post (FCP) was to be deployed with XXX Corps to support the fighting in the Reichswald Plug by processing requests from division for strikes by fighter-bombers. The FCP had in support an experimental Mobile Radar Control Post that in the event of poor weather could assist in directing aircraft to target areas.

A wing of 84 Group's fighter-bombers operated as a cab rank circling west of the Maas awaiting calls from the FCP. A system of 'contact cars' had been

Wherever possible, British and Canadian fighter-bomber squadrons operated from former Luftwaffe air bases captured during the autumn of 1944 rather than temporary airfields.

developed in Normandy, where once control of the attacking aircraft was handed over by the FCP, fellow pilots speaking direct to the aircraft by radio would direct the fighter-bombers to their target or recce area. Four such 'cars', normally tanks or armoured cars with suitable radios, were available for deployment as the advance progressed through the enemy position.

A system of continuous replacement at a rate of four aircraft every five minutes would ensure that there were sufficient aircraft airborne at any one time to support initially the four and later five divisions in action.

Initial fighter-bomber targets were, however, planned to be in depth beyond the artillery bombardment, with interdiction sorties to attack movement of enemy reserves, in particular reinforcement to the Nutterden and Materborn features, which were key to the early breakout from the confines of the Reichswald Plug.

H Hour

At 0915 hours, as the final phase of the barrage began, smoke rounds were fired across the front to provide cover for the assault troops from four of the five infantry divisions, as they completed their moves forward from their assembly areas in the woods. They threaded their way through the defensive positions of 2nd Canadian Division and shook out in the FUPs ready to cross their start lines at 1030 hours. A Canadian historical officer wrote:

> As H-hr approached, if anything, the noise increased, and a new note was added by the sound of armour moving forward and planes passing overhead. The combined effect produced a vivid picture of a war of machines – a war of calculated and terrible efficiency. A wounded soldier, with face covered by a field dressing, was directed to a nearby RAP, as pockets of smoke began to fill the contours in the ground. The historical officer and war artist were compelled to shout at each other in order to make themselves heard above the noise. Carriers rattled by, with red cross flags prominently displayed, and a tp of Cromwell tanks [*sic*] that had been camouflaged with straw against the walls of a demolished barn added their guttural roar to the din of battle.
>
> Churchill and Sherman tanks began to move east along the draw in square 7556, through the scattered debris of gliders that remained from the airborne attack of the previous September. At 0950 hrs the barrage, which represented the climax of the preliminary bombardment, was observed to be beginning. Capt Hunter and Capt Pepper proceeded down the draw to observe the armour and specialized assault equipment moving forward. Besides the orthodox types of tanks, there were Flails, Crocodiles, AVREs all with their fluorescent panels (for identification from the air) glowing like red hot plates against the dull background. A tank officer enquired anxiously about minefields but could not be satisfied. The armour lurched forward with all vehicles stripped for action – one tank still had a frying pan dangling from the back of the turret. An Air OP flew slowly overhead, and smoke shells continued to drop a short distance in front, as the deafening noise

AVREs negotiating deep furrows left by those ahead of them.

increased. Some enemy rounds dropped about 300 yards distant, and personnel took cover but the armoured advance went on without hesitation. There was an air of urgency and tense expectation evident everywhere as H-Hr approached.

The advance from the start lines across no-man's-land was preceded by a barrage 500 yards in depth, 'consisting of three lines of field artillery 100 yards apart and two lines of medium artillery superimposed, also 100 yards apart'. Rather than

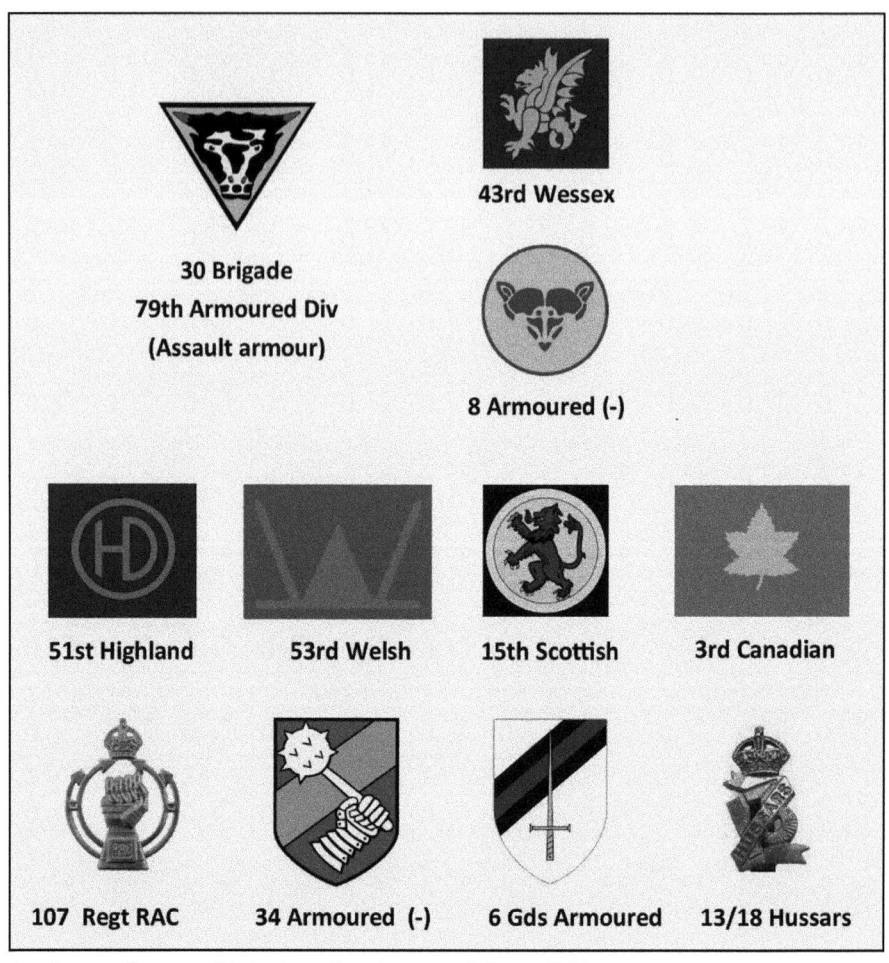

Attachment of armoured brigades and regiments to infantry divisions.

creeping forward it would move in blocks of 300 yards every 12 minutes. To allow the infantry commanders to control their advance:

> ... a minute before the end of firing on each block all guns on the front line ceased firing high explosive. One gun per troop then immediately fired one round of yellow smoke indicating that no more high explosive would land on that line and that the barrage would lift ...

This proved to be effective 'the lift of 300 yards enabled troops to make a tactical advance between lifts and made unnecessary the demoralising plod forward behind and at the speed of the normal barrage'.

Chapter Four

Attack on the Forward Position

General Horrocks was looking out over the open country and the German defences between the wooded Groesbeek Heights and the Reichswald, across which the leading units of his corps would advance:

> In the early hours of 8 February, I climbed into my Command Post for the battle; it had been constructed for me by the Royal Engineers and consisted of a platform half-way up a large tree. From here I could see most of the valley in front, and I was connected by line with a group of small scout cars below me at the bottom of the tree, each of which was tuned in on the same wireless link with a similar vehicle at the advance HQ of each of the divisions taking part. From my viewpoint I could follow the progress of the attack by the lifts in the barrage. Everything seemed to be going according to plan, though units began to complain (over the air) more and more about the state of the going ...

The barrage was likened to a 'wall of fire'. It was some 4,500 yards wide and 500 yards deep, falling across the front of the advance of the Welsh, Canadian and Scottish divisions, with some simple maths indicating that about 6,500 shells were detonating in every grid square per hour. A Canadian war artist recorded:

> At 10:29, as a line of yellow smoke-shells indicated the final minute before the barrage lifted, infantry and tanks began to pass through the 2nd Cnd Division's forward defensive line on that grey, drizzly morning, to advance into Germany. It soon turned out that the weather had taken side with the enemy, in the form of a wet that unavoidably slowed down progress of what should have been a fast thrust by a highly mechanized force to a mud begrimed crawl. Operation Veritable unavoidably began to run behind schedule.

The weather at daylight had been promising, allowing aircraft to get away to a good start on what was hoped would be a full day's programme of air strikes:

> Successful sorties were flown by the tactical groups with the object of disrupting communications between HOLLAND and GERMANY at TERBORG, ZEVENAAR and ARNHEM. KRANENBURG, where the enemy had an ammunition dump, was attacked but the weather soon deteriorated.

General Horrocks commented that the drizzle that set in as the morning progressed, made 'life even more unpleasant, if possible, for the unfortunate infantry-

General Horrocks up on his OP platform shortly after dawn on 8 February 1945.

men and preventing any support from the air'. However, thanks to the artillery barrage:

> The enemy was completely bemused, and very little resistance was encountered; our worst enemies that day were mines and mud. The continual rain [that started later] turned the terrain into a quagmire. Mud and still more mud must be the chief memory of anyone who fought in this battle.

53rd Welsh Division

General Ross' plan for his division's attack on the northern part of the Reichswald was to breach the Germans' forward defences, held by their old adversary 84th Division, which the Welsh had fought against around Falaise during the final phase of the Normandy campaign. 71 Brigade was to lead through the enemy obstacles and was also to secure objectives just inside the western edge of the forest. From this point, 158 and 160 brigades, right and left respectively, would take over the fight through the Siegfried Line to the eastern extremities of the Reichswald (see Appendix I for the Phase One grouping).

The initial attack by 71 Brigade was led across 1,000 yards of no-man's-land by the 4th Battalion, Royal Welch Fusiliers (4 RWF), with A and B companies in front, supported by two squadrons of 147 Regiment RAC, the Westminster Dragoons' flail tanks and the AVREs of 82 Assault Squadron RE. The RWF's advance was watched by one of the Intelligence Section signallers of 1st Oxfordshire and Buckinghamshire Light Infantry (1 Ox & Bucks), Private Milligan:

The divisional sign of the 53rd Welsh Division worn on the upper arm of battledress.

> I saw a railway 400 yards on my left with infantrymen moving along it [belonging to 15th Scottish Division]. A short way in front of them a line of Churchill tanks had started to advance. The plain was nearly 4–5 miles wide, nothing was growing on the fields, flat, brown and muddy. This bleak view was broken by one small farmhouse and three haystacks – all soon alight. A terrifying hissing rushing noise was our own rocket blanket.

Major Stothers, of the Royal Regiment of Canada, 4th Brigade, dug in near Groesbeek, recorded in his battalion's war diary that as the RWF moved forward, 'the tanks opened up with their machine guns. All buildings on the immediate front – houses and farms strung out along the roads all the way to the German border – are aflame or smoking.' The armour accompanying 71 Brigade was, however, soon in difficulty, as recorded by 34 Armoured Brigade's historian:

> The 'going' was such that 79th Armoured Division units failed to cross the start line on 53 (Welsh) Division's front, and that area was soon jammed with bogged flails, AVREs and Crocodiles. However, ordinary Churchills

Major General Ross, commander of the 53rd Welsh Division throughout the North West European Campaign.

mostly got over 4,000 yards of atrocious going with relatively few casualties from mines, and 147 Regt RAC led their infantry right up to the edge of the forest ...[1]

Leaving behind the squadron of flails and half a squadron of Crocodiles, the Fusiliers followed the lifts of the barrage but found most of the 180 prisoners they took sheltering in cellars and bunkers. One farmhouse yielded twenty-three stunned prisoners alone and, in another incident, Welsh soldiers escorting PoWs back to the battalion cage found themselves stuck in a minefield and in need of rescue. At 1215 hours, 4 RWF had reached the anti-tank ditch that extended across their front and found that the enemy's temporary bridge was still in place. This allowed the Churchills in that area to cross promptly, but with 79th Armoured Division's AVREs carrying fascines bogged in, unsupported, the infantry's

An AVRE bridge layer with a small box girder assault bridge.

advance could have been brought to a halt. For example, one of the Churchills attempting to cross the ditch unaided managed to bog itself in the soft soil up to its turret ring. Eventually narrower points were found, the ditch was crossed and the tanks motored on to catch up with the infantry.

Finally, two bridge layers managed to plough their way forward, providing crossings for the following units, but the approaches to these small box girder bridges were soon impassable quagmires. Having crossed the anti-tank ditch, Brigadier Elrington, commander 71 Brigade, committed 1st Ox & Bucks and 1st Highland Light Infantry (1 HLI) to advance to the Reichswald. A Pak 40 75mm anti-tank gun was one of the few weapon systems that came into action, firing five rounds at the slow-moving tanks without hitting them. Its sights were probably thrown out by the bombardment and the gun crew was quickly overwhelmed by the infantry.

By 1400 hours the Ox & Bucks had reached the edge of the forest, crossing into Germany, and were pushing on to seize the BRANDENBURG feature, a hill several hundred yards inside the forest. A total of 115 prisoners were captured by this battalion. Very few enemy dead or wounded were found. The effects of the barrage on enemy morale seemed considerable, but little physical damage was apparent. The brigade's war diarist wrote:

> Enemy resistance was practically non-existent and once into the Reichswald it ceased altogether, and the two battalions advanced to their final objectives strictly according to the time table. By 1530 hrs our battle was over, and the only change in plan had been to push 1 HLI on to the objective which was to have been taken by 4th RWF.

The task of securing a firm base in the Reichswald had been completed by 71 Brigade creating a lodgment in the forest from which the remainder of the

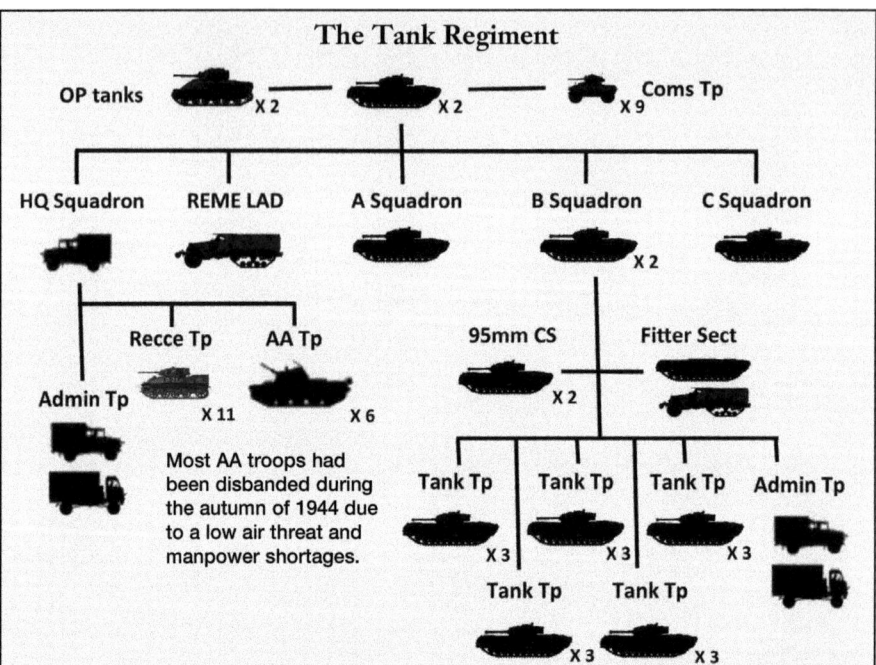

In contrast with the cruiser tanks (Cromwells and Shermans) of the armoured regiment, whose role was exploitation and pursuit, the tank regiment, with its slower-moving but more heavily armoured Churchill tanks, was organised for the support of infantry attacks. The individual regiments were grouped into brigades originally known as 'tank brigades', but by late 1944 they were being retitled as 'armoured brigades'. They consisted of two or three Churchill regiments but unlike those equipped with cruiser tanks, they did not have either an organic infantry motor battalion or a self-propelled artillery regiment and their slim brigade headquarters, certainly at the beginning of the North West European Campaign, was more for administration than command in battle.

Most tank regiments were cap-badged RTR, along with war-raised Royal Armoured Corps (RAC) regiments. The Household Division also provided battalions to crew the regiments of 6 Guards Armoured Brigade.

The majority of the Churchills mounted the 75mm gun but normally in one tank in three, the troop sergeant retained the earlier 6-pounder gun in the anti-tank role due to the development of the highly effective APDS round. In addition, two Churchill Mk 5 close support tanks were issued to each squadron headquarters. These tanks were armed with the Ordnance QF 95mm howitzer. This gun was a well-known 'lash up' using a sawn-off 3.7in AA gun barrel, a rebored 25-pounder breech and the recoil system of the 6-pounder. The primary ammunition was smoke and HE, both with a range of 8,000 yards. They also had a high-explosive anti-tank (HEAT) round, and the sighting system gave this a maximum effective range of 2,000 yards against armour.

Tank Support – 53rd Welsh Division

Affiliation of 34 Armoured Brigade squadrons to the battalions of 53rd Welsh Division during the initial phases of VERITABLE.

Supporting Tanks

71 Infantry Brigade 147 RAC
    4 Bn Royal Welch Fusiliers 4 RWF A Sqn
    1 Bn Ox and Bucks Light Infantry 1 OBLI C Sqn
    1 Bn Highland Light Infantry 1 HLI B Sqn
160 (South Wales) Infantry Brigade 9 RTR
    6 Bn The Royal Welch Fusiliers 6 RWF C Sqn
    4 Bn The Welch Regiment 4 WELCH A Sqn
    2 Bn The Monmouthshire Regiment 2 MONS B Sqn

The Mark VII 'Churchill I' Tank was designed to support infantry in the assault. By the time of the Battle of the Rhineland most of the Churchills' track guards had been removed or lost due to the snow of the Ardennes or mud of the Reichswald. Most replacements received in tank regiments were the Mark VII 'Heavy' Churchill, all of which mounted 75mm guns.

Infantrymen of 53rd Welsh Division awaiting orders to clear farms. Note the use of the slight cover of a tank track.

Welsh Division could deploy. Divisional Tactical Headquarters was just one part of the division that 'was greeted with a heavy enemy stonk which caused a number of casualties when it moved up to the edge of the forest at 1700 hours'.

In his first battle, Private Milligan driving one of the Ox & Bucks' Weasels, followed the division's advance into the forest and recalled that 'A young German lay dead on the road face down like a rag doll all awry as if without bones. His skin was wax-like with a yellow tinge. He was the first dead German I had seen.'

The Welsh concluded that the strength of the forward German defences on their front had been much overstated by the tactical overprint maps and agreed that mud was the main enemy, 'which in places in the forest had already proved too much for jeeps and Weasels'.

51st Highland Division

In the attack on 8 February (see map on page 84), General Rennie's Highlanders were to secure the south-west corner of the Reichswald, including a short distance into the woods, the southern part of the Freudenberg feature known as the Pyramid. Once this was achieved they were to cut off enemy positions in a salient located in the Kiekeberg Woods at the southern extremity of the Groesbeek Heights. The division's attack would also open the important, far less flood-prone, hardtop HEART route across the Maas floodplain from Mook to Gennep. The Highlanders were also to secure the first section of CLUB BLACK, which was planned to extend through the Reichswald as the advance progressed. It was, however, General Horrock's opinion that 'we could not use it until the forest had been cleared'.

The forward defences, including the Kiekeberg Salient, were held by the two battalions of the 1062 Grenadier Regiment. They were known to have been reinforced by 2 *Fallschirmjäger* Regiment only days before and were concentrated in the defences around the Pyramid,[2] which overlooked the ground to the north-west and to the south. A further reinforcing battalion was identified during the course of the fighting. The result was that of the four divisional operations

Major General Thomas Rennie is credited with revitalising the 51st Highland Division following its poor start to the Normandy campaign.

mounted during the morning of 8 February, that of the 51st Highland Division was the most difficult in terms of both enemy resistance and wet ground.

In common with the Welsh Division, the Highlanders' initial attack through the German positions was to be delivered on a single-brigade frontage. Brigadier Oliver's 154 Brigade was supported by 107 Regiment RAC, the flails of 1st Lothian Horse, a squadron of Crocodiles from 1st Fife & Forfar Yeomanry and the AVREs of 222 Assault Squadron RE. Oliver's plan for breaking through the enemy defences was to attack with the two battalions of the Black Watch (BW), the 1st Battalion to the left and the 7th Battalion on the right. These battalions were to break through the forward positions, while 7th Argyll and Sutherland Highlanders and, attached from 153 Brigade, 5th/7th Gordon Highlanders were to seize the Freudenburg feature within their boundaries.

At this point, 153 Brigade was to conduct a passage of lines and swing south heading for the Maas, cutting off the remaining enemy in the Kiekeberg Salient. All this was planned to be completed by dawn on 9 February.

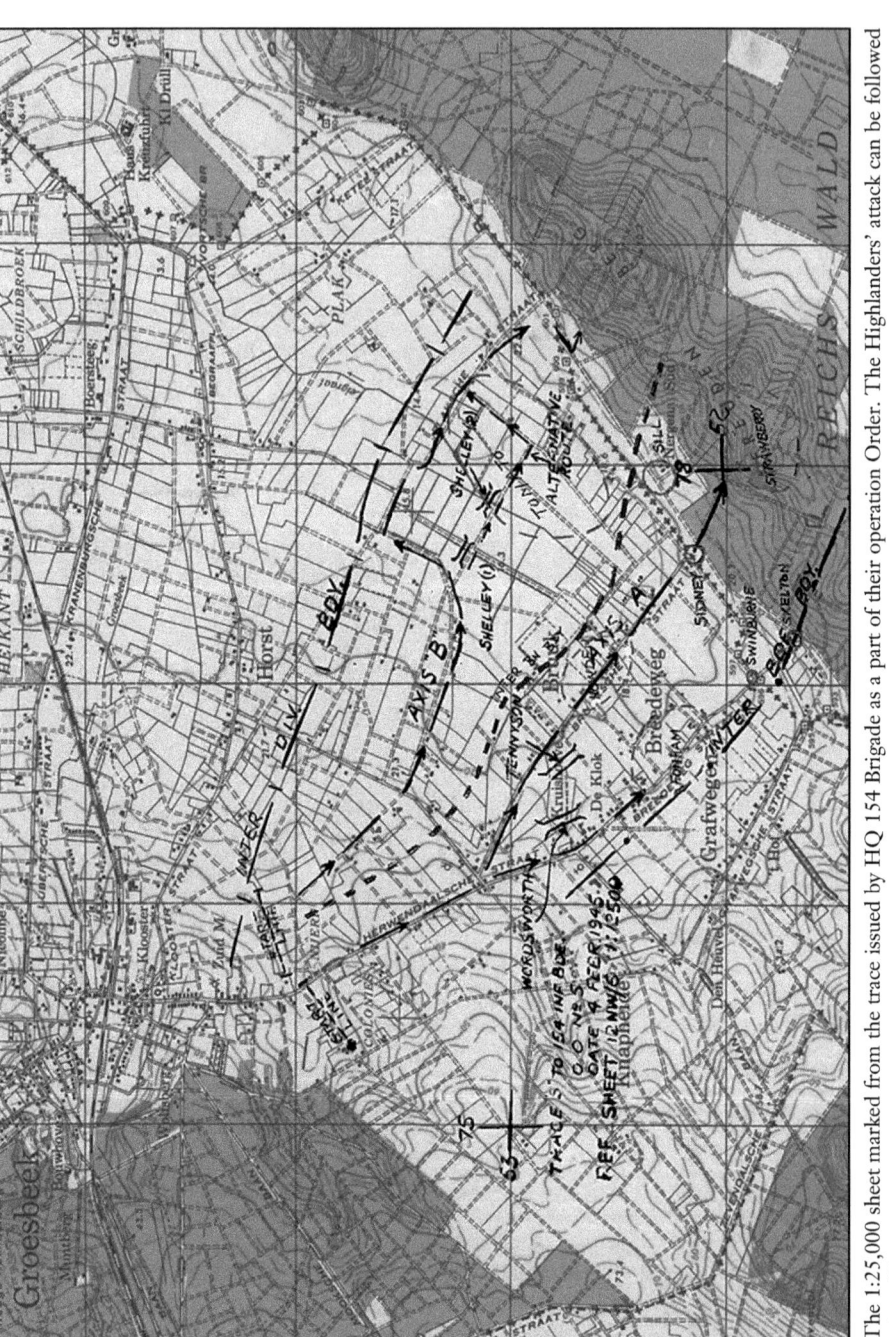

The 1:25,000 sheet marked from the trace issued by HQ 154 Brigade as a part of their operation Order. The Highlanders' attack can be followed using this map.

The Highland Division did not have the benefit of the corps' creeping barrage to cover their advance through the enemy position, but instead they had planned their own artillery tasks and a series of PEPPERPOTs. The attack was to be led by the infantry and Churchills to the Leigraaf anti-tank ditch that snaked through the German forward defences, at which point they would call forward the flails and AVREs carrying fascines and small box girder (SBG) bridges. With the Lothians' flails having beaten lanes through the minefields, the AVREs were to establish four crossing points as marked on the accompanying map (SHELLY 1 and 2, WORDSWORTH and TENNYSON). Once in place, the infantry and Churchills of 107 Regiment would resume leading the advance to the edge of the forest.

In addition to fighting through the forward defences, there was an additional tactical problem facing 7 Black Watch on the brigade's right; during the battalion's advance its open right flank was overlooked from the dominating high ground to the south and the scattered houses and farms of Knapheide and Grafwegen. This required the attention of the artillery planners, with PEPPERPOT shoots and smoke being required to both neutralise and blind the enemy.

Initially, 7 BW, supported by B Squadron, 107 Regiment RAC, advanced astride Herwendaalse Straat. Corporal Dyson commanded a Churchill named

As they were not involved in the first stage of the attack, 8th Armoured Brigade's 75mm guns were used in the PEPPERPOT shoots.

Buzzard in a troop that was supporting D Company. He recalled the opening moves of the attack:

> As we advanced, with the infantry of the 51st Highland Division hurrying forward purposefully, we were greeted by a truly unforgettable sight. On all sides, as far as the eye could see, were jerkin-clad men wearing tin helmets and carrying equipment on their backs, with trenching spades on top of their haversacks. Most of them had rifles at the ready and some were carrying Bren guns. In their midst the Churchill supporting tanks rolled forward, with exhausts emitting smoke into the cold air and their tracks cutting deep grooves in the soft green turf.
>
> Now we were on the move my butterflies disappeared, and the tenseness inside me gradually relaxed and gave way to a sense of exhilaration and excitement, mixed with a little trepidation. Our troop advanced slowly behind the Jocks of the Black Watch, who were warily probing their way forward in the direction of some ruined buildings about halfway between the start line and the anti-tank ditch. We wove our way in and out between the shell craters as if in a slalom. Smoke lingered all over the area, and the air reeked with the smell of spent explosives.

On reaching a road junction, B Company took the right fork and continued on Bredesweg Straat, while D Company advanced along Bruuk Straat on the left. Both routes were dotted with buildings and offered cover to German riflemen. Corporal Dyson continued:

The Black Watch cap badge.

> Looking through my periscope I could see no signs of the enemy in or near the first objective, but the Jocks were taking no chances. They advanced in leapfrog fashion from one shell hole to the next, taking turns to give covering fire with rifles and Bren guns, until they came within striking distance of the buildings.

Meanwhile, on 154 Brigade's right, Major Taylor, commanding 1 BW as his CO was on leave, advanced with his forward companies astride Axis B (see page 84); C Company left and A Company right.[3] Lieutenant Folley's troop of A Squadron, 107 Regiment, RAC, was supporting C Company:

> We had expected the start to be slow for us, because we were scheduled to wait around quite a bit while the funnies cleared lanes through the minefield. But bit by bit reports came back over the radio indicating that it wasn't the mines which were causing the delay, but the mud.
>
> The smooth green turf quickly churned up into black, track-clinging mud. One by one the Churchills sank on their bellies, their tracks spinning uselessly around in the bog.

Attack on the Forward Position 71

There was one road across the battlefield, but this had quite rightly been earmarked for essential wheeled vehicles only. To have put tanks on it would soon have made it as impassable as the rest of the ground.

I called up *Angler* and *Alert* on the 'B' set.

'This is going to be a drivers' battle,' I said. 'Pick your ground carefully and keep out of one another's track marks.'

'Wilco,' said Sergeant Robinson. 'What about getting out to the right a bit, by the road? It looks a bit more solid there.'

'That's King One's route,' I said, giving the daily code-name for Dick Richards' troop. 'But we'll go over there if it gets too bad here.'

And then a violent explosion echoed about the back of my head and looking over my shoulder I saw Dick's Troop Corporal (or rather his tank) leaning drunkenly to one side, a shattered track and a drifting cloud of yellow smoke betraying the fact that the enemy had mined the solid ground near the road.

'On second thoughts,' I radioed, 'we'll keep away from the road.'

But it was hard going. Bottom gear all the way, and the clinging black mud striving to tug us into the earth. Several times *Avenger*'s engine faltered and spluttered, and each time Crosby managed to nurse the big machine out of the bog.

And then the enemy began to recover from the six-hour bombardment. Eruptions of dirt indicated mortar and artillery fire coming down on our infantry and one or two of them started coming back, stolidly plodding along while holding a bloodstained arm or shoulder. Stretcher-bearers dealt swiftly and efficiently with those who couldn't walk, and still the Black Watch went forward until they reached a group of farm buildings where they were scheduled for a short halt.

As planned, just before midday, the battlegroup halted short of the main enemy minefield and the Leigraaf anti-tank ditch on a frontage of 1,200 yards astride the hamlet of Bruuk on the inter-battalion boundary northwards. However, all was not well with the assault armour, which was supposed to be breaching the minefield and laying bridges across the anti-tank ditch. Foley continued:

> We pulled into the buildings ... and I looked around for the Company Commander [Major Davies-Colley]. He was walking along a bit of a road, quietly smoking his pipe. With his little cane, and his red hackle on the side of his cap, he might well have been taking a Sunday morning stroll down Aldershot High Street, except that vicious little spurts of dust were cracking about his heels.
>
> He raised his stick in greeting when he saw Five Troop, and completely indifferent to the bullets kicking up the dirt around him he strolled across to *Avenger* and swung up to the turret.
>
> 'Going very well so far,' he said pleasantly. 'How're your funny-boys getting on with breaching that minefield?'

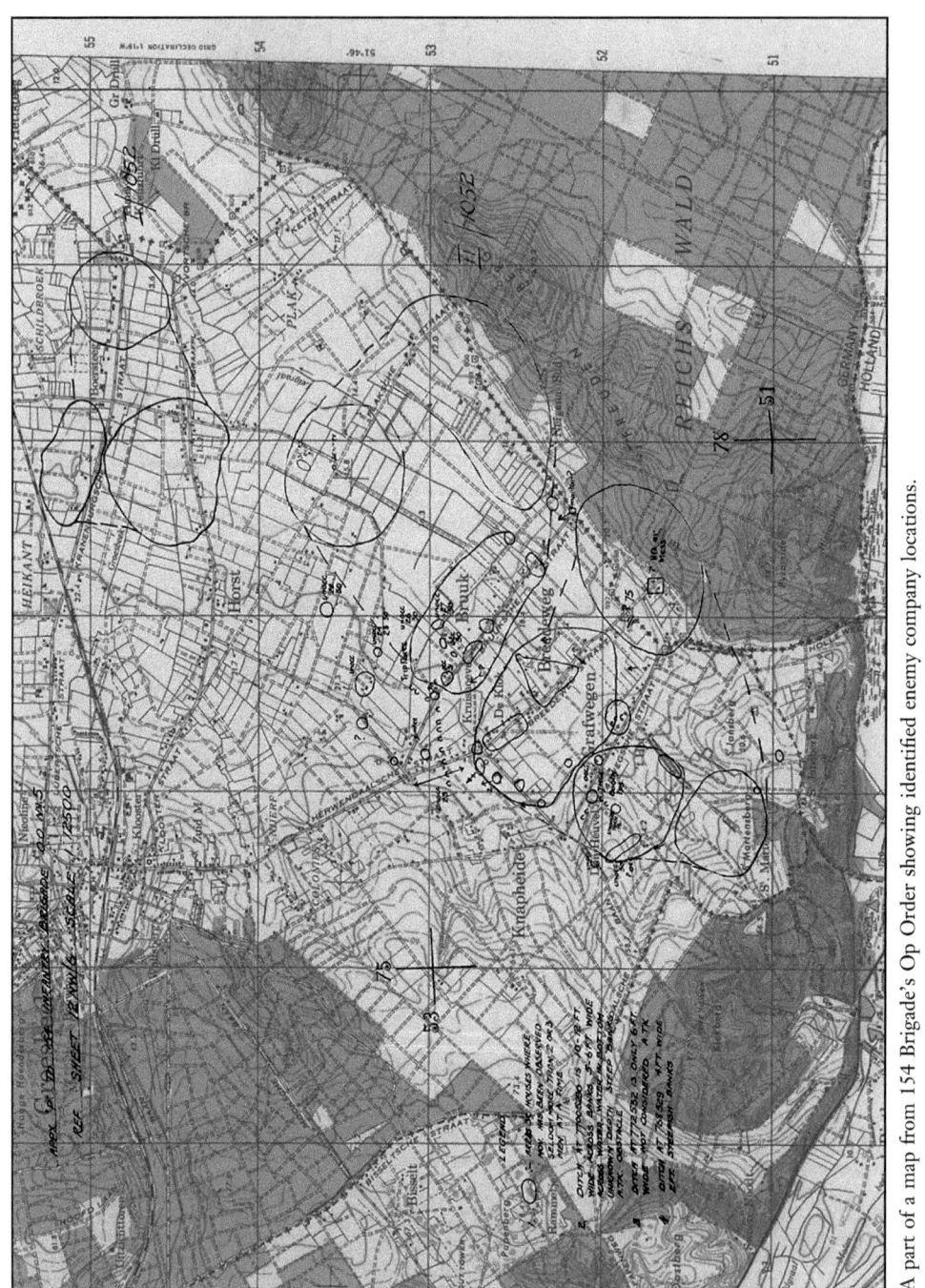

A part of a map from 154 Brigade's Op Order showing identified enemy company locations.

'They're all bogged,' I said gloomily. 'Look here, aren't you being shot at?'
'Oh, never mind that,' he said.' It's only got nuisance value.'

Enemy fire may have been just nuisance value to Major Davies-Colley but the percentage of officer casualties during the first phase of Operation VERITABLE across all four divisions was marked. The major continued his conversation with Foley:

> Well, it's a pity you can't get across that minefield. Looks like we'll have to go on without you.'
> 'Balls,' I said, and hastily added 'sir', because he was, after all, a Major even though it looked to me as if he would soon be a dead one. 'I'll see what the form is on the air.'
> I may have been mistaken, but it seemed to me that the Black Watch officer had little faith in our funnies, which was a shame because on the more solid ground to our right, where 'B' Squadron were fighting [with 7 BW], the mine-clearing and bridging tanks had done their job perfectly, despite some pretty stiff enemy opposition.
> But we decided to wait for a few minutes and, because I couldn't emulate the Scottish indifference to the spasmodic machine-gun fire, I juggled the three tanks around until we were in a position to fire at the front edge of the Reichswald, from where we judged the obstinate machine-gunner was operating.
> There was no sign of him, of course; I guessed he was probably sitting behind one of the scores of fallen trees we could see. But we blasted away happily at every likely-looking hiding place and the bullets stopped coming our way, so I suppose we must have done some good. But only temporarily.
> And then Ian came up on the air to say that we were going to use the road for a little way, and the funnies were in the process of clearing it.

The 1 BW companies resumed their advance at 1230 hours through the minefield and across the anti-tank ditch towards Objective TOMATO, with Lieutenant Foley's Churchills firing their machine guns over the Highlanders' heads as they made their way through the mines. The Churchills of 5 Troop spotted German movement on the edge of the Reichswald and engaged with HE, but the glass block in Foley's periscope was hit and shattered by return fire, which brought his part in the engagement to a halt until a replacement was fitted.

Earlier, we left 7 BW just short of their first objective, some ruined buildings at the end of Herwendalsche Straat. Corporal Dyson recalled D Company's commander, Major Lowe, coming back to speak to his troop commander, Lieutenant 'Johnny' Walker:

> There was a lull in activity while the Black Watch officer approached our troop, seemingly indifferent to any danger, and held his hand up to signal us to halt.[4] He climbed aboard Johnny's tank for a short discussion before jumping down and returning to his forward troops.

The Highlanders advanced through wrecked Waco gliders left after Operation MARKET GARDEN. Farms burn while the bulk of the Reichswald can be just seen in the distance through the murk.

The infantry company commander wanted us to hold our fire while he sent a raiding party into the buildings, so our tanks stood to and waited on further orders. The Jocks of the Black Watch rushed forward, bayonets fixed, with shouts and screams that could be heard above the other sounds of battle and disappeared into the buildings. They emerged with little groups of German prisoners with hands on their heads: they had apparently been there all the time, crouching in the cellars in a state of shock. The barrage had done most to reduce them to this condition, but the final straw must have been glimpsing the blood-curdling charge of the Jocks, with the cold steel glinting at the end of their rifles. It looked terrifying enough even viewed from the rear.

The next bound of the advance would take 7 BW and B Squadron to the anti-tank ditch. Corporal Dyson continued:

Our troop drove into the group of buildings while the RAMC lads were stretchering away some wounded Germans. I opened the hatch and took a look at the shambles all around. Some enemy corpses had been mangled by shells in the bombardment and were a gruesome sight – too sickening for one young Jock, who looked to be still in his teens. He was bent over spewing up as his companion, an unshaven, grizzled veteran, tried to comfort him. Looking up at me, he grimaced and remarked angrily, 'Och, 'tis bairns they be sinding doon ta us fer feeting, noo.' I could only agree that they seemed to be scraping the barrel for reinforcements ...

Shortly afterwards we continued the advance, amidst signs that the Germans were getting over the terror and shock of the shelling and starting to fight back. Sporadic small arms fire sent up spurts of earth among the infantry as they dashed forward, spreadeagling themselves under cover to fire at their targets. Our tanks took turns to help the infantry capture various pill-boxes, houses and barns leading up to the anti-tank ditch. The enemy were sending over 'stonks' of mortar shells, scattering the infantry as they dived into shell craters to shelter from flying fragments of shrapnel.

The Black Watch were suffering casualties now, and wounded infantry were mixed with the German prisoners taken back past us, with the more seriously injured stretchered back by medics. Dead men lay where they fell ...

The troop re-joined the squadron just a stone's throw from the anti-tank ditch, which stretched across the battlefield for miles. The infantry had gone to ground when we arrived on the scene, and we soon realised why: sporadic bursts of Spandau fire and the single cracks of snipers' guns were coming from a group of buildings near the anti-tank obstacle. The rapid fire of the Spandaus suggested there were three or four guns operating in the shelter of the buildings. The enemy strongpoint clearly had to be eliminated.

As D Company approached the anti-tank ditch via the Bruuk Straat axis, the enemy held their fire until the leading platoon was across the ditch and D Company's headquarters were within 50 yards of them. Corporal Dyson described the company's plan and action:

Once again, I saw the Black Watch company commander [Major Lowe] unhurriedly approach our leading tank for a short discussion. His apparently

A *Schumine* casualty awaiting evacuation.

nonchalant behaviour, amid enemy sniper fire spattering up little eruptions of dirt all over the area as bullets landed, was unbelievable! He intended to make an all-out assault to force a crossing over the anti-tank ditch and needed to plan the tank support with our squadron leader. The outcome of their meeting was that our troop was detailed to provide close support for the infantry. We grumbled resignedly over our bad luck.

Our troop advanced at the appointed time, and systematically fired HE shells from hull-down positions at the supposed lairs of Spandau teams. As our shots hit and exploded, sending fragments of debris flying into the air, we really thought we had put paid to the machine gun nests. The infantry assumed so too, as only sniper fire was now coming from the enemy and moved forward in little spurts towards the anti-tank ditch under cover of a smoke-screen from our shells. All seemed to be going well until the assault was halted in its tracks by bursts of Spandau fire. We could see to our horror that these claimed some victims, and the infantry were forced to withdraw hurriedly to avoid further casualties.

It was noted that: 'They picked off the company commander, Major Lowe, and two of his platoon leaders together with 5 men.'[5] This loss of officers threw the company 'off balance. It was not until the IO of the battalion, Captain Rae-Smith, arrived that some order was restored' and their objective (HOWDEN) at Bruuk was secured.

With the advance stalled, Lieutenant Walker informed the rest of his troop using the B radio that he was going to dismount from the protection of his Churchill and go forward on foot 'to see what the form was':

He returned to tell us that the Black Watch company commander was among those killed. We were appalled at the news: only a short while ago we'd seen him liaising with our commander. It might be said that his air of nonchalance under sniper fire was rather foolhardy; I prefer to believe that it

The view north-west from Bredesweg Straat across the typically open country dotted with farms that 7 BW advanced across on 8 February 1945.

was his way of inspiring his men and giving them confidence in his leadership. They had certainly shown it in the brave dash across the bridge, which ended so tragically when their commander was mown down by enemy machine gun fire.

The Black Watch had encountered unexpectedly determined opposition. They found themselves up against 1st Battalion, 1222 Grenadier Regiment, which had only arrived the previous night. It was later confirmed that this was part of a wider move by 180th Infantry Division north from the Maas to replace elements of 1052 and 1062 regiments and 84th Fusilier Battalion. The 1st 1062 had earlier been caught in the open by the opening barrage and had suffered heavy casualties.

Lieutenant Walker, despite being an Armoured Corps officer, remained on his feet and helped mount another attack. Corporal Dyson looked on from the turret of Buzzard:

> We watched, spellbound, as he went about the task. He moved between the infantry and us, directing our HE fire at designated targets. When he was convinced we had succeeded in putting the Spandaus out of action, we lobbed over a few more smoke shells and the infantry attempted another crossing. Buzzard's crew cheered in unison as the Jocks charged forward, this time amidst only desultory small arms fire, and succeeded in reaching the other side of the anti-tank obstacle in numbers and disappearing into the landscape. Our troop then followed them over to consolidate the position.
>
> The enemy was now concealed in a group of buildings on the far side of the ditch, but this next attack was rather an anti-climax after what had gone before. In a vengeful mood after passing fallen comrades in the stiff positions induced by rigor mortis, and supported by fire from our tanks, the Jocks infiltrated the buildings with bayonets fixed, and the enemy capitulated without firing a shot.

Meanwhile, 7 BW's B Company had been clearing the sundry buildings on their Bredesweg Straat axis and A Company took over the lead towards Breedeweg itself. With the armour struggling to get forward through the minefields to bridge the anti-tank ditch, the company's three platoons fired 2in mortar smoke bombs to cover their advance across the ditch. Breedeweg (Objective FONHAM) was soon being cleared by A Company. With the infantry across the anti-tank ditch, the Lothians' flails were called forward into action. B Squadron's war diary explains that:

> At approx. 11:30 hrs the 'OK' was given for WORDSWORTH [breaching team] to go forward and shortly afterwards permission was given for both TENNYSON and SHELLY to be started. WORDSWORTH was done on a tarmac road and went through fairly easily.

However, as already mentioned, the Funnies were in action but were in increasing difficulties. The track to the site of the proposed site of SHELLY 1 crossed some very wet ground, in which the AVREs carrying the SBG bridges had

A Crocodile passing a bogged in Churchill Mk V tank with a 95mm gun. Up armoured with track links, the weight of this tank would have been significantly greater.

bogged one after another and the 'road' referred to above was in fact little more than a country track 400 yards further north. It was, however, eventually cleared by the flails of 1 Troop, B Squadron, 1 Lothians, and proved to be firmer going for the following AVREs. The vehicles bringing forward some of the Highland Division's support weapons also used a crossing subsequently established in 53rd Welsh Division's area.

Lieutenant Foley's troop was tasked to cover the assault armour, but Sergeant Robinson's Churchill had become bogged, and a crew member was wounded while positioning the tow chains. He was one of six casualties suffered by 107's RAC tank crews that day.

With the funnies having established a crossing of the anti-tank ditch Lieutenant Foley contemplated the queue:

> all sorts of vehicles were waiting to cross it, from both sides. Flame-throwing tanks, half-tracks, infantry carriers, jeep-ambulances, were all queuing up to cross the steep-sided obstacle.
>
> Then I looked at the ditch and it didn't seem all that formidable to me. For a short stretch the sides of the excavation had been concreted, and it looked as if a Churchill might get over it with a bit of luck.
>
> I asked Crosby if he thought he could do it, and he climbed out of his seat and walked forward to look at it. In a few seconds he returned giving the thumbs-up sign, and I decided to have a go.
>
> The people queuing at the crossing gave a sardonic cheer as we motored slowly up to the ditch, and when *Avenger*'s nose dropped almost vertically,

The Churchill tank was designed to support infantry in the assault. Note the track links being used as appliqué armour.

and we slid head first down the concrete I began to wonder if I'd been very wise about this business. If it became necessary to tow us out of that ditch, Ian was going to have some very pointed things to say about Troop Leaders who deliberately drove into anti-tank obstacles. And then we were in the bottom of the ditch and the nose started to lift.

The anti-tank ditch wasn't as wide as *Avenger* was long, so that our nose was going up the far side while our tail was still coming down the other. Since a Churchill tank isn't made to hinge in the middle there came a point where we were completely horizontal, and apparently wedged in the ditch. But on the Churchill there is a handy device known as the 'neutral turn'; it consists of pulling on the tiller bar with the gear-box in neutral, and the result is that one track goes forward while the other goes backwards. (On a smooth surface I have seen a Churchill spin around on its own axis by this method.)

With the engine going flat out, Crosby swung the tiller bar to right and left, and *Avenger* wriggled madly like a horse trying to shake off an unwelcome rider. And then the tail dropped lower, the nose rose higher, and to a triumphant cheer from the watchers we clambered out on the far side of the ditch.

Alert and *Angler* successfully followed *Avenger* across the obstacle, and the troop set off to join 1 BW on Objective TOMATO, where the infantry had paused to reorganise. Foley continued:

> Then I heard a noise like a small boy dragging a stick along some iron railings, and a line of sparks dotted the side of *Avenger*.
>
> 'They've woken up,' I said, dropping down into the turret.
>
> Inside the turret the noise of the bullets ringing on the armour plate was magnified ten times. I grimaced and pressed the velvet-rimmed headphones tighter over my ears.

With 1 BW having reached their objective and, in the process, driven the German infantry back from the forest edge, the funnies were still attempting to clear and establish crossings of the obstacles. Eventually, Crabs of B Squadron, 1st Lothians, flailed 500 yards to the anti-tank ditch, detonating about thirty mines in the process, where a small box girder bridge was successfully laid by 222 Assault Squadron RE and opened at 1230 hours. The engineers also used an armoured bulldozer to fill the ditch 'with rubble, farm carts, fascines and a burnt-out enemy truck' to make a second crossing point nearby. Breaching team TENNYSON, however, had greater difficulties, as explained in the flail's war diary:

> This lane presented the greatest difficulties, presumably because the head of the road down which the flail path was to be made was practically blocked by two Churchill tks belonging to 107 RAC. Lt McGregor attempted to get his tp past these bogged tks but was himself bogged. He managed to get de-bogged again and, reversing to the rd junc at 761531, he started off again after a recce on foot and managed to get one tk (Sgt Cox's tk) onto the road. His other four tks were in difficulties ... While this was happening, Sgt Cox had gone on by himself and, after having exploded at least six mines, his tk was struck by a bazooka from a house on the left hand side of the road at 767528. The tk brewed up and, while the crew were evacuating, was machine-gunned from the house, Sgt Cox being killed as he attempted to bale out ... All these four men were evacuated by ambulance.

Further delays were caused by another Churchill running over a mine and blocking the route down to the bridge, resulting in TENNYSON, the centre breach, eventually being opened at 1900 hours. The left pair, in 1 BW's area, SHELLY I and II, were abandoned.

With WORDSWORTH open, the rest of 107 RAC was able to cross. Corporal Dyson recalled that:

> It wasn't long before the rest of B Squadron crossed over the bridged tank obstacle and joined us in the shelter of a copse. Looking back, we could see a long queue of vehicles waiting their turn to get across: flail tanks, Crocodile flame throwing tanks, bridging tanks, infantry carriers and supply trucks, all

Troops of 154 Brigade crossing into Germany at Breedeweg.

starting to pour through the breach in the defence created by the Jocks with the support of our troop. Surveying the scene, I felt a sense of pride at taking part in the assault which had made it possible. The final accolade came from Tom [his brother], who sought me out as soon as his troop joined us ... His congratulations were cut short, however, as we came under mortar fire which sent us scurrying back inside our tanks.

Once across the anti-tank ditch, B Squadron waited for A Company, 7 BW, and A Squadron to begin its advance and moved on with D Company towards the forest:

There was an immediate response from the enemy, concealed on the edge of the forest. Our infantry dashed forward from one bit of cover to another, under constant fire from Spandaus and snipers, but pressed on bravely and relentlessly. The tanks, rolling forward between stages of the advance, peppered the front of the forest with Besa fire. The going was heavy and some tanks got bogged down in the mud, so Johnny said it was by the luck of the draw that our troop happened to be in the lead when the CO of a company of Gordon Highlanders requested tank support for the assault on the enemy in the forest fringe. We preferred to believe that Johnny's daring leadership and tactically successful relationship with the infantry in the assault on the anti-tank obstacle had inspired the squadron leader to order our troop forward in close support once again.

The Lothians' war diary continued: 'Tanks of 'B' Sqn, 107 RAC, which after some difficulty managed to get across the AT-ditch, finally eased the company

[A Company] on to its objectives [SWINBURN, SILL, SIDNEY and SKELTON] at the forest edge.' Dyson continued:

> We were now only about two hundred yards or so from the forest, and the devastating effect the barrage had wreaked on the trees could be clearly seen through binoculars. Huge trunks of tall pines had been snapped and broken by the pounding and were lying on the ground or hanging down still attached by shreds. Shattered branches littered the forest floor. Here and there grey-clad corpses of German defenders stood out against the darkness of the debris beneath the trees; some bodies still whole, some in bits after being blown to smithereens by the tremendous bombardment that morning. The close-up view was grim, but the fast rat-tat of Spandau teams and sounds of rifle fire coming from the woods showed there were still a lot of enemy dug in.

With 7 BW having reached its objectives just inside the wood, 5th/7th Gordon Highlanders, attached from 153 Brigade, had finally been brought forward. They had spent a frustrating day following up behind the two Black Watch battalions and were only just moving forward as dusk was beginning to fall. The Gordons' leading companies crossed the Dutch–German border, entered the forest and advanced on Objective STRAWBERRY. Their war diary records that:

> C Coy were leading coy ... and moved down the right hand [Breedeweg] axis. Progress was slow as 7 BW experienced some difficulty on getting firm on their objective. There was also enemy interference from the right flank,

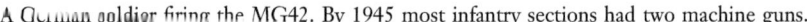

A German soldier firing the MG42. By 1945 most infantry sections had two machine guns.

which was open, though being dealt with by MMG fire and arty and proved a slight hinderance. C Coy reached its objective just before dark and suffered a number of casualties.

With C Company having secured an entry point into the Reichswald (see map on page 84) opposition on the approaches to the southern peak of the Freudenburg, some 500 yards into the forest, grew and the Gordons had a sharp fight to reach it:

> A Coy were then put through to penetrate into the forest but the leading platoon, after a battle at close quarters with a strong enemy force, could make no headway ... D Coy ... were being commanded by the [battalion's] 2iC Major Evans MC then made a left flanking movement across to the left of the axis to houses at ... [Objective SILL]. The move was a very successful one and when the company reported itself firm on their objective, a patrol from B Coy was sent through at 2100 hrs to recce the high ground [the Freudenburg] inside the forest. This very difficult patrol was safely accomplished and on its return B Coy was passed through D to establish itself on the high ground. This started just before midnight.

Lance Corporal McNeil recorded how on crossing the border and reaching the edge of the Reichswald: 'Most of my section paused for a celebratory piss on Germany. After years of war and all we had been through since Normandy, it seemed like an appropriate gesture.'[6]

Having secured their objectives on the edge of the forest, the battalion dug in under small arms fire from pockets of enemy, as well as increasing volumes of artillery and mortar fire. At 0300 hours, however, A Company, which had earlier withdrawn back through C Company, re-entered the forest and relieved B Company on the Freudenberg. Without difficulty except for the almost total darkness, this company headed deeper into the Reichswald, aiming for a cross-tracks that was their objective. Corporal Campbell of B Company recalled that: 'It was only by looking up and seeing the gap of slightly lighter sky that we could follow the track,' but as they approached their objective, they encountered the enemy in considerable strength. The Germans were, however, conducting a relief in place and 'several hundred enemy soldiers were milling around in the darkness in the area of the main track'.

Despite being outnumbered, B Company attacked and with the benefit of surprise caught the enemy unprepared. The enemy withdrew in confusion and the company took no fewer than 164 PoWs, with 'too many dead to be counted'. This action cost 5th/7th Gordons a single casualty. B Company had penetrated into an emerging German position and despite their success spent the remainder of an uncomfortable night at close quarters with the enemy.

By nightfall 1 BW was also in position on the crest of the Freudenberg a little further north. Overnight both battalions dispatched patrols deeper into the forest to keep the enemy at bay and dominate track junctions.

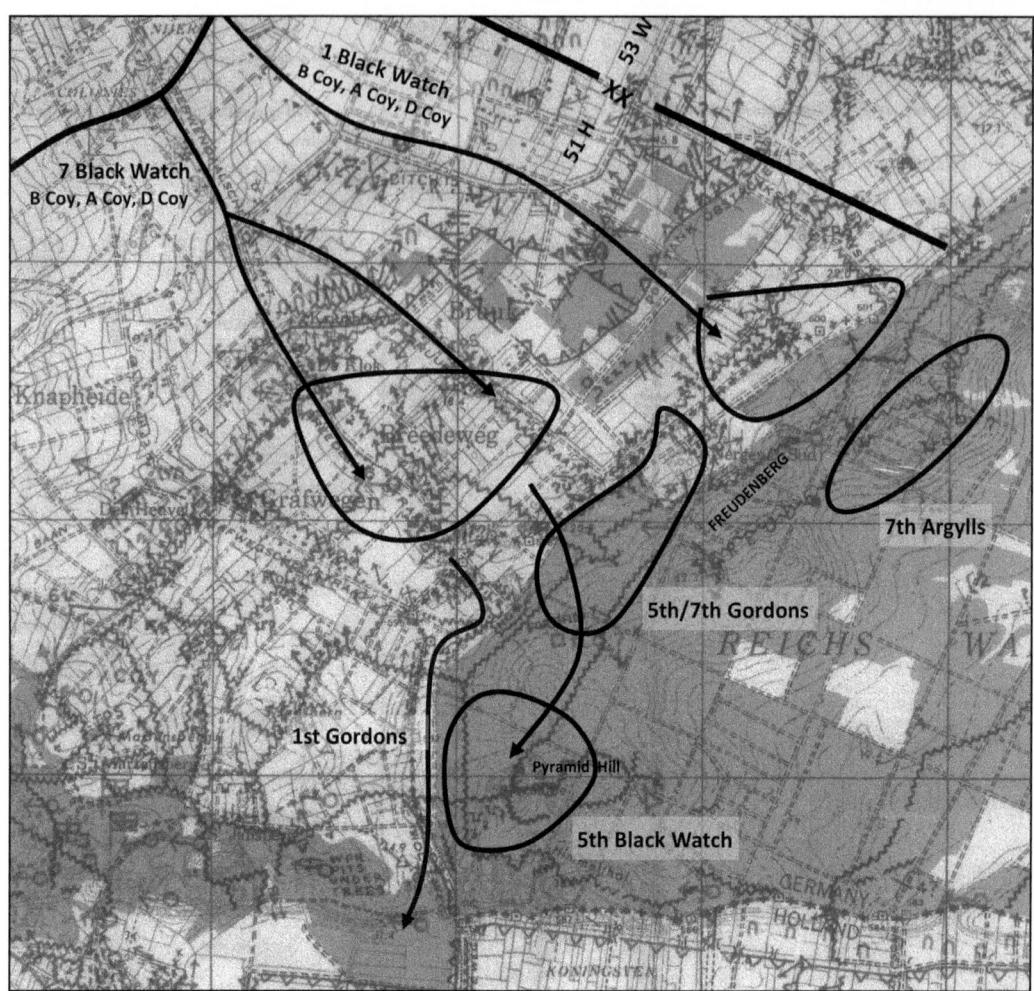

The 51st Highland Division's battalion locations on the night of 8–9 February 1945.

Later that evening the 7th Argylls, the fourth battalion under Brigadier Oliver's command, came forward through 1 BW and advanced further into the forest to secure an important cross-track on what was to become route CLUB BLACK. The regimental history records:

> The battalion entered the forest at approximately 11 p.m. and found the going very difficult both up to and in the forest itself, as all the tracks rapidly became a muddy quagmire. At this stage all transport had to be abandoned, and the troops had to carry extra loads in the form of wireless sets, etc.

Against negligible opposition, the Argylls were soon digging in, with D Company forward of the cross-tracks and B to their right. Battalion headquarters and A Company were at the cross-tracks. During the course of the night an enemy patrol approached the forward position but was driven off, leaving behind two men to be taken prisoner. After a lonely, wet and uncomfortable night: 'By 8 o'clock in the morning of the 9th of February, however, the necessary transport, together with one troop of Churchill tanks from the 107 RAC, managed to reach the battalion on the objective.'

153 Highland Brigade

The day that Brigadier Sinclair's 153 Brigade (1st Gordons and 5 BW) spent waiting to come forward to take over the battle from 154 Brigade affords a good example of the tensions they and other brigades in their situation faced during 8 February 1945.[7] Major Martin Lindsay,[8] of 1st Gordon Highlanders, started the day north of the River Maas:

> We left Groot Linden at 10 a.m. It was a nice morning and I hoped it would remain so. We had a two-mile march to the Mook bridge and were held up by traffic for the best part of two hours 200 yards short of it. I didn't much care for this as I thought the Hun was bound to shell the bridge ... For a time the confusion was considerable. However, we got moving at last and over the Bailey bridge across the Maas we went, five yards between men and 100 yards between vehicles. I think we all lengthened our stride and crossed our fingers while going over, but all was peace and quiet.
>
> It was another two miles to our assembly area in a wood behind the Canadians. As soon as the companies got spaced out either side of the track down the centre of it, a truck for each arrived with a meal ... I walked round the Jocks and noticed how quiet they all were. They had not eaten much. I felt much the same and had to force myself to take a second sandwich.

The badge of the Gordon Highlanders.

Major Martin Lindsay, second in command of 1st Gordons.

There was the usual noise, half whine, half whistle, of a shell coming over and the crash of it exploding in the woods beyond.

I could see that things were going rather slowly, as there was a long delay over launching the [7th] Argylls, who were next to us in the wood. So, I pottered over to Brigade HQ, which was a few hundred yards away... They told me that 154 had got most of their objectives and 5th/7th Gordons had just started, that there was a bit of stuff coming down on the road which was to be our axis, and some trouble from Grafwegen to the right of it in the form of one Spandau still firing, in spite of the pasting that place had already had.

It was getting on for 4 p.m. and we had been there for about three hours already. It is not pleasant hanging about waiting to move forward into battle, especially when the road you will have to pass down is being shelled... At 4.45 p.m. we were told to be ready to start at 5.30, so it was time to put on our pads.

I was nervous that we should be launched too early and have to hang about on the way forward under fire, while the battalion in front of us was held up. I mentioned it to [Lieutenant Colonel] Grant Peterkin, yet this is precisely what happened, though it is easy to understand his position with the Divisional Commander at his elbow pressing him to get on and capture the Kiekeberg. So when we had gone about a mile we came to the tail of the Black Watch, still 800 yards short of the wood.

I felt very miserable. There was quite a bit of shelling and hardly cover for a rat, since there was no ditch alongside this third-class road and the few houses had been reduced to little more than rubble. And thus, we remained for some four hours, when we might well have stayed where we had spent the afternoon and have had the evening meal as well.

After a day of waiting, during which several men were evacuated as psychological casualties, 153 Brigade finally advanced towards the dark outline of the Reichswald in full darkness and rain via the Bruuk Straat. Despite their objective being further south, they took this route as Breedeweg proved to be heavily mined and clearing it at night was a very slow business. Leading were 5th Black Watch, wheeling south from Bruuk towards their objective, the border fortifications around the Pyramid feature. Behind them, the 1st Gordons were ready to advance into the Stint Jansberg woods, which would cut off the Germans holding the Kiekeberg feature in front of 2nd Canadian Division.

Inevitably, with so many artillery pieces in action in a complicated fire plan that lasted all day, there were mistakes. On the receiving end of one such 'swinger' were the 7th Argylls. Major Graham was wounded by a round that landed 300 yards short but, having come to rely on the artillery, he commented that: 'We were just so glad to have it. We'd rather it was too close rather than too far away.'

Having spent the morning moving up behind 154 Brigade, 5 BW crossed their start line at 1300 hours led by A Company, which 'with little difficulty en route', thanks to the Germans having been driven or largely withdrawn from the forward

1st Canadian Rocket Battery's Land Mattress provided support across the corps' frontage throughout the day.

edge of the forest, occupied Pyramid Hill. So much for dismounted infantry, but for those companies following and vehicles bringing up support weapons and headquarters it was a different matter and they were only reported through 7 BW's defensive positions at 1845 hours:

> All roads and tracks were cut about by shell fire, and many were blocked by craters and fallen trees. This caused an increasing hold up to following troops who were frequently caught in the open by strong enemy counter-fire. Heavy rain and falling darkness added to the problems but the other companies and Bn HQ had all crossed the Start Line by 1845 hours and were in the forest.[9]

With the battalion established in the forest, B Company was tasked to cut the embanked and culverted road below Pyramid Hill (marked x on the map), which the Germans in Kiekeberg Wood were using to use to attempt to escape south. In darkness at 1930 hours: 'They captured 1 officer and 30 German soldiers, killed a number who refused to surrender and shot up a horse-drawn ammunition wagon which was towing a 150mm gun and trailer.' A patrol mounted by S Company's Carrier Platoon located an enemy headquarters just to the west of the Pyramid. 'They dismounted and shot up what turned out to be a German signals unit still in operation.'

Throughout the night 5 BW reported being 'in close contact with the enemy in somewhat confused situations'. Corporal Dow's diary gives a flavour of a tense night:

> Get busy and dig in, we are going to hold here. Sounds of machine gun fire and grenades to our left where our other platoon are. Finish digging in: longing for a smoke, have a crafty drag in bottom of a slit. Things were very quiet except for wounded German moaning out loud. All tensed up expecting enemy to come down track to their HQ behind us. They have to pass us first. Ensure everyone knows passwords and is ready to carry out drill. Put marker out in front of section aiming point. Tell Bren gunner to remain silent unless enemy passes marker. Settle down to wait. Butterflies in stomach. Not long to wait. Sound of voices shouting as they come down track. No need for Password, all shouts are in German. One grenade apiece, pins out. On command 'Throw' – heads down ... count five ... heads up ... chaos, shouts, screams, sound of men running back up track. Keep silent, keep down. Nothing to be seen in the dark ... silence for hours, then sounds of movement again down the track ... German voices ... repeat of last time ... more chaos; the Germans don't know which way to run but none get past our Section ... Dawn comes slowly and we are ordered back to get ready for next attack ... several bodies lying beside the track for someone else to recover.

By the following morning the battalion had rounded up seventy PoWs and along with the 150mm gun three 75mm Pak 40 anti-tank guns had been taken.

At 1800 hours 1st Gordons recorded in their war diary that they were held up behind 5 BW and ten minutes later the adjutant wrote:

> Plan changed and instead of the Bn passing through the wood we are now to go along the side and clean up houses at 766507.
>
> The Bn moved fwd with A Coy leading followed by B – C – D – Bn HQ and Carriers. The track [in the open just inside the German border] was in a very bad condition owing to heavy rain and also obstructed by two trenches which proved to be impassable to vehicles.

Many accounts of 1st Gordons' move on the evening of 8 February cover it in a short sentence, but this is to give a false impression of the difficulties of operations by night. Major Lindsay, who was sent forward to prove the route, again provides an insight:

> By this time, it was dark. There still seemed to be a good deal of rifle, Bren and Spandau fire about a thousand yards in front, just inside the Reichswald.

A familiar scene during the fighting in and around the Reichswald: columns of prisoners being marched to the rear.

We walked up the middle of the road, passing the dark forms of many waiting fighting men, sitting or sprawling at the roadside; many were fast asleep. I heard an officer talking and asked him what the trouble was, but as usual nobody at the back had any notion. All they could tell me was that the formation just in front of them had stopped. So on we went, till a lamp sign just short of the forest bade us turn to the right and soon we came to the Tac HQ of 5th Black Watch.

George Dunn was commanding and told me that they had met little resistance, all the shooting being on 5th/7th Gordons' front further to the left. His difficulty was that all tracks through the forest were hopelessly blocked by trees, felled both by enemy demolitions and our own shellfire; he had not been able to get a single vehicle into the Reichswald. But the companies were all getting into their positions without any bother. So I decided to go across the open along the edge of the forest; there was nothing to be gained by going round through the Reichswald now that it was too dark to be shot at from afar.

Followed by A and B Company Commanders and a small party to lay white tape along the route, I went on to have a look. We walked along a very muddy track, with the forest looking black and sinister on our left. By this time the moon was up, and with all the searchlights groping in the sky we felt rather exposed, strolling along there in the open. To the right of us was an

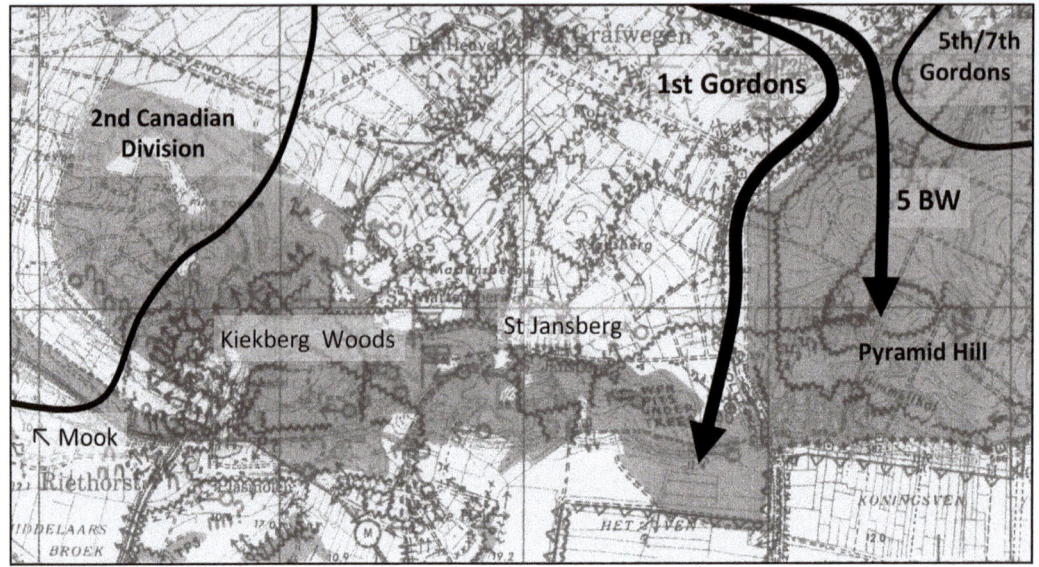

153 Brigade's advances on the evening of 8 February 1945.

open field, completely devoid of cover. We saw dead cattle 300 yards away, and I wondered whether any not so dead Huns might not see us. Our direction was parallel to the frontier. We were ten yards inside Germany. At the far end we found the two Black Watch companies digging in just inside the Reichswald, and they confirmed that all was quiet.

The two company commanders retraced their steps and led their platoons forward into their positions without encountering the enemy. B Company's clearance patrols soon brought back a few prisoners from the area in front of them, but D Company reported 'a lot of enemy' just in front of them. At 2340 hours, Battalion Tactical Headquarters was reporting that it was established in the woods. Under rain-laden skies it was, however, particularly dark inside the thick pine forest that night, and Colonel Grant Peterkin decided not to push further on but 'to make the best of it for the three or four hours that were left before dawn'. Most soldiers of the forward brigades had no food brought forward that evening and had to content themselves with emergency self-heating cans of soup. Some 500 of these cans had wisely been kept forward in a Weasel, thanks to 'good housekeeping'.

German Reaction

Reports of the preliminary bombardment reached the headquarters of 84th Division in Kleve before 0600 hours on 8 February 1945. General Fiebig, sharing the broad German opinion that the attack would be further south, believed that a Canadian operation of any scale was very unlikely because of the difficult going both in the forest and to the flanks. Thanks to the number of Allied troops appearing on the Groesbeek Heights, a diversionary attack on the Reichswald was, however, not unexpected and initially LXXXVI Corps did not consider it to be a serious matter. Consequently, it was only at 1045 hours, when reports

Armoured Recovery

The state of the ground in front of the Reichswald led to wholesale bogging in of armoured vehicles during 8 February and over subsequent days, with even Churchills and AVREs, which had an excellent cross-country reputation, succumbing. In some cases, this necessitated protracted attempts to recover them.

A Mk I Churchill ARV with a Canadian RAM Tank in the background. These were mostly used as OPs.

The Churchill Mk 1 Armoured Recovery Vehicles shown in the picture above were little more than Churchills with their turrets removed. So badly bogged were so many vehicles that it took two vehicles in tandem tow to break the suction between mud and belly plate and pull the casualty out. This was necessary as few REME ARVs at the time were fitted with winches. The danger was often that the ARVs had to get very close to the casualty to pull it, thus risking bogging in themselves!

First-line recovery of tanks fell to the Armoured Recovery Vehicles (ARVs), of which each tank squadron had one, commanded by a REME Recovery Mechanic sergeant. Second-line recovery was available at Brigade Workshops, where the Recovery Section held several more ARVs. To make up for the paucity of recovery assets, earlier in the North West European Campaign units used German tanks with their turrets removed as ARVs.

The Caterpillar D8 tractor.

By the winter of 1944/45 there were thirteen REME recovery companies and numerous heavy recovery sections found across 21st Army Group, which could be deployed as required, in this case to XXX Corps as the thaw set in and the difficulties were predicted. When recovery using the available ARVs was not possible, the Caterpillar D8 tractor with its 30-ton winch found in the heavy sections was used. Wheeled breakdown vehicles such as the Scammell 6 × 4 Explorer were also used. These vehicles, with earth anchors and other recovery and towing kit, were more than capable of recovering Churchills but it was a slow process. The main disadvantage in their use was that most were unarmoured. Also, because of the noise they produced, incoming enemy fire could not be heard. Several REME personnel received gallantry awards for carrying out recovery tasks under fire and many casualties were sustained.

The Churchill Mk II ARV, with a 25-ton winch, did not become available until just before the Rhine Crossing the following month, and even then in very small numbers, but their greater usefulness was welcome.

arrived that the forward defences had been penetrated, that any lingering doubts generals Schlemm and Fiebig may have had that this was the Allied main effort could be dismissed. However, by then it was too late to commit the scant reserves immediately available to best effect.

At 1300 hours, with the Allies entering the Reichswald, the situation was deteriorating further and Fiebig ordered the remnants of his forward battalions to withdraw and man the Siegfried Line defences. Execution proved to be almost impossible, due to the order to pull back not getting through, significant movement being impossible without heavy casualties from artillery fire, or because by this stage units could not disengage from the fighting. XXX Corps intelligence concluded, with some exaggeration, that: 'By the end of the day the whole of 1051 GR, one battalion 1052 GR and 84 Fus Bn had been captured or killed and all except three battalions of 84 Inf Div had been in action.'

Reaction at the higher levels of German command was also slow and the story of the night of 8–9 February 1945 could have been very different if General Schlemm had been allowed by General Blastowitz to proceed with 7th *Fallschirmjäger* Division's counter-attack. Having been planned to be launched from the Gennep area, it would have fallen squarely on 51st Highland Division and their incomplete hold on the western edge of the Reichswald.

The Numbering of Infantry Platoons

Unlike today when platoons are numbered in British battalions in companies A–C sequentially from 1–9, the 1943 system was significantly different, with the numbering starting in Headquarter Company and Support Company, followed by the rifle companies A to D.

Headquarter Company
No. 1 Signal Platoon
No. 2 Administrative Platoon

Support Company
No. 3 Mortar Platoon
No. 4 Anti-Tank Platoon
No. 5 Carrier Platoon
No. 6 Assault Pioneer Platoon

Rifle Companies

A Company
 No. 7 Platoon
 No. 8 Platoon
 No. 9 Platoon

B Company
 No. 10 Platoon
 No. 11 Platoon
 No. 12 Platoon

C Company
 No 13 Platoon
 No. 14 Platoon
 No. 15 Platoon

D Company
 No. 17 Platoon
 No. 18 Platoon
 No. 19 Platoon

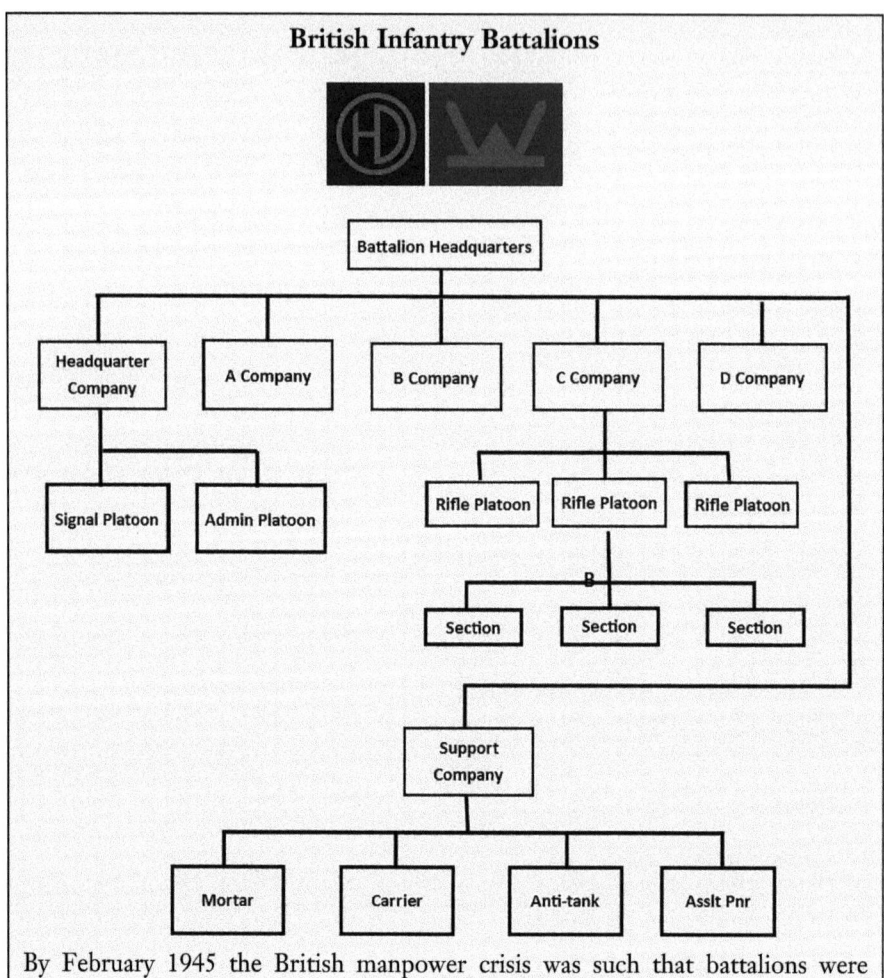

By February 1945 the British manpower crisis was such that battalions were authorised, if necessary, to reduce to a three rifle company ORBAT.

Chapter Five

Advance through the Reichswald, 9 February

On the 9th low-hanging cloud and heavy rain persisted well into the afternoon and not only curtailed air support but made movement as difficult as ever. [*Victory in the West*, Volume II]

The first day of VERITABLE had gone as well as could be expected bearing in mind the dramatic deterioration of ground conditions after the thaw. Equally positive was the fact that, so convinced were most German commanders that the attack on the Reichswald and across the Rhine floodplain was a diversionary attack, they had been slow to respond during 8 February. Consequently, only immediate reserves were reported by tactical air recce as moving to the support of the 84th Division. As one staff officer recorded, 'This could not last' and, as expected, on the morning of 9 February, German troops from across the Rhineland, elements of the 7th *Fallschirmjäger* Division in particular, were marching south towards Kleve and Goch, with the Allied air forces doing their best to interdict and slow enemy movement despite poor flying weather.

When questioned about the deployment of reserves after the war, General Schlemm explained to his interrogator how little influence, even as an army commander, he had over the conduct of the battle in the Rhineland:

> Once the battle was joined, it became obvious that the control of First Para Army no longer rested solely with Schlemm. Berlin had taken an interest in the matter, and Schlemm merely became a receptacle for the passing of orders. The Reichswald battle from that time on was to become for Schlemm a nightmare of excuses, entreaties and explanations. His first indication that he did not have a free hand came with the order that under no circumstances was any land between the Maas and the Rhine to be given up without the permission of Rundstedt, who would first ask Hitler. This prohibition on his freedom of movement considerably restricted Schlemm's options. He realized that if the Allies once captured the west bank of the Rhine, his complete army would be trapped. His own plan was to build a series of lines facing north, between the Maas and the Rhine, and retire slowly from position to position exacting as heavy a price as possible for every loss of ground. These tactics were not permitted, however, and 86 Corps was ordered to stand where it was and not yield an inch. As a result,

the British troops broke through vital positions time after time, forcing Schlemm to make a hasty adjustment to the new situation. In addition, a detailed explanation for each withdrawal had to be sent back.[1]

Schlemm later added that Hitler threatened to execute any commander who lost a Rhine bridge intact and that 'as I had a dozen bridges in my area, prospects of me living a long life seemed slim'.

There was, however, a fundamental problem facing the Allies, namely with VERITABLE's US counterpart, Operation GRENADE. The Germans had anticipated the American attack and, with the Roer dams still not captured by the First US Army, badly damaged these, releasing flood waters. Bradley's prevarication in January had come to haunt the Allies.

General Horrocks wrote:

It was now that I heard a really bad piece of news – namely, that on 9 February the Germans had blown the dam over the Roer, which meant that the Ninth US Army was faced by a wide strip of surging water which was quite unbridgeable. So their attack from the south had to be postponed. It was estimated that the floods would continue for at least two weeks. In fact,

It was only once the Roer's flow of flood waters subsided from 8mph could bridges start to be built.

it was not until 23 February that Simpson's leading troops were able to start crossing the Roer.

As a result, German reserves were able to concentrate against the First Canadian Army, condemning them to a hard and protracted battle.

The challenge for General Horrocks' XXX Corps during 9 February was to break through the Siegfried Line, which extended from overlooking the Maas floodplain through the Reichswald, across the Kranenburg–Kleve Road and onto the Rhine flats. The forest was regarded by the Germans as impractical for a major offensive and was, in their minds, a key feature of the Reichswald Plug's defences. Consequently, though enhancements to the defences had been made throughout the autumn, it was a lower priority than stretches of border further south. There were some concrete shelters in the Reichswald but most of the positions were revetted field defences. Attacks by XXX Corps on 9 February would be the continuation of the previous day's operations on a frontage of four divisions. These were: 3rd Canadian Division continuing their amphibious operations on the Rhine floodplain, which they had begun the previous evening, and 15th Scottish forcing its way on the strip of land between the forest and the floods. The 53rd Welsh and 51st Highland were to continue to fight through the Reichswald itself. The latter division also had objectives on the Maas floodplain south of the forest.

53rd Welsh Division in the Reichswald

After we had crossed the initial belt of organised defences, which included anti-tank ditches, *schumines* and fortified farms and villages, we now faced our biggest obstacle – the natural fortress of the Reichswald.

[Divisional History]

On the Welsh Division's left flank, the 15th Scottish Division were well ahead of the 53rd, having captured Kranenburg and reached the Siegfried Line at Frasselt by dusk on 8 February. Despite the considerable difficulties of getting the assault armour and tanks forward through the mud to breach the enemy's defences, by dawn the Scots were through and their dash to the vital ground of the Materborn feature was on.

Inside the Reichswald immediately to the right of 44 Lowland Brigade, the Welsh soldiers of 160 Brigade were also advancing. Their task was to push on adjacent to 15th Scottish Division, to the Stoppelberg and the north-easterly tip of the Reichswald between Nutterden and the Materborn feature. They would be followed by 158 Brigade, which would advance to the north and eastern faces of the forest and link up with 51st Highland Division.

Brigadier Coleman's 160 Brigade had spent most of the previous day waiting to pass through the division's 71 Brigade, which had attacked through the outer German defences and broken into the Reichswald. It had been planned that the brigade's leading battalions would follow through and attack the Siegfried Line defences along the Frasselt–Hekkens road by 1600 hours, but timing as elsewhere

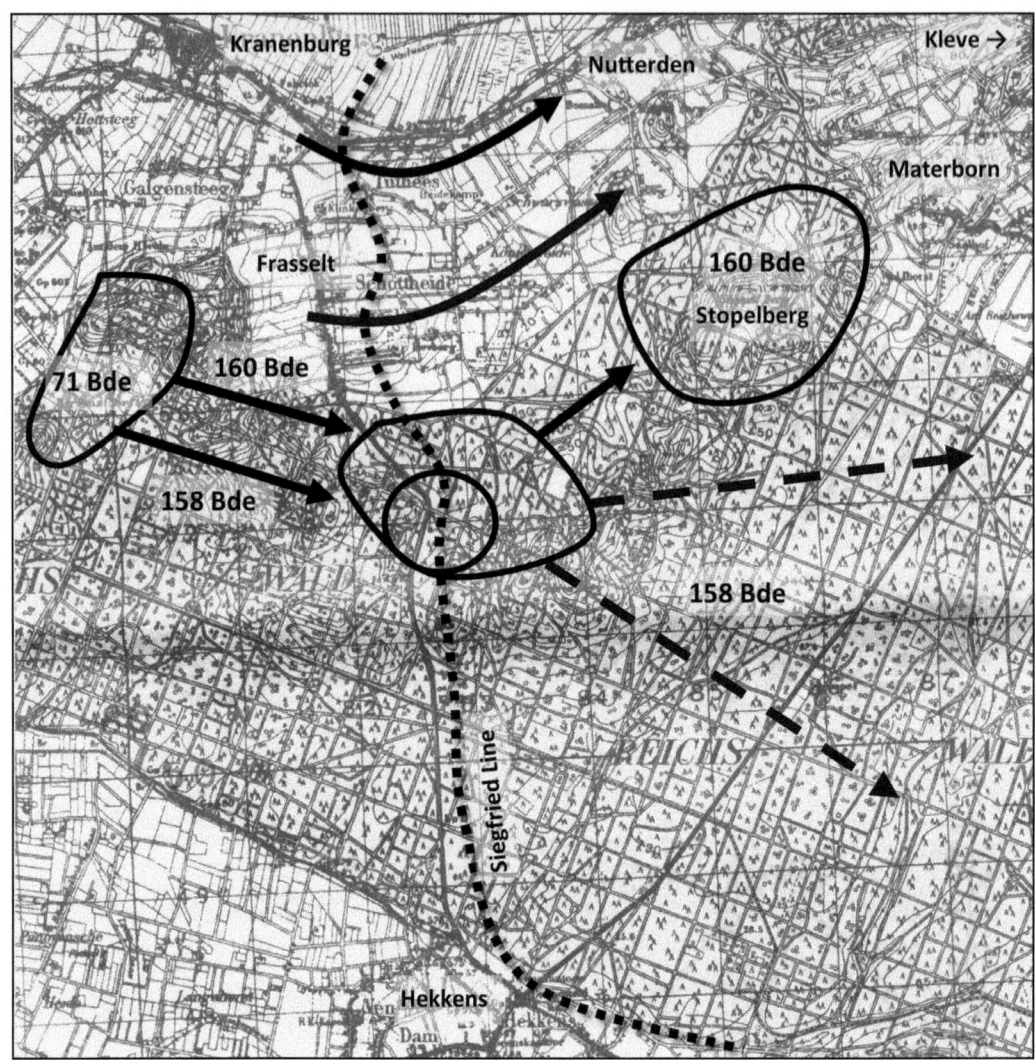

53rd Welsh Division's plan for the clearance of the Reichswald.

had slipped badly. Welsh war diarists all tell familiar stories of their move forward across the anti-tank ditch to join battle, which only began at 1630 hours. They laboured through mud with vehicles bogging one after the other. Consequently, it was not until between 1815 and 1915 hours that the advance from the western edge of the forest to a start line sited beyond the Brandenburg feature, let alone the objectives, could begin. The 4th Welch recorded that they: 'Passed through 71 Bde during night 8/9 Feb. Sight shelling on approach to SL.'

Inevitably, 160 Brigade's progress along the churned up forest rides and through the trees in darkness was slow. In this, the first part of their plan, they were allocated 1st East Lancashire Regiment from 158 Brigade as an extra battalion to help secure the Siegfried Line and act as a firm base for their own brigade. In short, they and 6th Royal Welch Fusiliers were to capture the defences on the Frasselt–Hekkens road, before 160 Brigade would continue the advance along the northern edge of the Reichswald to capture the Stoppelberg feature. They were to leave the 1st East Lancs to re-join 158 Brigade for their advance through the woods on the division's right flank.

The two infantry battalions in their advance to the Frasselt–Hekkens road were to be supported by C Squadron 9 RTR and A Squadron 147 RAC, but the latter could not get through the mud and traffic jams to join the East Lancs. Consequently, when the advance began at 2300 hours only 6 RWF had tank support. The history of the RTR records that:

> This manoeuvre had been thought out and practiced a fortnight previously. Moving on a single squadron front, tanks crashed through areas of plantation and were guided on foot where the trees were too solid to smash, but they arrived at the objective.

All four RTR troops advanced with the Fusiliers and due to the threat of mines, they avoided the tracks, with the tanks following one behind the other. The squadron reported the infantry appreciating 'their noisy movement that had been comforting and helpful in traversing dense woodland full of disorganised enemy

A Mark IV Churchill of 9 RTR, 34 Armoured Brigade, with the upgraded 75mm gun.

troops'. Consequently, with the Germans generally withdrawing, opposition on the 2,000-yard advance to the Frasselt–Hekkens road was light and their objectives on the Siegfried Line were reached at 0005 hours, some six hours behind schedule.

The German Siegfried Line defences in the forest proved to be far less formidable than glimpses through gaps in the canopy of pine trees showed on air photographs. In addition, they were thinly manned, and as the infantry and tanks approached resistance proved to be patchy. B Company of the East Lancs, however, had a stiff fight involving hand-to-hand fighting with bayonet and grenade to clear trenches and bunkers, collecting some fifty prisoners in the process. On the left of 6 RWF's advance, C Squadron reported resistance that 'needed dealing with'. As an indication of early signs of German recovery, local counter-attacks were launched against 160 Brigade but all were beaten off. By 0200 hours the anti-tank guns of the East Lancs and 6 RWF had arrived, and the battalion's forward companies were reporting being 'firm on the ground' 150 yards beyond the Frasselt road.

It was later discovered that the Germans had considered the Reichswald was itself sufficient to deter attack. One German officer taken prisoner confessed that: 'Our appreciation of the forest was that it was impassable to tanks.'

Major Lewis, commanding D Company, described the appalling conditions that 4 Welch had to overcome to follow the RWF into and through the forest:

> The single third-class road was blocked by bogged transport. Gangs of men worked feverishly to clear it. Any vehicle that could not move under its own power was abandoned and pushed into the swamp alongside. It was vital that no troops should be caught in this open ground at first light next morning [9 February]. It was raining hard and everyone was soaked to the skin. It was only with the greatest difficulty that weapons were kept dry and serviceable. At each halt men just lay down in the mud with the rain beating down on them trying to snatch a few moments of sleep. If they were near a burning building they crowded round it, regardless of text-book precepts about dispersion, to get some of the heat. Through a pitch-black night of driving rain, the column moved on fifty or a hundred yards at a time. The tanks in support had to take a different route and then try to find their proper place in the column. They were getting hopelessly stuck blocking the track. It was a tremendous struggle to keep any transport at all – yet it meant food, water and ammo. Inside the forest no track was distinguishable in the darkness. The start line for the attack – a lateral track in the forest – was reached at dawn.

After their torturous night march, at 0730 hours, approximately co-ordinated with 44 Lowland Brigade, it was light enough among the trees for 160 Brigade's advance north from the Frasselt–Hekkens road north to the Stoppelberg to begin. Now moving on a two-battalion front, 4 Welch and 2nd Monmouthshires (2 Mons) were supported respectively by the Churchills of A and B squadron of 9 RTR.

The 4th Welch advanced some 2,000 yards following the northern edge of the Reichswald to secure two features just inside the forest, with 2 Mons following behind them, starting at an hour and a half later at 0900 hours. Their task was to pass through 4th Welch and secure the wooded high ground of the Stoppelberg. Major Lewis recorded:

> The strain on the infantryman was terrific. After forcing his way through undergrowth or trudging in the pelting rain along tracks and paths ankle deep in mud, soaked through, tired out, he still had to be alert, never knowing from one moment to another when he was going to meet his enemy. Whenever an objective was reached, he had first to dig in, then spend four hours of the night on guard. Then he might, if lucky, get to doze in a water-logged trench.

So bad were conditions in the wood, 2 Mons and B Squadron attempted to come out of the forest into 15th Scottish Division's area near Schottheide but they were thwarted by anti-tank guns that were later dealt with by the Scots. The Churchills of B Squadron, despite the earlier passage of A Squadron along the edge of the Reichswald, also came under fire from a couple of artillery pieces sited in the open ground north of the forest. They were promptly engaged and knocked out by 95mm high explosive shells at a range of 2,200 yards.[2]

By 0903 hours, 4th Welch had 'assaulted and captured their objective (HOLLYHOCK) against slight opposition', taking 3 officers and 101 German other ranks prisoner. An hour later, 2 Mons passed through and had occupied the Stoppelberg by midday without a fight, much to their surprise.

Meanwhile, the remainder of 158 Brigade had another painfully slow march forward, led by 1st/5th Welch followed by 7 RWF. By 0700 hours they joined 1st East Lancs in the Siegfried Line defences, and 7 RWF relieved 6 RWF. This

The Churchill Mark V close support variant mounted the shorter-barrelled 95mm gun optimised for firing high-explosive rounds, rather than the 75mm or 6-pounders of the other gun tanks.

battalion, now mounted on the tanks of C Squadron, was at 1200 hours able to follow the well-ploughed route, taken by the rest of 160 Brigade. Two hours later the battalion had secured its objectives and was in position at the edge of the forest east of the Stoppelberg. 160 Brigade now held the area except for one small tongue of wood held by the newly arrived II Battalion, 16 *Fallschirmjäger* Regiment. This too was cleared after a sharp fight, in which and some fifty prisoners were taken:

> From this position 7 RWF were able to see German reinforcements heading north-east on to the Hekkens–Materborn road, which enemy infantry, motor vehicles, tanks and staff cars were still using ... and were able to harass this movement with indirect fire. This included a shoot directed by the squadron commander against a German infantry position, centred on four machine guns that were holding up 15th Scottish Division's advance.

When 158 Brigade was assembled, Brigadier Wilsey ordered his battalions forward at 1400 hours. With their carriers and the supporting tanks of 147 RAC still not having arrived, 1st/5th Welch set off to its objectives towards the north-east edge of the Reichswald. With a reduction in the availability of friendly artillery fire, and fresh German troops, it was clear that the enemy had continued his recovery from the weight of the previous day's attack. The Welsh Infantry encountered significant opposition from mortar and machine gun fire. This brought the advance to a halt but when the Churchills of 147 RAC finally arrived, a quick attack was launched, and completed the brigade's captured of its objectives by 1600 hours. Across the divisional area soldiers of the Welsh Division were continuing to round up prisoners but Germans were still emerging, mostly to surrender, from their hiding places in the extensive 'captured' area for several days.

Churchill ARVs in tandem dragging tanks of 147 Regiment RAC from the mud short of the Reichswald.

If the 53rd Welsh Division's advance had been achieved with relative ease, the same could not be said for logistic support. During the day the division's main supply route 'totally collapsed':

> The many mines, combined with the paucity of tracks through the Reichswald Forest, tended to canalize traffic and, together with the effects of the thaw and the frequent rain, resulted in an appalling deterioration in the mobility of units. Formations reported the utmost difficulty in meeting requirements of their forward troops, carriers were defeated and even the ubiquitous jeep found itself conquered. Eventually, recourse was again made to the WEASEL which had proved itself so valuable in the Ardennes. Every available WEASEL in the theatre was rushed forward and issued for use in the distribution of essentials where other vehicles would be useless.[3]

Attempts at filling ruts and quagmires with rubble and anything else that came to hand were only possible on a small scale, which was not enough, and even the combined efforts of the 53rd's Royal Engineers, pioneers and battalions that had carried out the initial attack failed to make a difference. Consequently, there was no other option but to divert the division's logistic traffic onto the Kranenburg road, along with that of the 15th Scottish Division, creating enormous traffic problems. With, however, only relatively short distances covered fuel was not the immediate problem, nor was food, as several days of Compo ration packs had been issued, although even these had to be brought forward by unit transport. The main challenge for the RASC was the rate of ammunition expenditure, particularly artillery natures. Large amounts of ammunition had, of course, been dumped well forward prior to the thaw, but these stocks were soon largely inaccessible, isolated amidst a sea of impassable mud created by the first vehicles attempting a collection from them. Other ammunition dumps were lost to the rising flood waters and led to First Canadian Army introducing rationing of artillery ammunition.

51st Highland Division

Even though separated from the 53rd Welsh Division to their north by little more than 1,000 yards, during 9 February, the 51st Highland Division was effectively fighting its own battle isolated by the thick forest. The Highlanders of 154 Brigade had broken into the Reichswald the previous evening but with the attack running well behind schedule, their objectives had not been fully secured.

To the right, 153 Brigade, after a day of waiting throughout the 8th, had finally entered the western extremity of the Reichswald and Kiekeberg Woods. By midnight, however, it was apparent that it was so dark amidst the densely packed pine trees that it was in most cases impossible to continue operations that night. Not only that, hardly any of the brigades' vehicles could get through the mud, and radios and support weapons had to be man packed forward. Around dawn, however, the Churchills of 107 Regiment RAC that had withdrawn to leaguer and replenish, returned managing to drag some of the missing vehicles forward, for instance, the 1st Gordons' battalion headquarters. Having missed their evening

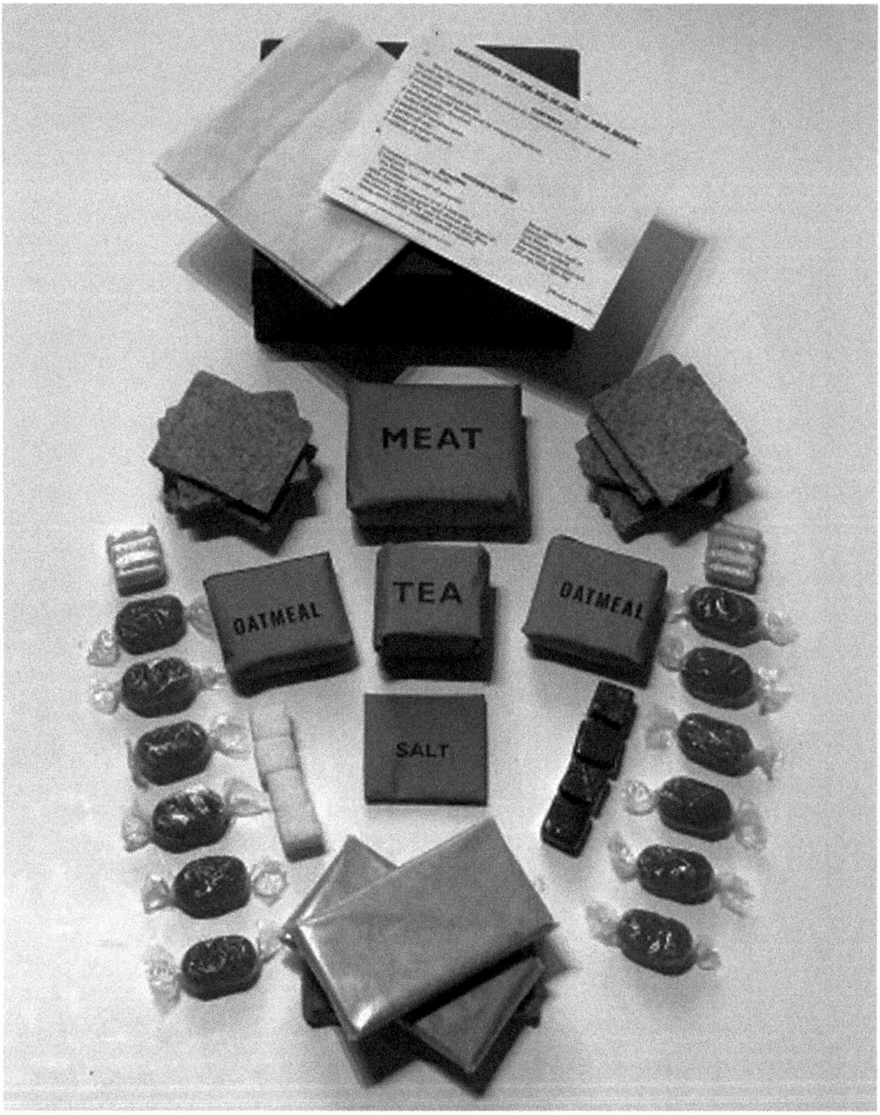

The contents of a British twenty-four-hour ration pack.

meal, the Jocks were relieved to find that the tanks had also brought up their breakfast in 'hay boxes' to within a mile of company positions.[4]

The division's intent was to complete the previous day's tasks before pressing on east through the Reichswald and south out onto the Maas floodplain, which unlike that of the Rhine, although wet, was not as flooded. With 152 Brigade finally being able to come forward, they were to fight their way along a forest ride called the Kartenspielerweg, and capture the villages of Hekkens and Kessel,

Food prepared at the Battalion's Q staff would be kept warm in the Insulator 6 Gallon or 'hay box'.

along with the crossing of the River Niers at the latter village. From the Kiekeberg Woods, 153 Brigade, with 1st Gordons right, 5 BW left and 5th/7th Gordons as brigade reserve, was to strike south out onto the flat ground, where they were to secure the river line and the vital hardtop road between Mook and Gennep (Route HEART).

With operations paused until 0900 hours, the war diary of the 1st Gordons describes the resumption of clearing through the Kiekeberg Woods towards 6 Canadian Brigade's forward defensive line:

> The day started with two simultaneous mopping-up operations. B Coy with the Carrier Platoon mopping up St. Martensberg and all enemy posns to the north and NE of it as far as Grafwegen, while D Coy cleaned up the valley to the west of their posn. B Coy had no trouble and took some 150 prisoners but D Coy were fired on from entrenched inf in the valley and were held up, the leading Pl Comd (Lieut Fraser) being killed. As the guns of the supporting Fd Regt would have to fire directly towards the axis of advance, it was not possible to use arty until B Coy had returned and were pulled back in line with the Jansberg buildings. A sharp shoot was then put down on the valley and D Coy repeated their operation, supported this time by a tp of tks. They completed it successfully and returned with a dozen POWs to their original posns where they were best placed for their next attack.

As far as 1st Gordons were concerned: 'The next phase of the operation was to take the network of deep trenches and dugouts on the far side of the valley. C Coy proceed to occupy this without opposition after an arty concentration.'

Meanwhile, further north in the main body of the Reichswald, A Company, 1st Black Watch, was sent up from 154 Brigade's reserve to assist B Company of

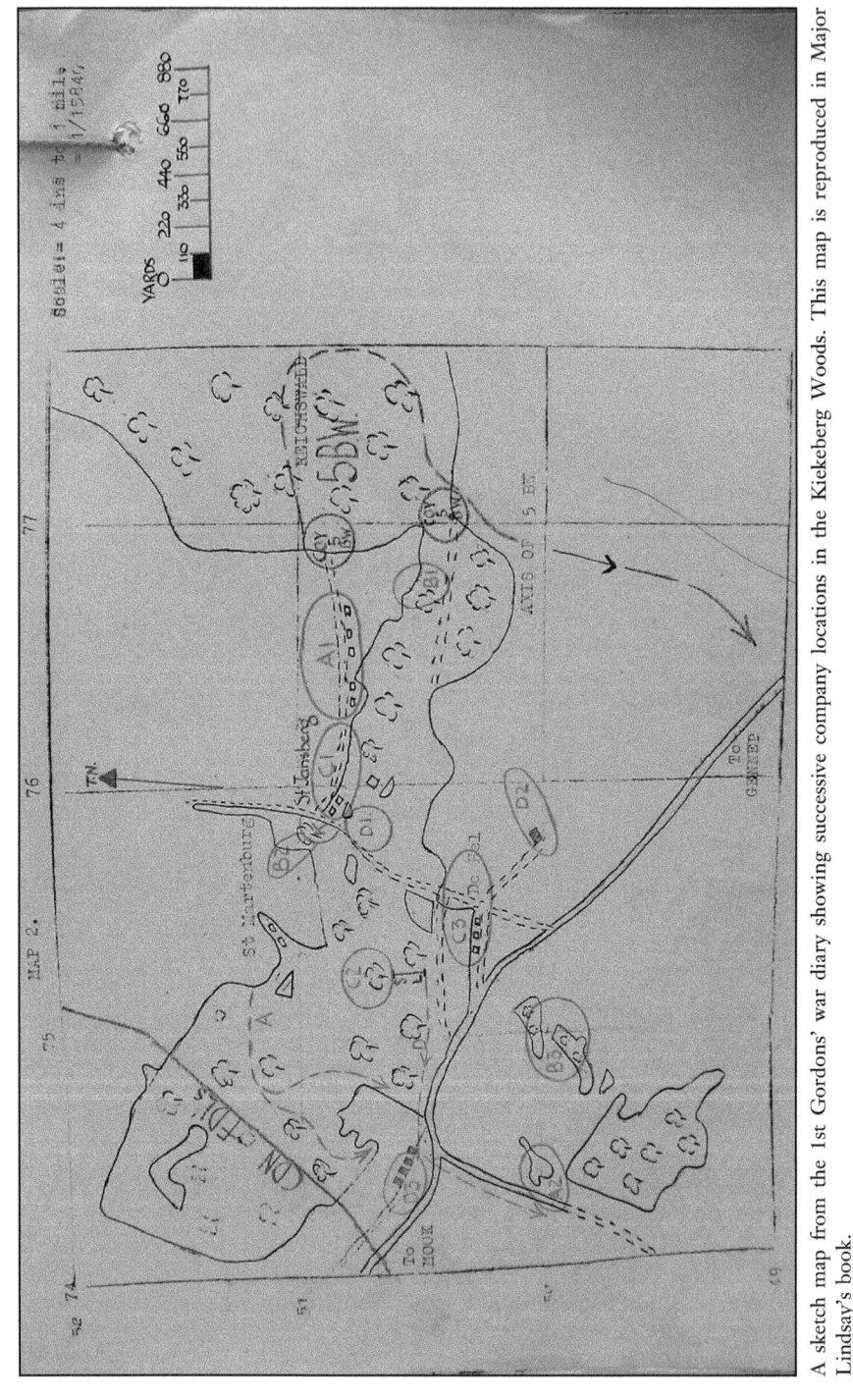

A sketch map from the 1st Gordons' war diary showing successive company locations in the Kiekeberg Woods. This map is reproduced in Major Lindsay's book.

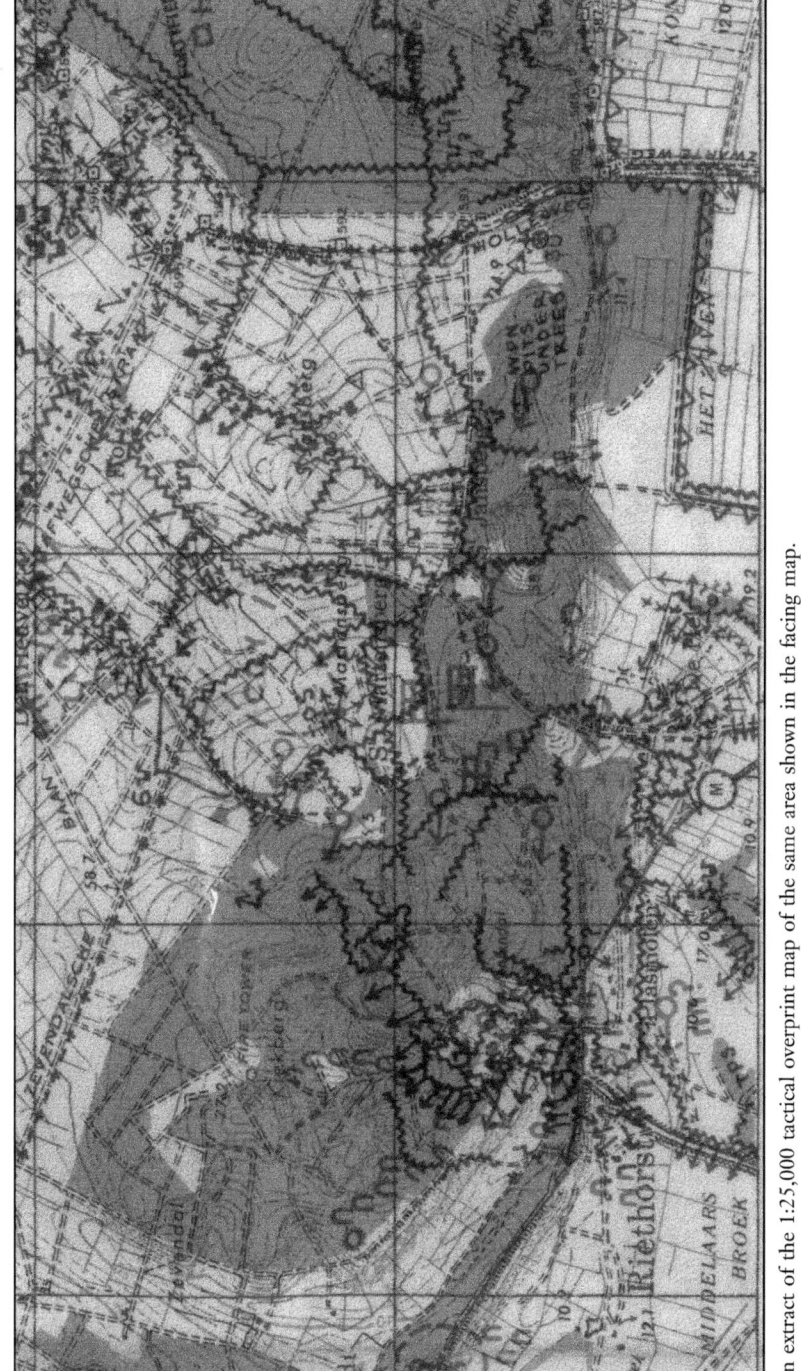

An extract of the 1:25,000 tactical overprint map of the same area shown in the facing map.

the 5th/7th Gordons in their forward position. This battalion, following their night advance deeper into the forest beyond the Freudenberg, had been at close quarters with the enemy for some hours. When the Black Watch arrived the Germans, however, stood and fought, inflicting eleven casualties, both killed and wounded, on A Company, before withdrawing to the east.

At the same time, 154 Brigade's reserve battalion, 7th Argylls, along with its transport and a troop of Churchills, had by 0800 hours managed to come up alongside 5th/7th Gordons' main position, occupying the northern end of the Freudenberg. The 7th Battalion's historian, writing of their action later that morning on 9 February, recorded that:

> It was no easy task to find one's way through this extensive, featureless forest, and indeed at times the location of the battalion was in doubt. Up to this time no enemy had been encountered or observed, which perhaps in away was a good thing, as conditions were unpleasant enough without enemy interference, but when the battalion started to advance again at 10 o'clock to a further objective, several Spandau posts were immediately encountered. The Churchill tanks went into action at once, and very quickly cleared up these posts without difficulty before the battalion reached their objective.

With the previous day's tasks completed, 153 Brigade was to swing south out of the woods and forest onto the Maas floodplain, where they were to clear the flat ground, which was dotted with villages and copses. As he was preparing orders, Major Lindsay received a signal from Colonel Grant-Peterkin commanding the brigade, in the circumstances exerting surprisingly gentle pressure. 'I am sure you are doing everything you can to open the Mook–Gennep road as soon as possible, as it is required for the Corps axis. We want sappers to be able to work on it as soon as it is dark.'

During the afternoon of the 9th, 1st Gordons' C and D companies advanced parallel to each other, south to the edge of the woods at Del Hel overlooking the Maas floodplain and the Mook–Gennep road (see map on page 112). Major Lindsay wrote:

> I watched this attack from a wonderful observation post ... Dany Reid [D Company] reported that he had seen about sixty Huns going into it [a copse south east of Del Hel], in addition to those previously there, and all were starting to dig hard. There were no less than nine of us there to witness the slaughter when we turned the 25-pounders and 4.2 mortars on them before the attack.

Major Lindsay had carefully planned the attack phase by phase, with fire support not only from the mortars and guns of the field artillery but of the supporting tanks as well. As a result:

> It was a wonderful sight to see D Company race across the open ground and onto their objective, with enemy mortar fire coming down just too late

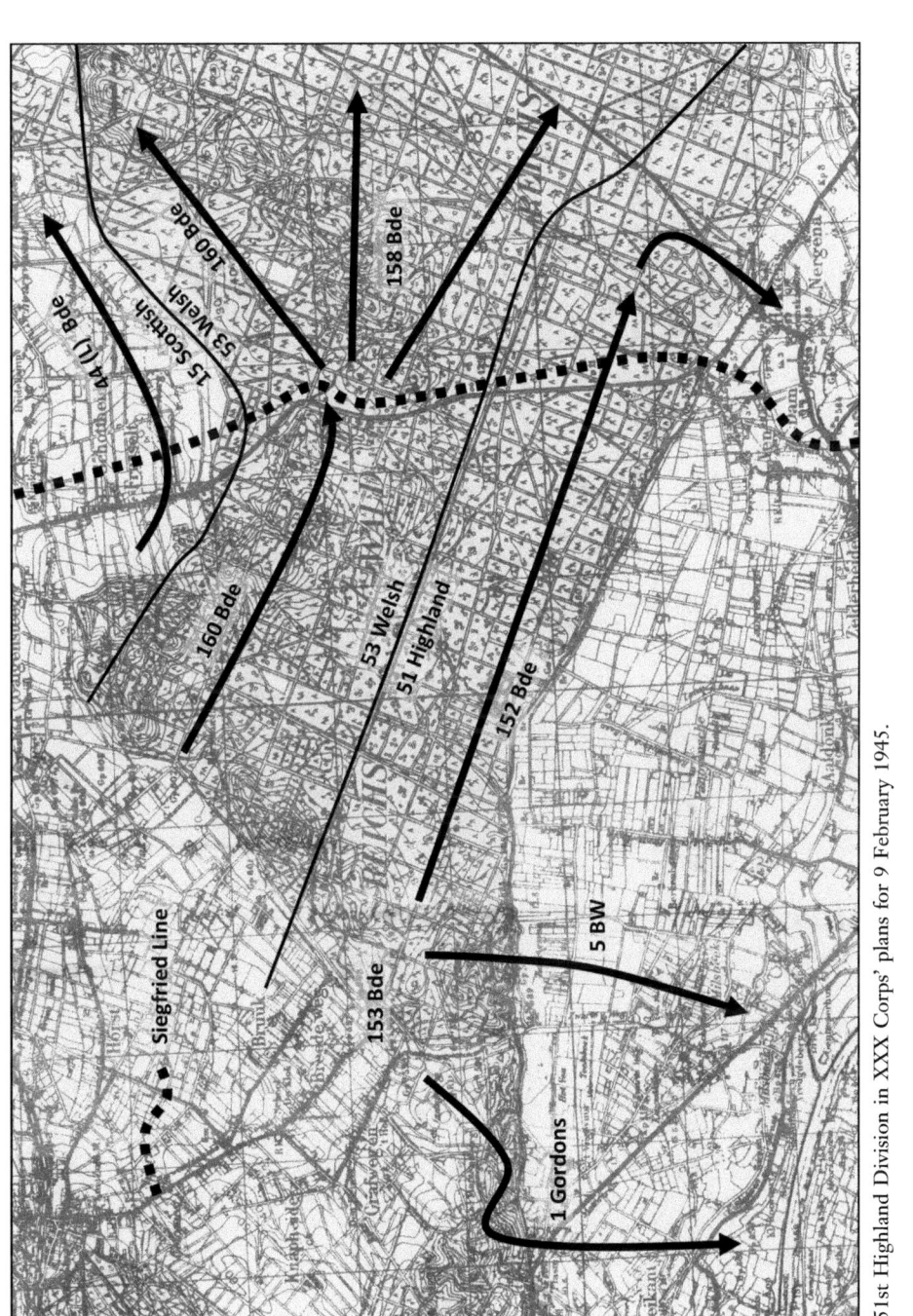

51st Highland Division in XXX Corps' plans for 9 February 1945.

Churchills of 107 Regiment RAC (King's Own), 34 Tank Brigade, at the edge of the Reichswald on 9 February 1945.

behind them. From the observation post we could see the Hun streaming back in little packets into the wood beyond. It was a gunner's dream but unfortunately there was so much traffic on the air at the time that we could not get through to the guns.

C Company, however, had a stiff fight to capture Den Hel, which unknown to them was a German battalion headquarters. When the company advanced, without radio contact, the sound of battle was soon heard at the Gordons' battalion headquarters. That C Company was locked in battle was soon confirmed by the arrival of stretcher bearers at the Regimental Aid Post:

When I joined Alec Lumsden down at the bottom he told me that a young officer of nineteen, whom we had been rather worried about, had been splendid: he'd apparently made up his mind that he had no chance and might as well die bravely – at any rate, in the face of intense fire and with one or two wounded shrieking with pain, he ran forward, leading his platoon until they had charged in and taken the position.

Of the resulting close-quarter fighting in Den Hel, Company Sergeant Major Morrice recorded:

> I was able to get our company piper – Piper McLaughlin – into a trench and he played the pipes. It had a great effect on the Germans. We fixed bayonets and charged and were able to round them up. We captured an enormous number of prisoners at their headquarters. I caught the CO of the battalion and disarmed him myself.

By now the number of prisoners in the Gordons' hands was nearly 300 and Major Lindsay commented: 'So far everything had gone according to plan and all the companies reached the objectives ... But I might have guessed that the luck was soon to break.'

On the battalion's right flank, A and B Companies were also in action clearing German positions in several copses near the village of Heikant, which were in front of the defences of the Cameron Highlanders of Canada. B Company had advanced at speed from Den Hel at 1700 hours and, despite coming under mortar fire, the battalion's FOO reported that at 1900 hours: 'The wild highland cries we could hear above the general din, told us that the Company had launched a bayonet charge through the copse.' A Company's attack, however, was not going well.

The Riethorst/Plasmolen country 1st Gordons fought over during 9 February 1945.

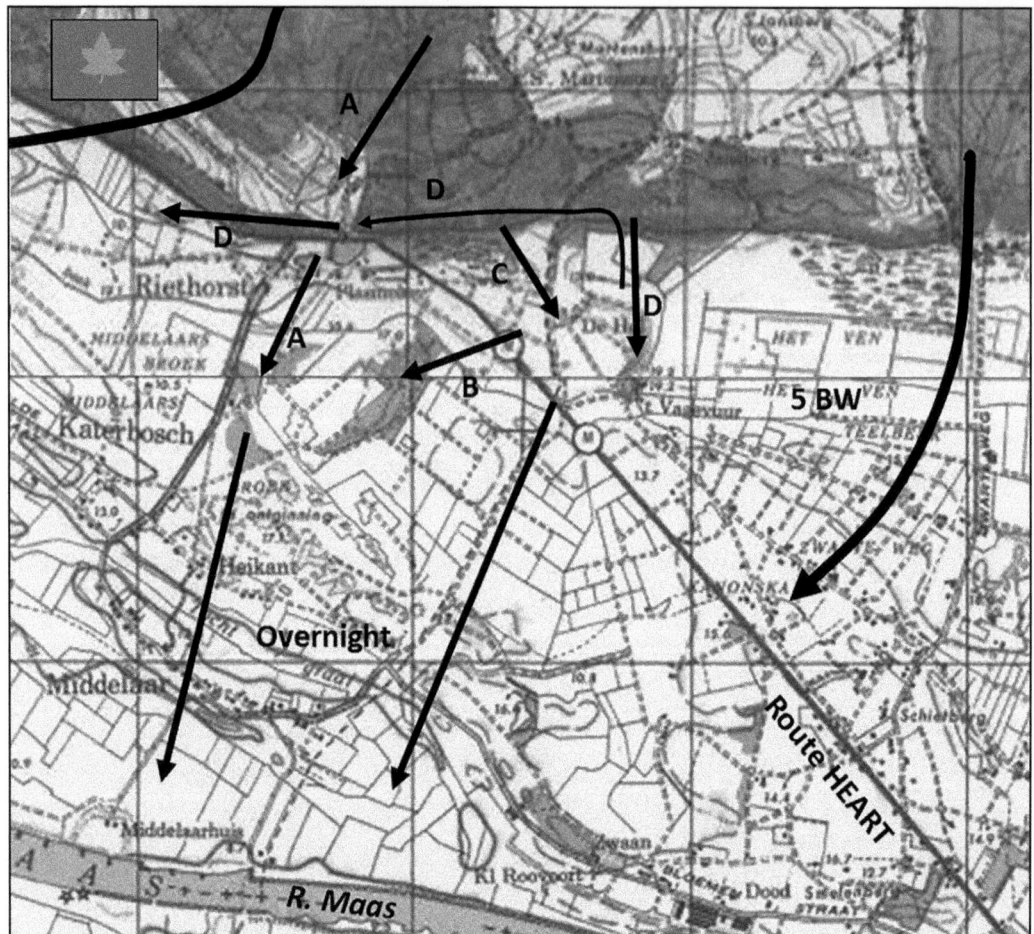

The area of the floodplain fought over by 1st Gordons.

A simple statement in the war diary dashed Major Lindsay's hopes. '1640 A Coy held up at 749508' by a previously unidentified German strongpoint astride the Mook road. He wrote:

> I had had no news of them for nearly three hours and hoped that they had mopped up that strong point and were now in their final position. So judge my dismay when Dennis said that his company had failed to take it, that it was very strongly held and protected by mines which had caused him several casualties, and that they had been finally stopped by at least three well-sited Spandaus.
>
> This gave me a very nasty jolt and I had to do some rapid thinking. I told him that I would attack with another company from due east, along the ridge, as soon as it was dark. Then the line went dead.
>
> I did not like it at all. But the position simply had to be taken. I remembered the message I had received an hour before. I knew that both the Divisional and Corps Commanders were waiting for the news that 1st Gordons had opened up the road. Failure was unthinkable.

The war diary continued: 'The CO decided to send D Coy along the main road (MOOK–GENNEP) to attack the enemy in the rear' (see aerial photograph on page 111 and map on page 114). With daylight fading fast, this would be a night attack for D Company, which had already carried out three attacks that day. They would, however, be supported by the firepower, mobility and (limited) armoured protection of the Carrier Platoon. Major Lindsay continued:

> It seemed to me that the responsibility for this attack was altogether too great for a company commander ... so I decided to take personal command of it. I told Alec [the battalion's second in command] to take over the rest of the battalion. By this time the [5th] Black Watch were down in Kanonskamp, so the general situation [on the left flank] was good.
>
> Danny Reid and I decided to use a start-line running northwards from a German command post which had already been cleared. So we marched round towards it in single file, along a narrow path at the foot of the very steep ride, with trees on either side of us: Macpherson's platoon in the lead, then Danny and I, then the remainder of the company, followed by Moir and his carrier platoon.

As the company moved in single file along a path west from Den Hel, they were ambushed by an enemy section position that had not been cleared during earlier advances:

> They must have been asleep, for one-third of us had already passed them. There was an instantaneous crash of automatic fire from the column and every one of them fell, riddled with bullets. It was all over in about two seconds, and our only casualty was Macpherson, slightly wounded in the leg. Actually, it was a most efficient performance on our part ...

This was, however, not a good start even before the FUP had been reached and as D Company wound its way along the steep southern slope of the Kiekeberg, they were slowed by taggle of trees blown down by the Allied bombardment. 'Every hundred yards took us about fifteen minutes, and the confusion was indescribable.' Lindsay continued his account, confessing serious doubts. 'What an awful balls up of this I've made,' I thought to myself, having lost all control. 'It's going to be a ghastly failure.'

An outbreak of fire from a defensive position in and around a building to their front told Lindsay that they had run into the enemy. He recalled that: 'It was fearfully dark among the trees in spite of many flares behind the Canadian lines. Much red tracer was also going up beyond ...' It was the natural inclination to wait and attack in the morning but with the need to open the Mook road 'it had to be done':

> A light mortar kept slamming down close to us on our left. Everybody was a bit frightened, except perhaps Danny [Reid]. I heard him moving from platoon to platoon, full of confidence, putting them in position and giving

Moving in single file was not only necessary through the more tightly spaced trees but elsewhere to minimise casualties from mines.

The defences overprint map and A and D companies' fight for Riethorst.

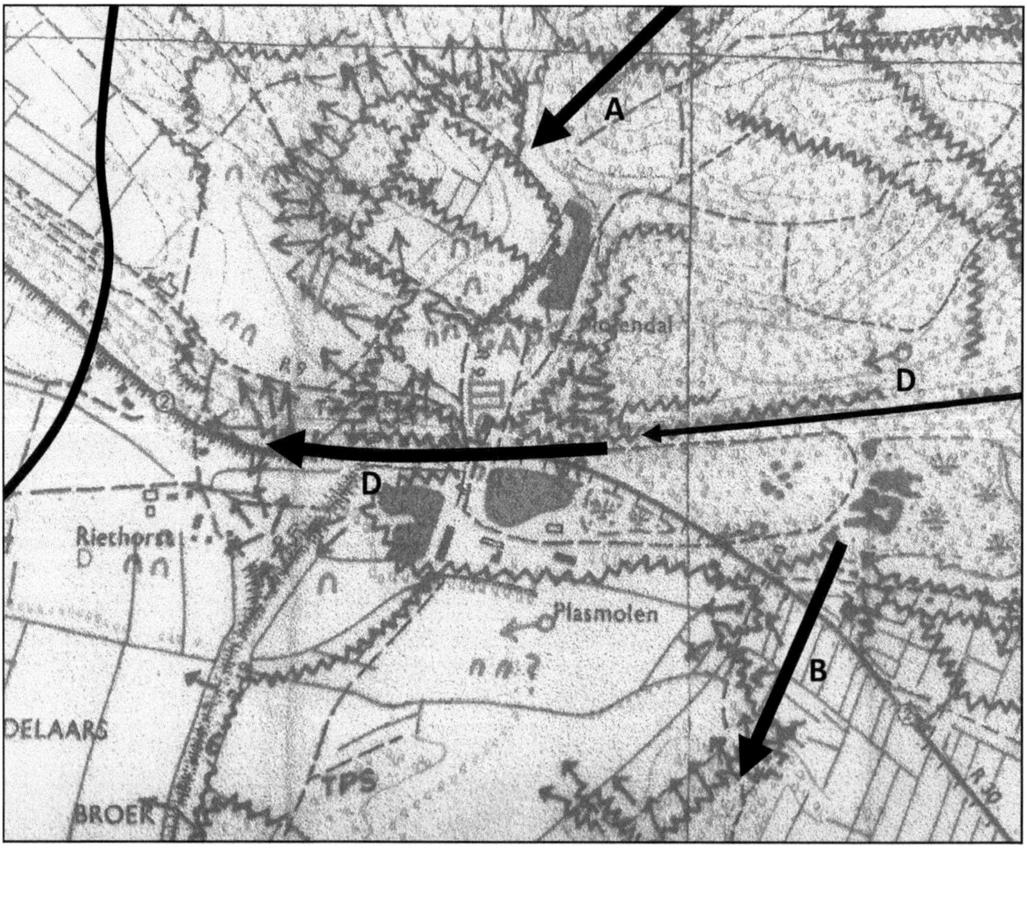

orders. Then the leading platoon moved forward. 'Get on, you bastards, what the hell are you doing hanging back on the right?' I heard his loud voice shout.

There was a cheer and bursts of Sten and a wild surge forward, and in a moment a shout of 'Kamerad!' and a column of Huns, seventy-one in number, came running out with their hands up. They said there were no more of them, but I told Danny we must go right through the position as far as the Canadians.

As the leading platoon fanned out, climbing over piles of rubble interlaced with a honeycomb of trenches, there was the obvious danger of fratricide with the Canadians. To warn them of the approaching friendly force, Major Lindsay ordered the company pipers to play the regimental march but 'I feared that our friends would not hear it, so we went forward shouting "Canadians!" at the top of our voices.' Overnight, 1st Gordons cleared a further 2,000 yards south to the banks of the River Maas, which they reported being in their hands at 0600 hours on 10 February.

On 153 Brigade's left flank, 5th Black Watch had captured Pyramid Hill the previous evening and, as with the other battalions in the forest, the soldiers had endured a short but tense night. Their part in the plan was to swing south out of the forest, across a floodplain and, swinging south-east, capture the small town of Gennep lying between the rivers Maas and Niers. Private Tom Renouf recalled:

> In the dank and misty early light, we reached a ditch running along the southern fringe of the forest and then followed it to our new start line. As we left the forest, the [5th] Camerons prepared to take our place.
>
> We were glad to be out of that forest and remained in our ditch until about midday. But then came a new terror, when we took the highly unusual step of attacking in extended order, strung out across an open field instead of advancing in single file to present less of a target. Normally, we would be right behind each other, gingerly marching up a road or hugging a tree line or a ditch. But here we were, spread out across an open field, with no cover. It was very strange and uncomfortable. We felt so exposed, like grouse on 12 August.

The battalion was, however, covered to a degree by a barrage of HE and smoke and thickened up by the fire of the Vickers guns of the 1st/7th Middlesex, who had during the morning occupied fire positions along the southern edge of the Reichswald. Without this support it is inconceivable that 5 BW's advance would have been possible.

Captain Jack Schwab, an artillery FOO of 127 Field Regiment RA who was providing 5 BW with the necessary artillery fire support, recalled the advance out onto the Maas floodplain:

> We had to attack over 2½ thousand yards of open country, quite flat with our left flank open, and the place where I had to leave the forest over a little

A Vickers machine gun in action firing an indirect barrage during the opening phases of Operation VERITABLE.

bridge was heavily mortared by the Boche. After the infantry went up under smoke from us and heavy medium shoot from ten Regts, I took my jeep up the road. It was a bad moment waiting there but on we went flat out, closely followed and preceded by Spandau bullets from our right flank. They whistled overhead and at the road in front, but we got there and reached C Coy. Sometime later they attacked, for which I provided an HE stonk followed by a really most effective smoke screen. I went with the Coy Comd … We got there – quite good shooting at houses with the PIAT gun was a feature …[5]

So effective was the fire support that Private Renouf commented: 'Even though the bullets zinged all around us, we did not suffer a single casualty. It was nothing short of miraculous.' His conclusion was that they were up against second-rate

German troops and that: 'Instead of picking out one poor sod and concentrating their fire on him until he dropped, they fired willy-nilly, spraying bullets across the line without any accuracy and with absolutely no effect.'

> We stalked steadily forward in a crouch. I was saying my prayers and hoping for the best. Before we got very far, the enemy opened fire from all directions. The quaint, red-roofed farmhouses that were scattered in front of us were all bristling with German machine guns. They must have thought it was the Führer's birthday when they saw us spread across the field.
>
> It was petrifying. I wanted to drop to the ground and burrow down as far as I could. But Bob Fowler, revered as our 'Immortal Sergeant', was completely cool. He kept shouting: 'Six to eight yards between each man. Spread out! Keep moving! Keep moving!' He was the best soldier in the British Army, as far as I was concerned. A stern disciplinarian, he still managed to be friendly and highly respected by the platoon. He was wise and efficient, and looked after us like a grandfather. I would have followed him over a cliff.
>
> The bullets were whizzing past us, hitting the ground and spurting up dirt in front of us as we walked towards the guns. But we kept going, battling the natural instinct to hit the deck, as Bob urged us on and steadied our nerves ...

Captain Schwab, veteran of campaigns in North Africa, Sicily and north-west Europe.

> We reached the first farmhouse and kept up withering fire with rifles and machine guns while we crept forward and chucked grenades through the windows. Then we crashed in and took the surviving Germans prisoner. As soon as we had secured them, I collapsed against a wall with sheer relief that we had made it to safety.

This was, however, only the first bound of the advance. 'Soon, we were off again, heading across more open fields towards the next farmhouse,' and by dusk they had secured the fourth farm complex. Here they were ordered to halt. This advance had taken the leading companies, A and B, to positions on the Mook–Gennep road by 1600 hours, 1,000 yards north of the river.

Captain Schwab concluded his account of his day with 5 BW:

> I established an OP in the church steeple which I'd persuaded the PIAT to spare! Excellent view and I got some grand shooting on the Maas bank where we got about 100 Germans all retreating from 1 Gordons on our right. We were by then right behind them. The shells broke up what looked like a possible counter-attack and then good old B Coy came up to the road – a hundred yards in front of me. We were again mortared, and machine gunned. So far nothing to eat since breakfast of tea and bread and jam but had some bacon at 1600. Icy wind in the church tower.

152 (Highland) Brigade

During 8 February, 152 Brigade had, like much of the rest of the division, spent the day waiting but now it was their turn to conduct a passage of lines through 154 Brigade's positions on the Freudenberg. General Rennie's plan was that while 153 fought their way towards the edge of the Reichswald, Kiekeberg Wood and out onto the Maas floodplain, 152 Brigade would advance further east into the forest along the axis of the 7-mile-long Kartenspielerweg to the Kleve–Hekkens Road. From there they would subsequently wheel south to secure the area of Hekkens, Kessel and the crossings of the River Niers. The extract below from the brigade's Operation Order No. 12 explains how the brigade's three battalions, one after the other, supported by C Squadron 107 Regiment RAC and three machine gun companies of the 1st/7th Middlesex, were planned to advance through the Reichswald.

> INTENTION
> 4. 152 Inf Bde will adv on D + 1 and will
> (a) Clear the SOUTHERN edge of the REICHSWALD on the axis rd junc 773518 – Xrds 827496 [Kartenspielerweg].
> (b) Secure and gain control of the area KESSEL 8547 – Xrds HEKKENS 8348 – Xrds 846490.
> (c) Deploy 1/7 Mx to give flank protection on SOUTHERN edge of the REICHSWALD.

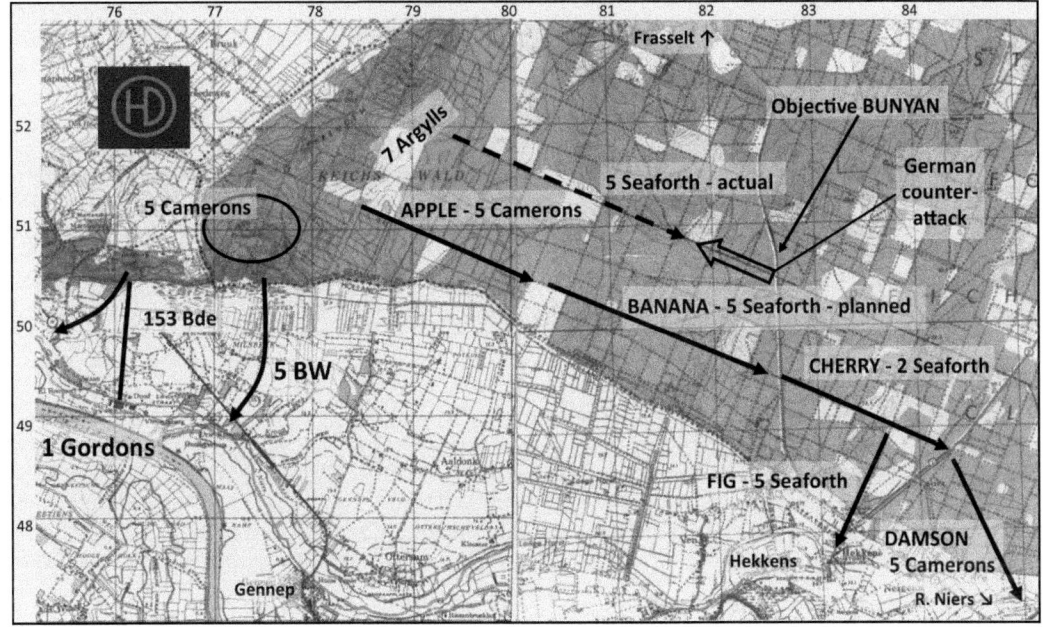

The planned advance through the Reichswald by 152 (Highland) Brigade.

METHOD
5. Gen. Adv will be carried out in five phases as under –
(a) Phase I. CODEWORD – APPLE.
   5 CAMERONS will adv through 154 Bde and secure gen area 8050.
(b) Phase II. CODEWORD – BANANA.
   5 SEAFORTH will pass through 5 CAMERONS and will secure gen area 8249.
(c) Phase III. CODEWORD – CHERRY.
   2 SEAFORTH will pass through 5 SEAFORTH to secure gen area 8449.
(d) Phase IV. CODEWORD – DAMSON.
   5 CAMERONS will pass through 2 SEAFORTH to secure br 419470.
(e) Phase V. CODEWORD – FIG.
   5 SEAFORTH will capture HEKKENS 8347.

This was an ambitious set of tasks that even in good conditions would have been challenging, but given the mud that at best slowed the tempo of the operation and at worst bogged in both tracked and wheeled vehicles, it was indeed a tall order.

The first phase of the attack (APPLE) was delayed by 5th/7th Gordons, who having reached the southern knoll of the Freudenberg ridge just inside the Reichswald the previous evening, had struggled to secure the area during the hours of darkness. Consequently, it was not until 1000 hours that 5th Queen's Own Cameron Highlanders were able to conduct their passage of lines and advance on the Kartenspielerweg. The battalion was led by D Company, followed in order by B Company, Tactical HQ and A and C companies. The Germans had clearly anticipated the axis of attack and had prepared defence in depth along the length of the track based on a series of *fallschirmjäger spandau* posts, which only withdrew when attacked, having inflicted a delay. It was obvious from the outset that the advance east would not be quick or easy, or indeed achieved in a single day as planned.

A troop of 107 Regiment RAC's Churchills supported D Company and helped make short work of the first enemy position, but they had only advanced 200 yards before a large demolition crater in the ride brought the tanks to a halt. Now advancing on their own, another 300 yards further down the ride D Company encountered determined *fallschirmjäger* opposition and without the tanks the advance was halted.

The density of the forest's trees made it a slow business for platoons to manoeuvre off the axis to deliver flanking attacks or fire support. Thus, the fighting tended to become a series of mostly frontal attacks on the German machine gun positions, depending on the size of the enemy positions, by platoons or whole companies, the latter only if there was room to deploy. Some enemy positions were supported by *sturmgeschütz* of various types, which, confined to tracks, tended to withdraw as the Highland infantry approached through the trees.

Lieutenant Ross Le Mesurier, a Canloan officer[6] who commanded a platoon in Major Callender's B Company, described the fighting:

> Without tank support which had become bogged down, machine-gun, snipers and mortars took their toll throughout the morning of the 9th. My head was creased by a bullet, then a piece of shrapnel hit my back. Later on

AVREs, flails and bulldozers waiting at the rear of the column to remove obstacles and fill craters.

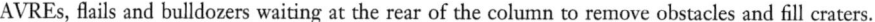

another fragment hit my upper left arm, which stiffened up. The day dragged on, progress was slow, and darkness came early. It also started to rain. Our company wireless operator was badly wounded, in great pain, his uncontrolled moans seemed to draw gunfire.

Eventually D Company was halted and, realising that they were up against a strong enemy position of trenches and bunkers, the commanding officer deployed B Company to outflank the enemy position to the right. In manoeuvring around the flank, they encountered further enemy positions and 'a very spirited engagement followed in which they accounted for many of the enemy'.

As the Camerons were still unable to resume the advance on the axis, C Company, commanded by Major Melville, was brought forward along with the tanks. They promptly engaged the enemy defences with high-explosive shells at close range and Melville led a bayonet charge, which overwhelmed the Germans to his front. At the same time Major Callander led B Company in a charge. The citation for the bar to his military cross reads:

> Owing to the thick country it was impossible to call for close support artillery fire. Major Callander's company suffered heavy casualties as he formed his men up for the attack. Displaying supreme courage and with complete disregard for his own personal safety, he moved about in the open under continuous fire organising the assault. Once organised he personally led the leading two pls into the assault over a fifty yard clearing. Major Callander was the first to reach the enemy position with a handful of men and with these men behind him accounted for ten of the enemy dead and wounded.

Lieutenant Le Mesurier recalled the brutality of the fighting and one of the enemy dead:

> My company commander, Major Donald Callander, yelled out, 'For God's sake, Ross, do something'. The wind was blowing towards the Germans, so I cocked a phosphorous grenade to throw it. It was hit by a bullet or a piece of shrapnel and burst in my face which was covered with blobs of burning goo ... I rubbed handfuls of snow mixed with mud on my face to stop the burning. Some Germans began advancing towards us. Our firing forced them to go to ground. A few of us charged them firing from the hip. My Sten gun jammed, so I freed my shovel. They started to run and we chased them. I hit one with the shovel blade in the neck. He hit the ground in a heap. I swung at another but he ducked and it glanced off his shoulder.

During the aftermath of the attack, while reorganising C Company, Major Melville was hit by a shell splinter and was evacuated along with thoroughly demoralised German wounded and prisoners.

The advance was resumed after midday with D Company and tanks continuing astride the ride clearing successive enemy posts, while B and C companies to the left threaded their way through the forest. However, after another 1,000 yards

A casualty being treated at a 51st Highland aid post at the edge of the Reichswald. Note the German prisoners in the background being escorted to the rear.

Advance through the Reichswald, 9 February

they came under heavy fire from a *fallschirmjäger* position sited at a cross-tracks. As an attack was being prepared C Coy:

> appeared on the scene with one of his platoons, and without further ado, dashed out towards the centre of the enemy position shouting to his men, who followed like a pack of hounds. Everyone expected him to become a casualty, but instead, those of the enemy that escaped bayonetting surrendered and the cross-tracks fell into the Battalion's hand.

Sergeant Sands of D Company described the nature of the fighting:

> We continued to advance along a track with the tanks on our right flank, until we reached a cross track, which was taken mainly due to 'C' Company. Snipers were still firing at us from all directions. It had taken the Battalion all day to advance 1500 yards. The Germans were mainly Paratroopers, mostly fanatical, who kept firing until wiped out, usually at point blank range, with hand to hand fighting not uncommon.
>
> At one point we had run out of ammunition, and we finished off one position, attacking and killing the occupants with our trenching tools. It was a particularly bloody affair, but they were never going to surrender. Those defenders suffered a particularly violent and bloody death. You know, you can actually take a man's head clean off his shoulders with a trenching tool. We spent that night consolidated in the cross track area ...

By 1600 hours the battalion had reached objective APPLE and were mopping up the area, having in the words of the battalion's history made:

> A penetration of 1500 yards into the forest ... this against determined opposition. German paratroopers fired until wiped-out at point blank range, while snipers who had not been flushed by the leading troops resolutely continued firing from the immediate flanks and rear.

Meanwhile, waiting most of the day for the code word BANANA, the soldiers of 5th Seaforth 'stood shivering among the shattered trees where the ground was littered with German dead and prayed that the advance would come soon'. Captain Borthwick of the battalion's intelligence section recalled that:

> It came at 1600 hours, and in an unexpected direction. The Camerons were having trouble along their ride, the winter daylight would soon be fading, and our objective was the Hekkens/Kranenburg road, which ran north and south through the middle of the forest all of six thousand yards ahead. If we could not pass through the Camerons, some other way would have to be found. In the end we advanced along a parallel ride half a mile to the north, where 154 Brigade had reached a point only a thousand yards short of the road. This would take us to our objective just as quickly, and it was hoped that later we should be able to turn south down the Hekkens road and rejoin our original axis. It was late by the time we had gathered all the information

we could from the forward troops of 154 Brigade and moved the Battalion up into their area; and when we moved off into the unknown, we had only one hour of daylight in hand.⁷

The Seaforths were ordered forward through 7th Argylls, who had advanced to the east of the Freudenberg. By now, however, the mud across the Groesbeek Heights and along the forest rides was worse than ever, defying the efforts of those labouring to establish a route forward:

> One result of this was important: we could take with us no supporting arms, no mortars, no anti-tank guns, no machine-guns. Our link with the rear was one slender channel of mud. We had only the weapons we carried in our hands, plus artillery support from outside the forest; and, worse still, we had no tanks. The Argylls, the battalion through which we were passing, had a troop, but it had no orders to accompany us; and it looked as if we should have to advance with no close support whatever until the personal element made its appearance in the paper plan and Colonel Sym discovered that the tank commander's father had been a Seaforth. The Colonel, praising the tradition of the county regiments, found himself the temporary owner of three Churchills.

Advancing on a ride parallel and 1,000 yards north of the Kartenspielerweg that cut across several spurs of high ground in the forest, the battalion made good time 'through the evil, threatening Reichswald':

> There was no wind, and in the silence of the forest they [the tanks] seemed to make a tremendous noise. B Company led and cleared a big quarry on the right of the track. The forest closed in again, and we began to drop down into the valley which lay between us and the Hekkens road.

The thought in the mind of the Seaforths was that the country was ideal for ambush. 'It had been inevitable ... Yet we were wrong. As we were soon to discover.' The delay in 5th Seaforth getting forward to begin their advance as dusk fell seemed to have convinced the Germans that 'the Argylls represented the limit of our advance for the day'. However, while the Seaforths had been cautiously covering the last 1,000 yards, the Germans had been busy organising a counterattack on 5th Camerons. 'Just to complicate matters, their axis of advance was our ride, and their start-line our objective, the Hekkens road. The two attacks met head on.' Borthwick continued his account:

> B Company had two platoons beating the forest to the right of the ride, and one to the left. The tanks were undamaged but stopped, so that as the company attacked it drew fire away from them. Spandaus opened up at fifty yards' range, Brens replied, and the forest was filled with muzzle-flashes and streams of tracer. Neither side could see much, but we had the advantage in that we were in battle order and expecting trouble, whereas most of the Germans were still forming up on the Hekkens road and only their advance

A well and truly bogged carrier of 51st Highland Division.

guard had started to move down our axis. Still, it was a sticky ten minutes. Only the leading company was in a position to fight. The rest of us lay behind trees, peering into the shadows and watching the tracer tearing through the branches. In the lulls there was total silence. Then would come the crump of a grenade, and the shooting would flare up again.

B Company's commander was killed, and the attack was in danger of stalling but picking the tanks up from the Argylls was a stroke of luck and made all the difference:

> We heard them rumble forward, the sound of their heavy Besas [machine guns] cutting clear above the rattle of the other machine-guns. The Germans stood only two or three bursts, and then fled. C Company went through with the tanks, caught the counter-attack still trying frantically to form up on the road, and scattered it. Once again there was silence. We were left in peace to dig in astride our ride by the edge of the road, a thousand yards farther into the Reichswald than any other unit in our part of the forest.

With 5th Seaforth reaching the Hekkens road, 152 Brigade had taken its second objective, all be it a little further north-east than planned. Meanwhile,

2nd Seaforth had been brought forward into the forest around dawn and, after a long wait, echeloned to the right rear behind the 5th Seaforth, was ordered to advance on the original axis. They passed through the 5th Cameron Highlanders, who were digging in astride the axis at dusk. They were held up by machine gun fire after about 500 yards and were ordered to consolidate their position and 'stay put till morning'.

Consequently, 5th Seaforth remained out on their own as the forward element of the brigade, deployed in a tight all-round defence little more than 200 yards across, 'peering outwards through the darkness to front, flanks, and rear'. In front of them, the Germans had the well-established trenches of the Siegfried Line several hundred yards beyond the Hekkens road, and for the Seaforth soldiers 'straining eyes and ears into the night for moving shadows or the snapping of a twig' it was an unpleasant night:

> The forest was absolutely still. There was no wind. Every now and then we heard the distant rumble of our guns, then silence, then the growing wail as the shells passed overhead and crashed down behind the German lines. Then silence again. German planes passed over, flying low, seeking out our gun-lines. We saw the sky behind us light up as the flares dropped and heard the crump of the bombs. The planes flew home. We settled down to watch and listen again.

The 51st Highland Division, despite the delays of the previous day, had during 9 February made up some time, mainly thanks to the relatively poor resistance. However, when one takes into account the limited support from the tanks and Hobart's Funnies, the infantry fighting without the usually lavish support was highly creditable. As was the case the previous evening at the divisional and

A Highland Division patrol at the edge of the forest on 9 February 1945.

The Kartenspielerweg, the axis of 152 Brigade, is today a tarmac cycle track.

brigade headquarters, the orders process ground on into the night, revising and refining battalions' missions for the following day.

For the Germans there was one piece of good news and that was that as the US Army made its belated advance on the Roer dams, the Schwammenauel Dam's turbine machinery had been blown as the 78th US Infantry Division closed in. The resulting sustained release of water put the River Roer into spate for two weeks, forcing the postponement of Operation GRENADE. As a result, First Canadian Army would for the time being face the undivided attention of the Germans in the Rhineland.

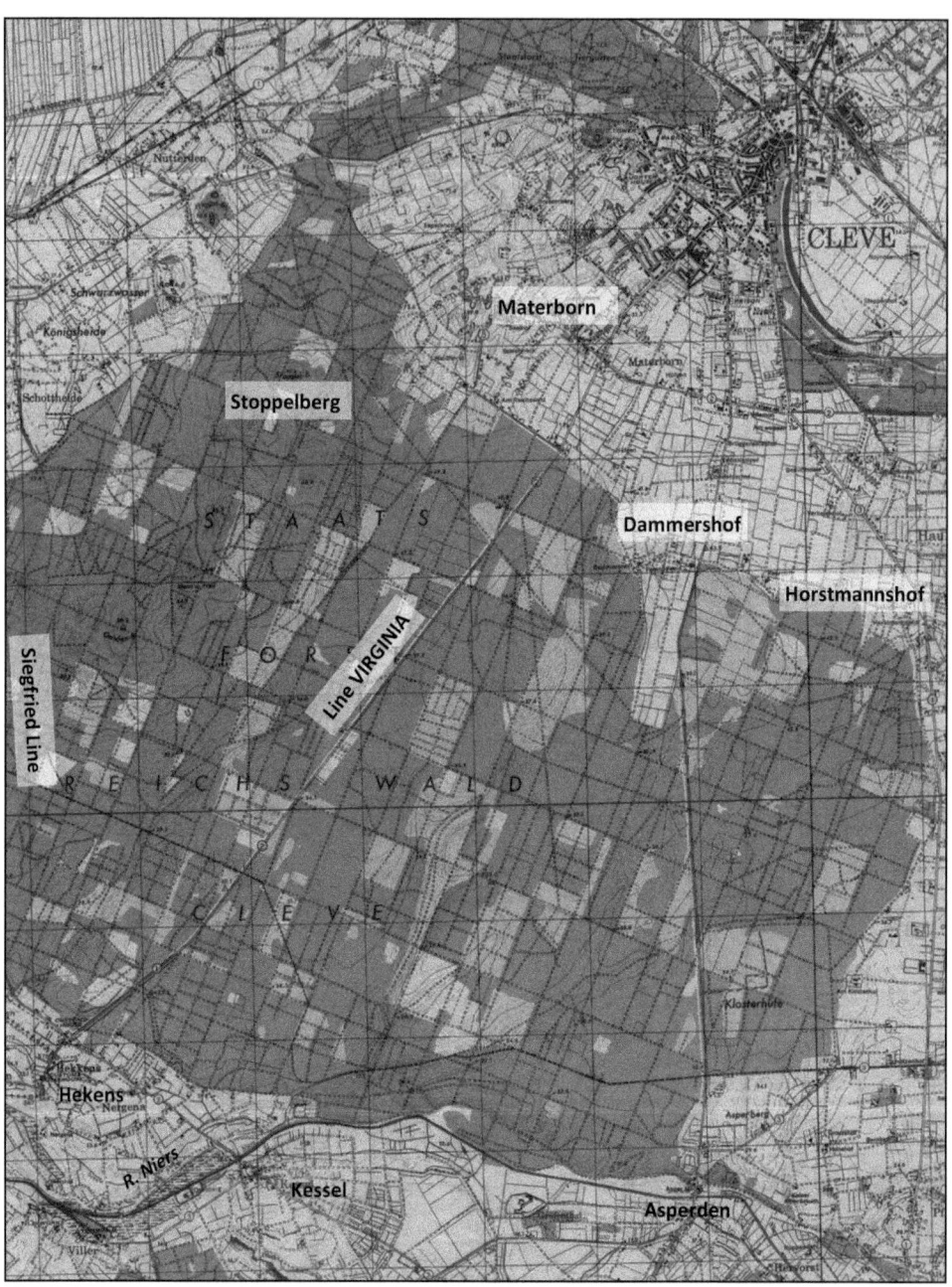

The eastern part of the Reichswald.

Chapter Six

The Reichswald and the Maas Plain, 10 February

During 9 February the fighting in the Reichswald had taken 53rd Welsh Division to the north-easterly corner of the forest adjacent to the 15th Scottish Division on the Materborn feature. The 51st Highland Division's 152 Brigade had, meanwhile, only advanced against stiff resistance as far as the Frasselt–Hekkens road and the Siegfried Line. At the same time, the Highlanders' 153 Brigade cleared the Kiekeberg Woods and fought their way out onto the floodplain and on to the banks of the River Maas. With the Highlanders behind schedule and focused on opening the southern axis into the Rhineland by securing the hardtop road (Route HEART), and capturing the bridges over the River Niers at Kessel and Gennep, this left a large portion of the Reichswald still to be cleared by the Welsh.

Route HEART, to the south of the Reichswald, out on the Maas plain, had gained additional significance for the breakout into the Rhineland due to the northern axis, the Nijmegen–Kleve road (Route PEARL BLACK) becoming submerged as the Rhine floods deepened, and was therefore unable to take anything like the volumes of traffic anticipated. Route HEART's significance was further enhanced by both the projected CLUB RED and CLUB BLACK divisional supply routes through the Reichswald being impassable.

On the Corps' northern axis, 15th Scottish Division's leading battalions had only just beaten the German reinforcements to the Materborn feature. This good news was, however, interpreted by General Horrock's headquarters as 44 Lowland Brigade had captured Kleve, rather than just having a slim and tenuous hold on the high ground overlooking the city. The result was that overnight 43rd Wessex Division was released to begin the breakout but ran straight into German counter-attacks in the southern suburbs of Kleve. In the resulting traffic jams the following brigades of both divisions were paralysed for most of the day. As for the defenders, General Schlemm, despite reinforcements being rushed from the Twenty-fifth Army north of the Rhine and the belated committal of XLVII Panzer Corps, was under pressure to hold Kleve and contain the Allies.

During the Normandy campaign a combination of ULTRA decrypts, signals intelligence and air recce provided warning of the approach of powerful formations, against which the power of the Allied air forces would be directed. In the

Grounded. Fighter-bombers of the Second Tactical Air Force awaiting a break in the weather.

case of VERITABLE, as recorded in a Headquarters XXX Corps situation report up to 11 February, the weather did not co-operate:

> AIR SUPPORT – VERITABLE – 10/11 FEB
>
> This was a very annoying day. In the morning the weather was bad but it was possible to fly armed recce and to carry out blind bombing with the MRCP [Mobile Radar Control Point] MOYLAND and TILL adm [administration] areas given by a PW and bombed before on 9 Feb were bombed in this way between 1100 and 1200 hrs. No targets in direct close support of forward troops were however received until after 1400 hrs. From then on, a spate of targets from 43 Div, 51 (H) Div and 3 Cdn Div coincided with a turn for the worse in the weather. Bases were becoming fog bound and conditions in the battle area were such that the MRCP could not be successfully operated. So with great regret the engagement of targets which would have helped the infantry on had to be abandoned.[1]

In short, the weather precluded both close air support to the battle and the interdiction of XLVII Panzer Corps, thus allowing the Germans a breathing space to recover from the surprise of being attacked through the Reichswald.

53rd Welsh Division

General Horrocks believed that his Army commander, General Crerar, was much underrated and recorded a couple of aspects of his style of leadership that had particularly impressed the British general. 'Every day after the battle started, he [Crerar] would fly over the front (a somewhat dangerous operation) in a small aircraft, and then came to see me wherever I might be. I grew to like him very much …'

In common with the practice of his commander coming forward to 'sniff the battle', Horrocks also spent a considerable amount of time away from his headquarters visiting his divisions. During these daily visits to headquarters and units, in conversation with staff officers, commanders and their soldiers he 'read the battle'. Horrocks recorded his impressions of one such visit to the Welsh Division in the heart of the Reichswald:

> One day when visiting the 53rd Welsh Division in the Reichswald, I almost stumbled over two young soldiers crouching in a very muddy trench. They were all alone and could see none of their comrades, who were also concealed in foxholes nearby ... These two young men were desperately lonely; how much harder is the lot of the infantryman today, compared with, say, his great-great grandfather on the battlefield of Waterloo, where the infantry would be formed up into squares with their officers and NCOs all around them. There would then be shouting, noise and excitement in the air ... Now, owing to the power of modern weapons, more and more fighting takes place at night. Yet nothing in their previous life had prepared these young soldiers for their loneliness and the darkness, as the greater proportion of them lived in large, well-lit towns or, at any rate, in villages.

For General Ross' soldiers of the Welsh Division, 10 February was a day of consolidation. Other than patrolling and issuing orders during what was 'A very wet day', the 53rd Welsh spent it:

> regrouping with two objects in view, namely to establish a 'front' along the Kleve–Hekkens road, and to position the division in a favourable manner to continue the advance in a south easterly direction and clear the rest of the forest.[2]

To secure the Kleve–Hekkens road, in the afternoon 160 Brigade was ordered to extend southwards to positions adjacent to the Materborn feature to aid 15th Scottish Division. At 1800 hours, 4th Welch with A Squadron, 9 RTR, under command advanced through the lines on the Stoppelberg and reported being firm astride the road at 2200 hours.

Meanwhile, 6 RWF, probing west to establish a link with the 51st Highland Division with a substantial two-platoon-sized patrol, had a brief but sharp encounter with *fallschirmjäger*. This first fight with enemy paratroopers during VERITABLE resulted in twenty German dead but only two prisoners.

The day was, however, far from quiet. In the large area of forest that the division had already 'captured' there were plenty of Germans who were either lying in wait to snipe at opportunity targets or to infiltrate east out of the Reichswald, or to simply surrender once the battle had moved on. The whole area had been well-managed woodland mostly divided up into rectangular blocks of some 200×700 yards by a series of tracks, some surfaced with a layer of stone scalpings and others simply earth. The forest was far from as uniformly dense as portrayed on most maps. It had blocks of trees that had been felled, and there

Two soldiers of 6 RWF dug in during the fighting in the Reichswald.

Operations of 53rd Welsh Division during 10 February 1945.

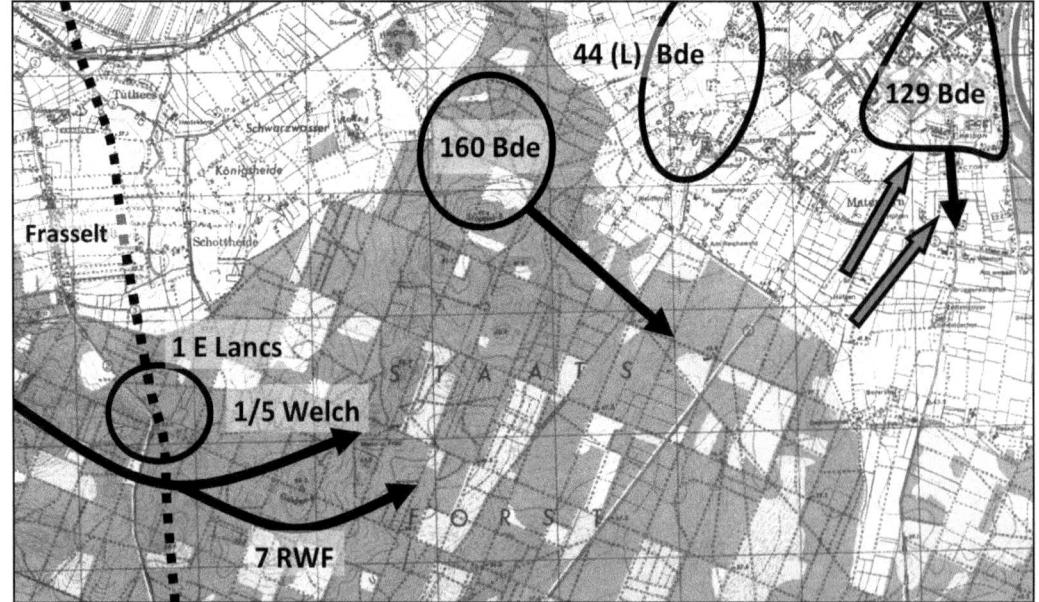

were dense blocks of saplings, underbrush and pines, in addition to more open areas of mature deciduous trees and pines. All, however, offered opportunities for enemy resistance. German cohesion in the Reichswald had obviously been spoilt by the initial bombardment and subsequent fire plans that had helped the Welsh Division's battalions onto their objectives:

> The Reichswald was awful in just about every way! The weather and mud we had seen before plenty of times since Normandy but the trees, endless trees were a different matter. In places they were so dense and dark that we could only thread our way through in single file and then be brought to a halt by a tangle of trunks and branches. Where we could we avoided the tracks, because they were often mined, and junctions were covered by fire and more schu mines [sic] planted in the verges where we would predictably take cover.[3]

Consequently, there was a flow of casualties from snipers and ambushes, along with shell and mortar fire by both night and day. Mortar bombs and shells detonating up in the trees not only brought whole boughs down on the men below but in addition to the shards of steel, large wood splinters caused serious injury. With the Jeep ambulances unable to reach the front on the Kleve–Hekkens road, the wounded increasingly faced a long carry through the mud on stretchers back to ambulances. Private Huntley, a RAMC stretcher-bearer, recalled:

> At first, the trees were so dense it was literally black. Later, after much shelling, the woods became a skeleton. The shrapnel had stripped the branches from the trees; there were just the trunks left. Then it became light, but there was no protection from the shells exploding overhead, not even in the trenches.
>
> You could hear this cry going up, all along the front, a cry for help. You didn't know where to go first. You had to feel in the dark where his wound was and put on a shell dressing or tourniquet. There was no chance to do anything more, not even to administer a shot of morphine. We just had to get him out fast and get back to the next one, lying there waiting his turn.
>
> You just couldn't let yourself think about it. You couldn't dwell on the fact that you were carrying a man whose legs had just been blown off or who had some really devastating wounds from shrapnel. If you thought about it, you'd never do it.

German prisoners in the difficult circumstances in the Reichswald were used to help evacuation of both British and their own casualties.

The Kartenspielerweg track, which had been cleared of mines, had been quickly taken into use by the vehicles of the division, but in the pouring rain, this route equally quickly dissolved into axle-deep mud. The divisional axis soon became progressively more unusable, eventually to all but Churchill tanks of 34 Armoured Brigade. Even the Churchill could only reach the Reichswald thanks to committing every available spare body to road making across the Groesbeek Heights.

The density and age of the Reichswald's trees varied from area to area but as shown here, where the forest had been heavily shelled, going was always very slow through blown-down trees, shell craters and the mud.

Lieutenant Beal of 9 RTR wrote of regimental headquarters' main activity that day. 'A Brigade RASC column had succeeded in getting through to regimental areas,' and from there 'RHQ tanks ferried much needed petrol and ammunition round squadrons.' For four days the Welsh Division was at the end of an extremely tenuous supply and evacuation line.

51st Highland Division

Having cleared the ground south from the Reichswald to the River Maas, General Rennie overnight swung his axis of advance to the east, in order to continue the opening up of the southern flank of the Reichswald for the development of Route HEART, code name for the alternative corps' axis.

The divisional objective, to be taken by 153 Highland Brigade, in this phase of the operation was the bridge over the Maas tributary, the River Niers, at Gennep. Meanwhile, 152 Brigade were to continue their advance east through the southern portion of the Reichswald towards the town of Hekkens and the bridge at Kessel. Patrols mounted by the armoured cars of the divisional reconnaissance regiment, 2nd Derbyshire Yeomanry (2 DERBY YEO), were directed on Zelderheide between the two thrusts of the infantry.

153 Highland Brigade

The plan for 153 Brigade on 10 February was for 5th/7th Gordon Highlanders to advance from their overnight position on the edge of the Reichswald to the north-west and seize the Niers bridge at Gennep via the main road. With the

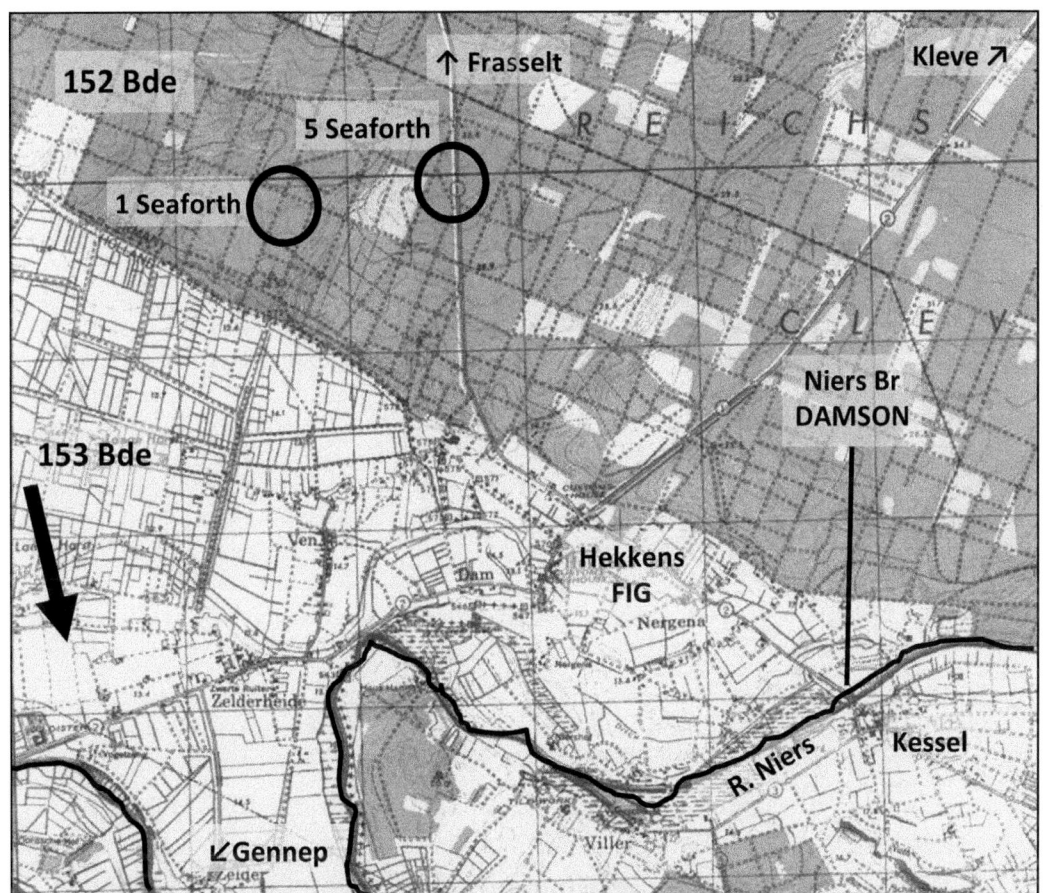

Positions of 152 Brigade's leading elements at dawn on 10 February 1945.

bridge in their hands, they were to exploit south and clear the route towards Goch. The battalion made substantial gains south on the axis towards Gennep and the River Niers during the morning but was ultimately frustrated.

In the centre of the brigade area leading the advance were the recce cars of C Squadron of 2 DERBY YEO. The squadron was directed on the village of Aaldonk and on to the banks of the Niers. Initially 2 Troop's advance went well, reaching Ottersum without incident, but here they came under machine gun fire, which caused little delay, and the next village, Zelderheide, was found to be clear. The officer commanding C Squadron, Major MacNaughton, reported on Lieutenant Partridge's action, which was now directed on Hekkens. Leaving Zelderheide, the troop commander radioed through that a minor bridge just east of the village was blown up as he approached:

> I enquired whether there was any danger of the road flooding and their retreat being cut off, but Lieut Partridge replied that there was no likelihood of this. He also reported R. Niers to be in flood. I ordered him to proceed cautiously and his next report was of two men running to houses at 831476 [the outskirts of Hekkens]. The Tp was then off the air for 10 minutes.

The Tp Ldr then reported two cars have been hit by anti-tank gun which I can't spot. I have the crew ...

At that moment, his own car was hit and no more was heard of the Tp until Sgt BROWN ... returned on foot to own lines.

Lieutenant Partridge was wounded and taken prisoner but was subsequently released. The remainder of the squadron was ordered to clear the ground between the Reichswald and the Niers but in growing darkness this was eventually called off.

Meanwhile, leaving their positions on the edge of the Reichswald at 1000 hours, 5th/7th Gordons had taken minor roads to the Mook–Goch highway, which they then followed to the south-east with B Company leading. They were mounted on the Churchills of B Squadron 107 RAC, and Corporal Dyson commented that in open country 'it was a little more our line of work than fighting in the confines of a pine forest. In a series of leapfrogging actions, the squadron's troops made slow but steady progress towards the river crossing [at Gennep].' The Gordons' war diary described the fighting near the bridge and its destruction:

> B Coy reached its objective, [at the junction 1000 yards short of] the bridge ... without incident and sent a patrol commanded by 2/Lieut Stephens MM down the road to OSTTERSUM [Ottersum], which it reached and reported clear. A Coy were then passed down the road through B Coy with orders to cross the bridge over the River Niers just outside the town and form a bridgehead in GENNEP. The leading platoon had almost reached the bridge [about 300 yards away] when the enemy blew it up and our men were pinned down by heavy MG fire from the buildings on the far side of the river. Smoke was laid by the artillery to enable the platoon to be extricated, an operation that took an hour to accomplish.

The extraction from the area of a café was significantly helped by a 17-pounder gun mounted in an M10 Tank Destroyer of 61st Anti-Tank Regiment, commanded by Sergeant Vousden. The citation for his Military Medal reads:

> Although the area was completely open and swept with fire from Gennep, Sgt Vousden, without hesitation, moved to a position in the open from which he could engage the enemy posts.
>
> With cheerful determination he inspired his detachment to support the infantry in this difficult operation. He proceeded to plaster the enemy posts with HE and AP from his 17-pdr and succeeded in neutralising the *Spandau* posts.

The Gordons' war diarist continued:

> C Company were then ordered to pass through A, which was established around the road junction [see map] and enter OSTTERSUM. The enemy were, however, able to cover this stretch of road from their positions across the river in Gennep and the road was entirely devoid of cover. Tanks were

An M10 Tank Destroyer of a divisional anti-tank regiment mounting the 17-pounder gun

The first attempt to capture the Niers bridge at Gennep.

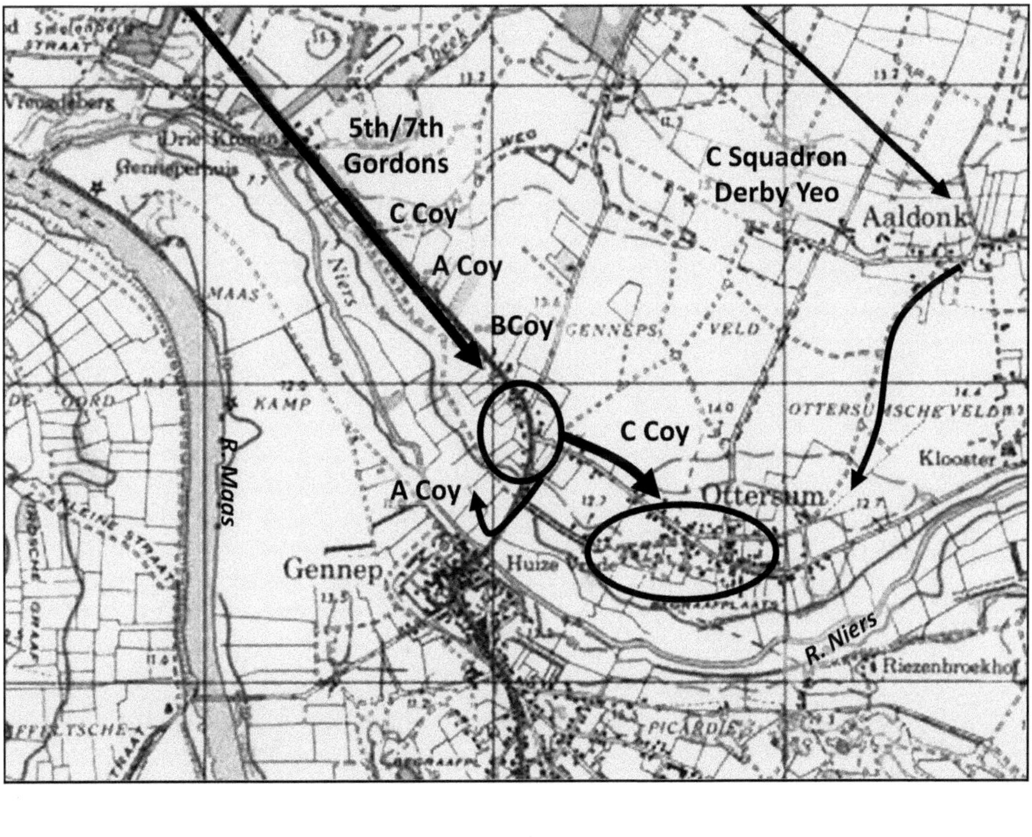

The Niers looking north-east towards Zelderheide. In early February the river had broken its banks and the country well over 100 yards to either side was flooded, with rain and melt water still coming down the Maas.

brought up and the coy moved down the road behind the cover of the tanks and entered the village. No opposition was encountered, although shelling and mortaring by the enemy was quite heavy. D Coy joined C Coy in OSTTERSUM after dark and apart from recce patrols down to the bridge with REs no further action or movement took place.

During the afternoon, to the east of Ottersum, 2 DERBY YEO managed to clear the villages in the centre of the divisional area to the west of the River Niers.

152 Highland Brigade

The second day of VERITABLE had seen 152 Brigade fighting south-west along rides through the Reichswald against stern resistance from *fallschirmjäger*. Of the brigade's three battalions, 5th Seaforth Highlanders reached the Frasselt–Hekkens road in the Siegfried Line defences 1,000 yards forward of its sister battalion, 2nd Seaforth. Having spent an uncomfortable night in a tight all-round defence, matters did not improve with daylight, as recounted by Captain Borthwick, the battalion's intelligence officer:

At 0900 hours the Germans discovered where we were, and for the rest of the morning they shelled us heavily every thirty minutes. In the afternoon they stepped up the pace and shelled us every fifteen minutes. Hundreds of shells and mortar bombs fell in or around the Battalion area; and, as many of them burst in the trees overhead, we had casualties. At one time during the morning one of our tanks ditched itself and made a great deal of noise revving up its engine to climb out again. The Germans, thinking we were about to attack, loosed off bank after bank of rocket-bombs which they had dug in in readiness for our final assault [on the Siegfried Line] – a good thing, possibly, as once fired they were irreplaceable and we were all underground when they landed; but there were at least a hundred and fifty of them, huge things a couple of feet long and as heavy as a man could carry, many burst in the trees, and they were accurate. Single bombs blew full-grown pine trees out bodily by the roots. We heard the squeal as each bank was fired; then the moan, multiplying itself as the flight approached; then the crashes all round us as they burst; then silence, and the doleful cry of 'stretcher-bearer, stretcher-bearer.' Farquhar Macrae [the RMO] could find no cover at the crossing of the ride and the road where most of the casualties occurred. He lay in the open, binding up the wounded while the salvos were still coming over; and the stretcher-bearers, too, worked in the open to bring more to him.[4]

The brigade's objectives for 10 February were the crossroads village of Hekkens and the Niers bridge at Kessel, originally planned to have been taken during D+1. The operation on this flank was now running a full day behind schedule. Phase 1 (APPLE) had been completed the previous day, but by the time 2nd Seaforth took over the advance it was dark, and the advance was halted short of the phase 2 objective, BANANA. On a track through the forest, running parallel to the Kartenspielerweg, 5th Seaforth had reached the Frasselt–Hekkens road (BUNYAN), where they waited under fire for their next part in the battle.

On 10 February, 152 Brigade was to resume fighting their way forward to the Frasselt–Hekkens road, continuing to use the 7-mile long Kartenspielerweg forest track as their axis of advance. The 2nd Seaforths were to complete the

The *Wurfkörper Spreng*, a close cousin of the *Nebelwerfer*, was a rocket-propelled munition with a 148lb warhead.

capture of BANANA, from where 5th Camerons were to take over the advance to the Phase 3 objective, CHERRY, on the Kleve–Hekkens road, a further 2 miles. From here they were to swing south out of the forest. As the battalions advanced, the machine gun companies of 1st/7th Middlesex were to continue deploying on the edge of the Reichswald covering the brigade's right flank.

The renewed advance began at 1130 hours preceded by an hour-long bombardment of BANANA and then as 2nd Seaforth advanced supported by C Squadron, 107 Regiment RAC, the artillery isolated the objective. The order of march of the battalion was C Company, followed by D and Battalion HQ and then A and B companies. With the vehicles of F Echelon bringing up the rear, the two forward companies were each supported by a troop of Churchill tanks. The commanding officer had also requested Crocodiles to flame bunkers and other points of resistance. These were provided by A Squadron, 1st Fife and Forfar Yeomanry. Lieutenant Foley, a Churchill troop commander, described the fighting from the armoured perspective:

> Slowly we fought our way through the interminable Reichswald Forest. And each day the great trees steadily dripped rain on to us and succeeded in blotting out most of the grey daylight.
>
> Our three Churchills proved very effective de-foresters; trees of quite respectable sizes were pushed flat and we managed to show the Germans that they were just as wrong in counting the Reichswald as an anti-tank obstacle as we had been in regarding the Ardennes as one in 1940.
>
> We took it in turns to break the trail, sometimes with unexpected results. Like the time we were grinding our way forward with the infantry, and all was suspiciously quiet. A screen of Scotsmen flung out in front reported that the Germans had withdrawn, but that there were signs of self-propelled anti-tank guns on the rides which crisscrossed the forest.
>
> So we avoided the rides and took it the hard way straight through the trees.

Foley's advance encountered limited opposition, but the tension was great for both infantry and tanks:

> Wet and uncomfortable, we were doing our 'tip-toeing elephant' act along one of the winding tracks which led through the forest. At each bend we expected to be greeted by a nasty explosion, and have the tank burst into flames beneath us, or at least blow a track. Cautiously I poked *Avenger*'s nose around each bend and, when nothing happened, ambled forward to the next bend to repeat the process.

Report line BROOKE was reached at 1200 hours, but resistance stiffened and progress slowed, as explained by the Seaforth's regimental historian:

> The two leading companies came under enemy mortar and artillery fire when about 600 yards from their objective and deployed C Company astride the axis, D Company to the right of it. They then met with considerable small

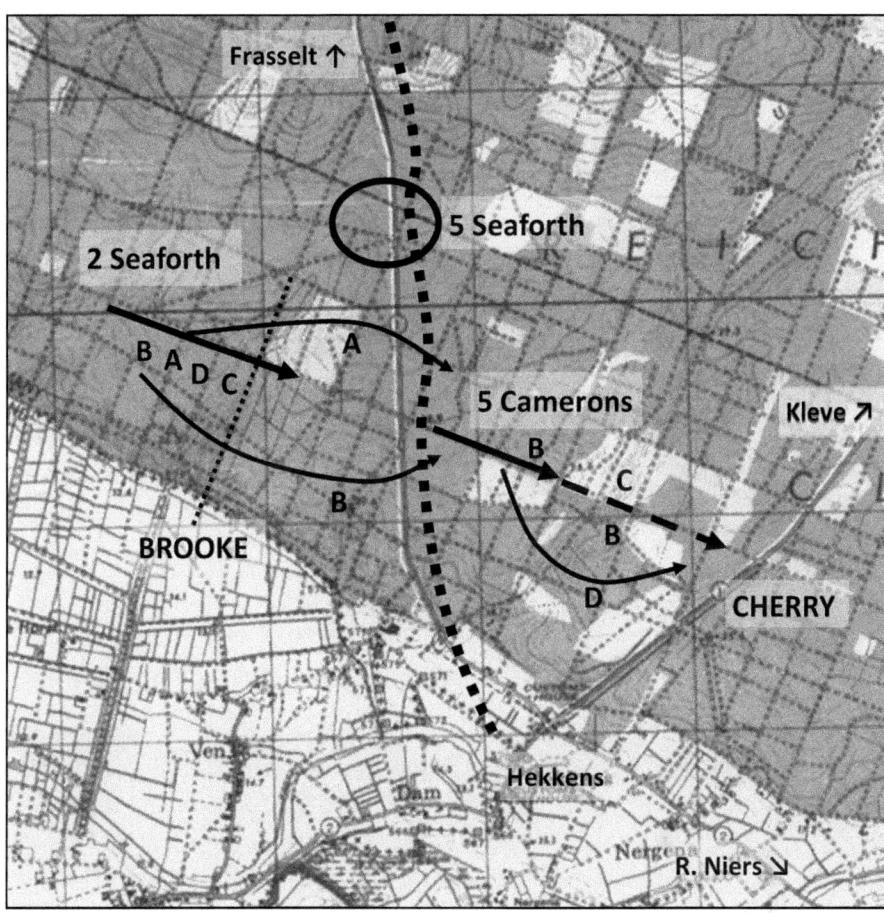

Operations of 152 (Highland) Brigade in the Reichswald on 10 February 1945.

arms fire from the enemy, dug-in on, and in rear of, the main road and an anti-tank gun opened up on the leading tanks, temporarily immobilizing them.

The leading companies having suffered significant casualties, the Seaforths' fight through the main Siegfried Line defences now began. As mentioned above, a Churchill was a knocked out and with C and D companies fixing the enemy's attention astride the axis, A Company manoeuvred around the right flank to gain the line of the Frasselt–Hekkens road. B Company subsequently performed a similar role to the left and shortly after 1400 hours the battalion broke into the forward enemy defences, but the solidly constructed bunkers proved to be difficult for the infantry to overcome. The gun tanks played their part, but it was the Crocodiles of 2 Troop that made the difference, despite concentrated enemy fire and having little room to manoeuvre off the Kartenspielerweg. One of the two

Crocodiles in action was forced to withdraw when some of its flame fuel was deflected back from a tree and set light to kit stowed on the rear of the tank. With the infantry having reformed, the advance resumed into the enemy's depth position. The troop commander's Crocodile, with the close support of a platoon of Seaforths to protect it from *Panzerfaust* fire, was able to punch a hole in the defences some 300 yards deep, flaming points of resistance as they advanced. The 2nd Seaforths reported that Objective BANANA was in their hands and mopping up was under way, but ammunition stocks after the protracted fight through the Siegfried position were low. By 1600 hours the battalion had rounded up seventy-six prisoners.

Once again, with just a few hours of daylight it was the turn of 5th Queen's Own Cameron Highlanders to leapfrog through to take the advance forward to Objective CHERRY at 1530 hours. Within a couple of hundred yards, it became apparent that their advance had culminated before it was through the German defences. The Camerons had been halted at a fire-swept clearing, with the enemy positioned in cover beyond. B Company was 'immediately ordered to push through this enemy pocket' but, as the regimental history describes:

> C Company following met firmer resistance and was held up while D Company, pushed round the right flank, found the going very sticky. The

The reserve company, B Company of 2nd Seaforth, and a Crocodile of 2 Troop on the Kartenspielerweg.

turning-point in this action was the gallant conduct of the crews of two Crocodiles, who followed the companies into action with great verve and effect, the Commander of one Crocodile, with a blood-stained bandage round his head, mouthing fearful oaths from the turret of his tank!

This was Lieutenant Dudley of 4 Troop and once again the forest was too thick to allow the deployment off the track. His citation for the Military Cross describes the action:

> Lieut. Dudley with his flame thrower Churchill saw that his weapon could be the deciding factor. Displaying supreme coolness and courage, he drove his tank through a thick patch of wood from a flank in support of the Infantry. At the time the light was failing and he had no Infantry round him as protection against the many enemy Bazookas, which had already become apparent. His tank pushed on, felling trees on either side, until he reached the clearing and could fire his flame at the enemy positions. The flame broke the enemy morale and the Infantry were enabled to dash forward and mop up the position.

The action by the Crocodiles enabled C and D companies to clear through the enemy, and 'left them to the mercies of the 2nd Seaforth, who [following up] duly mopped them up'. The Camerons' historian wrote:

> The Battalion's advance continued for another 1½–2 miles before darkness fell. The crash of grenades, 2-inch mortar bombs, and *Panzerfausts* in front indicated B Company in action at this time: they had surprised some Germans casually laying mines at a cross-tracks – the Battalion's objective – quite oblivious of the Company's arrival. The night was pitch black, bitterly cold, and a drizzle had begun to enshroud everything. Each man had to hold on to the bayonet scabbard of his fellow in front to avoid losing himself!

Unlike the previous evening, the company quartermaster sergeants managed to get through from B Echelon back in the woods on the Groesbeek Heights. Of most interest to the soldiers, they arrived 'with a hot meal, after a difficult journey over almost impassable tracks, lengths of which had to be covered with trunks of pine and larch to make the going possible for the 3-tonners'.

The fighting in the forest against the hardened infantry of *Fallschirmjäger* Regiment 20 had been both slow and costly, in contrast to other stretches of the Siegfried Line elsewhere in the Reichswald. While Hekkens was under observation by 2 DERBY YEO from the south, neither of the day's objectives, the cross-roads nor the Niers bridge at Kessel, had been taken, pushing VERITABLE further behind schedule.

Gennep, Night 10–11 February 1945

Meanwhile, 153 Brigade, having had the Niers bridge demolished in front of the 5th/7th Gordons, immediately started preparing a renewed attack, this time by

5th Black Watch. After a reconnaissance with his company commanders, Lieutenant Colonel Bradford decided to cross the swollen River Niers, now some 200 yards wide, near to its confluence with the Maas using assault boats. Once it had formed a bridgehead the battalion was to advance a mile west on a spit of land between the rivers and deliver a night attack on Gennep, thus avoiding a potentially costly assault crossing. Moving up behind the Black Watch were 1st Gordons, whose task it was to expand the bridgehead into the extensive southern part of Gennep.

The battalion's war diary records that at 2300 hours the first platoon of D Company crossed to clear the far bank and secure the bridgehead, with the main crossing beginning at 0030 hours. Lance Corporal Renouf recalled: 'We were ferried across in motor driven assault boats. D Company crossed first. Then the rest of us followed in groups of ten, without meeting any fire.' From the bridgehead D Company made its way silently along a narrow strip of unflooded land and 'several Spandau positions had be to overcome and it was a long time before the coy reported itself in position at LESLIE', an outlying farm, which

The attack of 5th Black Watch across the River Niers and into Gennep on the night of 10–11 February.

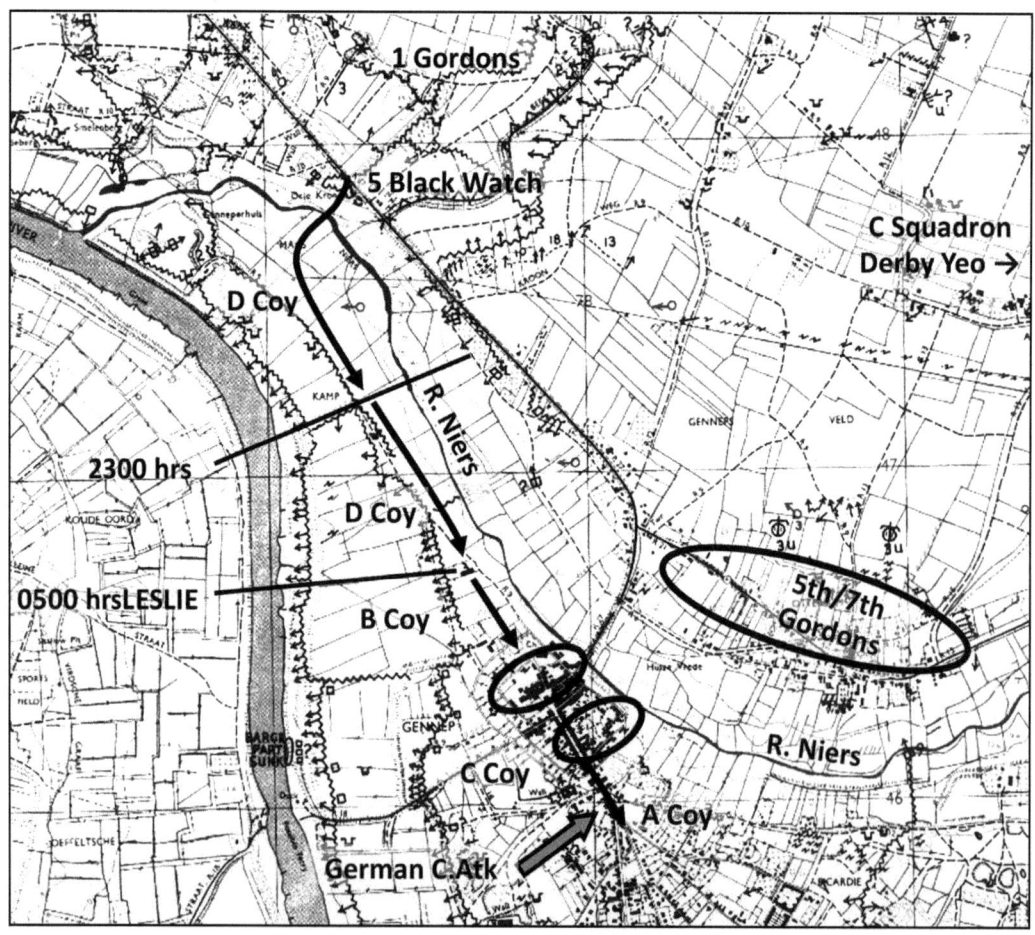

was to be the firm base for the attack. Here just before 0500 hours, D Company almost walked into an enemy outpost. Private Walker described the action:

> When the sky was momentarily illuminated by a flash of a shell, we were shocked to see a German platoon right in front of us. A tremendous firefight erupted and I was hit by three bullets, thankfully all flesh wounds, before we drove the Germans away. My corporal was killed, though the platoon managed to take the farm. But as soon as we got inside the farm we were hit by mortar bombs. The Germans were so expert with the mortars and had such excellent communications, that they were firing at the farm almost immediately.

Despite the firefight a degree of surprise was achieved, probably because the defences were facing the Gordons across the river, and at 0730 hours B Company were ready to attack. However, with the barrage falling short, they were delayed by ten minutes. The Jocks 'attacked with great spirit' across the last 400 yards of open ground and, having broken into the northern outskirts of Gennep, 'prisoners soon started coming in'. Against 'considerable resistance', they fought their way into the town as far as the church before wheeling left on to the road to the blown bridge. The site of the bridge was secured but the enemy held a substantial industrial building that dominated the area and fire from houses overlooking the river delayed the engineers' construction of the Bailey Bridge. The Germans were eventually driven out of the building by the fire of tanks and self-propelled guns.

The attack through the bombed out ruins of Gennep had thus far benefitted from momentum that prevented the Germans from organising a co-ordinated

This bridge is a replacement for the one blown up in front of the Gordons. The substantial building and church tower survive.

resistance. A and C Company, following closely behind B, quickly took over the advance further into the town. Lance Corporal Renouf was with C Company:

> We passed through their position and entered the main street of Gennep. Major Graham Pilcher's C Company went up the left-hand side, dashing from house to house, while those of us in A Company went up the right. All of the shop windows had been blown out and the roofs were close to collapsing.
>
> We eventually reached a shop whose whole frontage was missing. I stormed inside and found three Germans. One was crying in agony with a broken femur while the other two were trying to help him. They were clearly second-line troops – older and terrified, they did not want any trouble and were relieved to be taken prisoner. I said, 'OK, get out,' and pointed down the street to where they had to go. I had no time to escort them – we needed to clear the house and get moving. They plonked the injured Jerry on a plank and picked him up, but when they reached the street, his leg fell clean off and he let out a terrified scream. Poor chap. If I had remembered my Boy Scout training, I would have tied his legs together. I silently chastised myself but then shouted at them to carry him away. We had to carry on.

Having fought through some 300 yards of the town to a crossroads, C Company swung left onto Picardie Weg and the cleared the houses of the snipers from the area of the river. This left A Company to continue the advance in a south-easterly direction:

> As we marched towards the town hall, clearing more houses as we went, checking the basements and the bombed-out attics, things were starting to heat up in Gennep. Halfway up the main street, we turned left onto a road called Picardie. Fifty yards of open ground separated each property from its neighbour, so it was a mad dash to find some cover and then regroup for the next domestic raid. The Germans, using their staggeringly good lines of communication, had already organised back-up. Unfortunately for us, these reinforcements were the big boys, crack paratroopers, who appeared from nowhere. The resistance stiffened immediately, and before we knew it, they were counter-attacking. It was clear that they were steeled for battle, and we feared for our lives as they pushed us on to the back foot. These were highly skilled, well-drilled professionals, ready to kill or be killed. They evoked frightening memories of our hand-to-hand fighting with Himmler's SS troops in Normandy.

With 5th Black Watch having seized a bridgehead across the Niers at Gennep, there were by now definite signs that the Germans were recovering their balance and had committed elements of 2nd *Fallschirmjäger* Division to the fighting. Expanding the bridgehead and, of course, holding their gains against the inevitable counter-attack would be the next challenge for 153 Brigade to face.

Chapter Seven

The Gennep Bridgehead and the Hekkens Crossroads, 11 February

On VERITABLE's northern axis, 3rd Canadian Division completed the clearance of the flooded polder land and prepared to take over the city of Kleve, which had been cleared by 15th Scottish, while the Wessex Division swung south but made slow progress against mounting opposition. With the American Operation GRENADE stalled by the flooded Roer, the Germans were still able to concentrate against XXX Corps. However, critically short of fuel and spare parts, even though the weather was unfavourable for much air interdiction, XLVII Panzer Corps only made slow progress north. Consequently, German reinforcements for Schlemm's struggling defenders only arrived to confront the Allies piecemeal during 11 to 14 February.

Gennep – The Fight Continued

On the southern axis, with the River Niers bridge at Gennep having been blown as 153 Brigade approached during 10 February, overnight 5th Black Watch had crossed the Niers and with B Company leading had broken into Gennep. Still before dawn, A and C companies had taken over the fight some 300 yards south of the main street. Having reached a junction, A Company continued to advance down the main road toward the railway, while C Company swung left onto Picardie Weg to clear 'The housing estate'.

C Company had only progressed a short distance on their new axis when the reinforced Germans launched local counter-attacks. This, of course, being at a point in the battle when the Black Watch were still advancing on Picardie Weg, they were, consequently, not deployed for defence, thus the fighting took on the character of a meeting engagement. Private Renouf wrote:

> The paratroopers rushed the rear of the cottages we had just taken. We fought back and held some of the houses, but we had to abandon others as we were forced to retreat. The Germans overran 8 Platoon in number 21. Our lads threw smoke grenades, and some escaped through the front door and windows, but six of them were trapped in the cellar, where they had gone for a smoke. The Germans took them prisoner.

148 *The Battle of the Reichswald*

As the paratroopers continued to rush through the back doors and windows of the cottages we had occupied, we decided our best option was to take up new positions across the street.

At that point, Major Eric Mathew told me to run back and tell the commanding officer that we had met some serious resistance. As I sprinted to the battalion command post on the main street, I wondered how I had drawn the short straw to become the company runner … To survive this dangerous job, you needed to be quick and strong, sufficiently athletic to scramble over ruins and ditches, reliable, able to think on your feet and resourceful.

Renouf found Colonel Bradford outside the house where he had established his headquarters conferring with his subordinate commanders. 'I watched as the officers agreed on a way forward and then dashed back to their positions. These were all impressive leaders, but Bradford was a cut above the rest – a man at

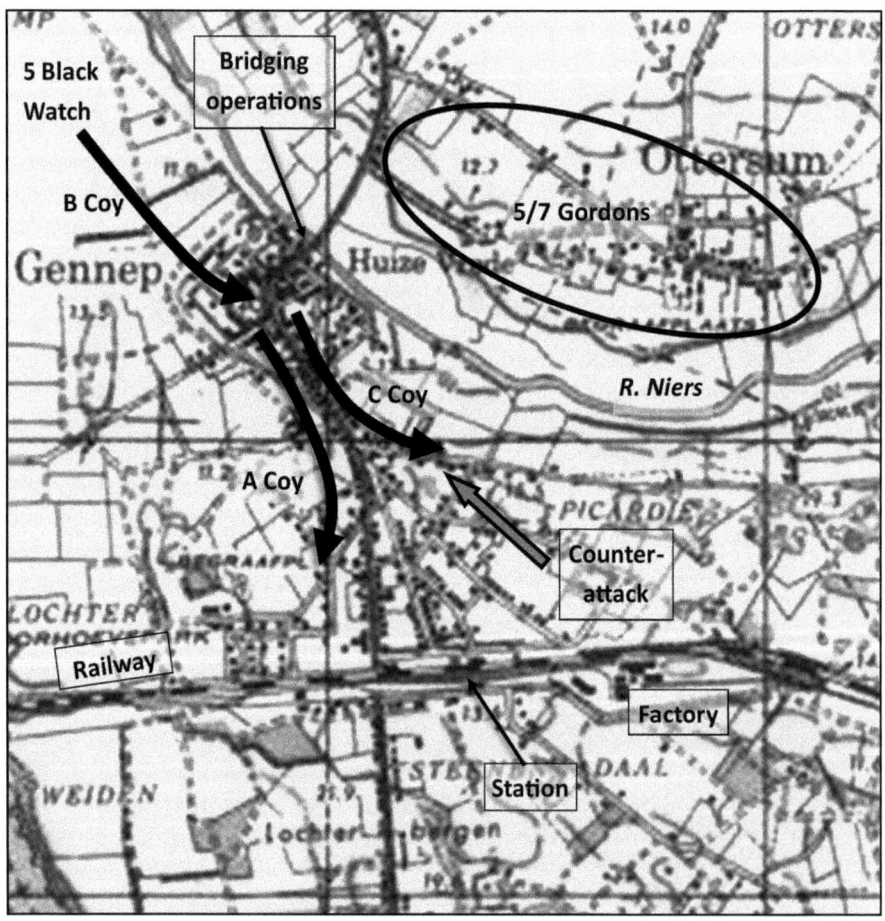

Operations of 5th Black Watch to clear Gennep during the morning of 11 February 1945.

the peak of his military powers.' Colonel Bradford had the previous evening returned from leave and 'was dressed immaculately', in contrast to his battle-grimed soldiers:

> When we arrived, Bradford consulted with Mathew and then gave the men some friendly encouragement. His mere presence and courageous bearing – not to mention his spick and span appearance – restored morale at a crucial moment in the battle. No amount of Sandhurst training could instil that level of stature in a man. I accompanied him back to the HQ and then returned to the front, where my comrades were already engaged in a tit-for-tat gun battle against the Germans across the street.

Private Reid, of 7 Platoon, A Company, was also fighting with the *fallschirmjäger* at close quarters a little further south:

> I was in the ground floor of a house with a very large front window. The Germans had occupied the cottages across the road, less than fifteen yards away, and we were firing point blank at one another. Corporal Robertshaw came into the room and as I shouted to him to keep down, a Spandau burst came in through the window and killed him outright. He was an older, married man. He seemed to have had a premonition that he would be killed and had given me his wife's address, which I passed on to Lieutenant Scott. I and three others carried his body in a blanket back to battalion HQ.

One of C Company's Bren gun teams photographed in action during the fighting in Gennep on 11 February 1945.

150 The Battle of the Reichswald

The fighting in the cobbled streets of Gennep went on all day. Renouf expected the *fallschirmjäger* to reinforce and launch a further determined counter-attack, but 'Major Mathew had the company well deployed, and he was determined to hold his positions'. In this situation, although they duly attacked, the enemy, in little more than company strength, lacked the combat power to overcome the Black Watch.

A heavy expenditure of ammunition is always expected as part of fighting in urban areas, and this was no exception. With the battalion running low, the war diary records that 'some DUKWs and Buffaloes had become available, and essential vehicles and ammunition was brought over'.

The battalion's war diary recorded that: 'In the late afternoon 1 Gordons advanced through C Company [5 BW]' supported by B Squadron 107 RAC. Major Lindsay established his headquarters in the main street within a 100 yards of 5 BW's but he 'heard our two companies doing a lot of shooting so I ran up to see what it was all about, dodging from back garden to back garden, and in that

Major Pilcher and officers of 5th Black Watch in a cellar in Gennep during the battle.

way up the street. The leading platoon was crossing the gaps between houses under cover of smoke grenades.'

These were 1 Gordons' platoon closing up behind A Company 5 BW on the main road south and Major Lindsay:

> having judged the strength of the opposition, I decided to take strictly limited objectives astride the main road as far as the level-crossing and to get the four rifle companies firm there; then, after that, to strike outwards and clear up the whole area north of the railway before going further.

With the leading platoons advancing through the Black Watch, Major Lindsay watched the attack of one of his company commanders who:

> was very cool and keeping excellent control of his company, never moving more than one platoon at a time. With him he had the commanders of the two following platoons, so that he could show them just where the platoon in front was working and from what point they were required to take on. I was also impressed with the coolness of one or two NCOs who could tell me exactly where it was not safe to loiter and from which houses the shooting was coming.

Corporal Dyson, commanding an A Squadron Churchill, recalled that: 'Our squadron advanced, the infantry dealing with very determined strong points. Houses farms and buildings until we reached the outskirts of Gennep.' Here the close-knit troop of fifteen men lost their troop commander, Lieutenant Jonny Walker, who, having motored forward, was decapitated by an armour-piercing round that skimmed over the top of his turret.

The Gordons were able to fight their way to the railway crossing but on their left the station area remained in enemy hands, with the Germans in a 'large factory just across the railway line. C Company was occupying a big yellow milk factory about seventy yards this side of it and they had duels, PIAT versus bazooka [*panzerfaust*], which broke a lot of glass but did not seem to hurt anybody.' The night was far from quiet as, 'there were odd *Spandau* parties roving about in most of the rest of the town ...'

The final German attack fell on the Black Watch's A Company at about 1900 hours, but although delivered under cover of darkness, with only fifty *fallschirmjäger* it once again it lacked sufficient strength. Despite their losses that saw NCOs taking command of platoons and the Germans coming to close quarters, A Company were able to beat the enemy back. By the end of the day the war diary reported that 174 prisoners of war had been taken.

Bridging the Niers

The sappers of XXX Corps' infantry divisions were fully committed to road making and ferrying. Consequently, Lieutenant Cantley's troop of engineers was detached from the Guards Armoured Division for the task of building a Bailey

An aerial photograph marked with the advances of 1st Gordons through the southern part of Gennep to the railway line.

bridge across the Niers for the Highland Division and subsequently his own division, at Gennep:

> When I reached the bridge[ing site] with my armoured section, having ordered the troop to follow on, there was not a bloody kilt in sight! Not very nice at all. With the assault boat on the top of the halftrack I got a Bren gun team over the other side, but we couldn't see anything ... When the troop arrived, we started to clear the site of debris and the blown bridge for the Bailey ...

which was to be a 'double/single Bailey. The bridging column arrived between 1100 and 1200 hours and then the Germans realised what was happening and started to mortar the sappers. Fortunately, for Lieutenant Cantley's troop there was not much hard ground and the shells that fell in the polder did little harm, but those that burst on the road forced the suspension of the offloading of the trucks. First the wreckage of the blown bridge had to be cleared:

> We just carried on with the charges and we got all these on ready to blow. We were ready to put the detonators in; until that time, you string up your detonating fuse and all that, ... until you put that [the detonators] into the

The Gennep Bridgehead and the Hekkens Crossroads, 11 February

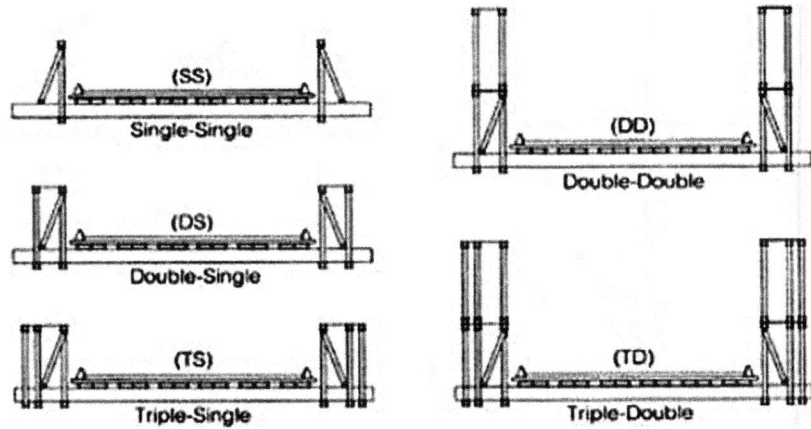

The Bailey bridge could be built to match the requirement. A bridge constructed of a single set of panels could bear the weight of light vehicles up to about 9 tons, a double, tanks and trucks of up to 40 tons and a triple the heaviest vehicles.

charges very little will happen. If something really does hit a charge it might go off, but the chances of it are not so much, but immediately you put the detonators in, you're in trouble. So Sergeant Dixon takes the left hand girder, and I take the right hand girder, and we're both crawling up this girder putting the detonators into the charges and we get stonked. That's not terribly happy when you're lying on that with that happening. Fortunately nothing happened.

With the abutments eventually clear of the wreckage of the blown bridge, under continuing artillery and mortar fire the engineers worked through the night of

A typical double-single Bailey bridge.

What appears to be Lieutenant Cantly and Sergeant Dixon preparing to blow the remains of the bridge prior to building their Bailey bridge.

10–11 February to get the bridge open at 1030 hours the following day. Later, however, to be a useful crossing on the division's main supply route in subsequent phases of VERITABLE and for the build-up to the Rhine crossing, the bridge was upgraded to a double triple, capable of carrying 60 tons.

The Hekkens Crossroads, 11 February

The previous day 152 Brigade had continued to fight their way south through the Reichswald but by nightfall they were still over a mile short of the edge to the forest. Having waited all day and with 7th Argylls taking over BUNYAN, 5th Seaforth, reorganised into three companies, was to advance the final leg to Hekkens. Captain Borthwick recalled: 'At 0100 hours on February 11, C Company led off cautiously down the [Frasselt–Hekkens] road, with D and A following, and a heavy barrage sweeping the ground ahead of them; and as far as the bend in the road they met nothing.' In the pitch black of the forest, however, with heavy rain falling, 'Progress was slow and there were many halts, but nevertheless we were advancing, and our hopes began to rise.'

The battalion reached the edge of the forest and approached the anti-tank ditch that ran along the length of the southern boundary of the Reichswald. Here they were halted, as Borthwick explained:

> After half an hour the leading section approached the anti-tank ditch, and as they went forward to investigate it all hell broke. Spandaus opened up all

along the front, straight lines of tracer were striking the trees and flying off in all directions, grenades burst. They went to ground in a ditch by the roadside, with the Germans still firing at point-blank range. There was a hurried consultation, carried on in whispers in case the Germans would hear it, and a section was sent to work round the flank and discover the enemy strength; but before they had gone far, four more Spandaus opened up and pinned them. There were more consultations, more expeditions; and always there were more Spandau. The Germans were in the [anti-tank] ditch in strength and try as we might we could not get to grips with them.

The Seaforths, in the anti-tank ditch just short of the Hekkens crossroads' main defences, were in an unenviable position. They were pinned down at close quarters by a strong enemy position on higher ground beyond. The situation was further complicated by the fact that the tanks, already delayed by the mined road and now a sapper bulldozer that was to have filled the anti-tank ditch for the Churchills, were driven back by an anti-tank gun covering the exit from the

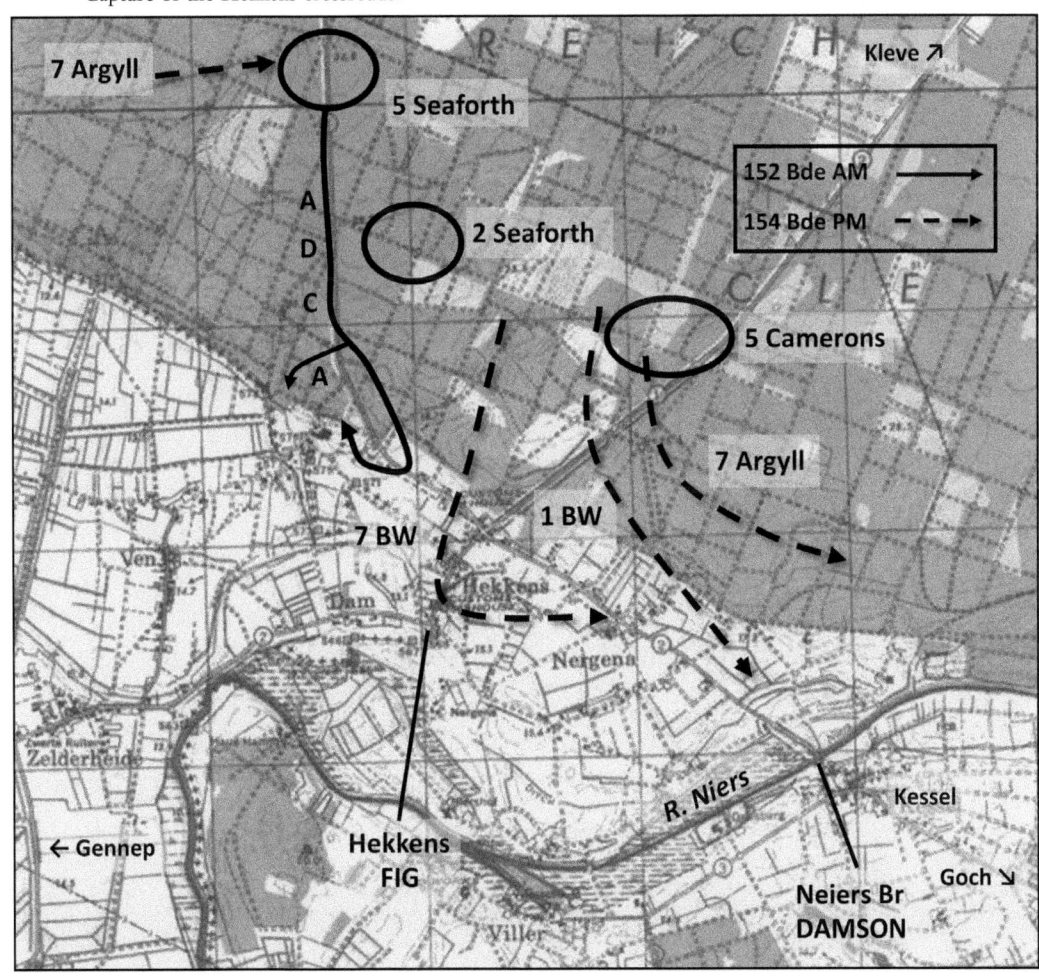

Capture of the Hekkens crossroads.

woods. Without tank support to help shoot the Seaforths forward, there was no option but to commit the reserve company to break the deadlock:

> 'A' tried to work round the right flank and made good progress at first. Spandaus fired here and there, but the answering brens drew gradually away from us as the company advanced, and we began to hope. Shouts of *'Kamerad! Kamerad!'* came through the darkness; and then, just as 'A' Company seemed to be breaking through, a murderous burst of defensive shelling and mortaring came down on top of them and pinned them. They could go no further. All along the line the Spandaus broke out again, worse than ever.

The enemy were attempting to infiltrate forward. At this point the CO was wounded but remained with the headquarters when the second-in-command was seriously wounded. The battalion's tactical headquarters was so close to the forward ditch that they could hear the NCOs giving fire control orders, and conditions in that ditch within grenade range of the enemy were indeed unenviable:

> The ditch was deep, but not deep enough to stand in. There was so little room that at one time men were lying on top of each other three-deep to keep under cover. Outside, the fixed lines of the Spandaus were firing tracer at stomach-height; and the only safe way forward was to crawl along the ditch, over all the bodies. In places the piles of humanity were so deep that even this method left the crawler exposed. The stretcher-bearers, unable to stoop and carry simultaneously, did magnificent work in carrying the wounded back through the hail of bullets in the open, but many of them were hit.

Having been ordered to remain in position, the Seaforths:

> Then began a long and anxious day ... Shortly after daylight the Germans concentrated every weapon they had, and for hours on end we were shelled and mortared and grenaded. The Spandaus were firing almost continuously, now so deadly that it was impossible to move in the forward positions. Shells were bursting in the trees, not in ones or twos, but by the score, throwing great splinters of steel and wood at the men lying prone in the ditch. We heard *the pop-pause-pop pause-pop* of the mortars, flattened ourselves and counted twenty; and down they came all round us, bursting in the treetops, on the road, everywhere. There was a nasty little yellow rifle grenade, too (it was one of these which had wounded the Colonel) which we had not met before and did not want to meet again.

Casualties across the battalion mounted inexorably, 'and still the storm of high explosive continued'. After three hours, the Churchills of 107 RAC got through in time to help break up an enemy attack but a German anti-tank gun firing straight down the road made life so dangerous for them they were forced to

A German bunker on the edge of the Reichswald near Hekkens. The thick roof of soil and tree trunks provided cover to all but a direct hit by a medium shell.

withdraw. Captain Borthwick concluded that late in the morning, having been ordered to withdraw:

> The tanks returned a little later and kept the German heads down while we drew back into the forest. And that was the end. Our job, though we only then realised it, was done. We had not taken the Hekkens crossroads, but we had pinned down every German capable of defending them and another brigade had been able to walk in behind the backs of the defence.

Opening XXX Corps' main supply route, Route HEART ROUTE, remained General Horrocks' priority for developing the battle into the Rhineland but by now the Seaforths and the rest of 152 Brigade had been fighting for three days and had culminated, being thoroughly exhausted. General Rennie, therefore, deployed 154 Brigade, which had been in reserve since the break in battle of 8 February. Brigadier Oliver received his orders to take the Hekkens crossroads at midday. In revising the divisional plan to make the capture of his Phase V objective, the Hekkens Crossroads (FIG), his main effort, rather that the Kessel Bridge (Phase IV DAMSON), General Rennie recognised that with reinforcement by the *fallschirmjäger* he was realistically unlikely to be able to capture DAMSON intact (see map on page 155).

Having received his orders, Brigadier Oliver's problem was that he had only a few hours of daylight in the woods during which to carry out battle procedure and launch the attack; it was obvious to him that he had to abbreviate both. To achieve this with an H Hour of 1530 hours, after a brief reconnaissance, he made the simplest of plans possible. Hoping that the Seaforths' attack on the axis of the Kranenburg road would have fixed enemy attention, the plan has been likened to a First World War-type infantry attack rather than the sort of operation the Highlanders had generally carried out.

The brigade was to attack astride the Kleve–Hekkens road, using a convenient cross-track as their start line, with 1st Black Watch on the left and 7 BW on the right. The 7th Argylls were to sweep through the forest in a south-easterly direction in order to provide flank protection to the main attack. For his fire plan Brigadier Oliver had all of XXX Corps artillery that was in range (four field and nine medium regiments and six heavy batteries). The heavies and the medium guns would fire on the objective, the adjacent Siegfried defences and likely enemy forming up points, while the divisional field artillery would fire a creeping barrage ahead of the advance.[1]

The battalions' commanding officers and orders groups[2] were rushed forward by Jeep, leaving their companies that had the previous evening been brought up from the western edge of the Reichswald to get their kit on and march 2 miles to their FUPs. They arrived at just thirty minutes before H Hour, allowing little time for either recce or orders.[3] Corporal Whitehouse of 1 BW recalled:

> Just past the [5th] Camerons we rested briefly ... Squaddies wandered into the thick undergrowth to answer nature's call, but I went among the trees

for another reason. I thought of all my mates lost on the long haul from Normandy's beaches. In that lonely retreat I became completely overwhelmed by it all and broke down, sobbing bitterly. But there were no tears, which might at least have helped me shake off these feelings of abject despair, triggered no doubt by the sight of the Camerons' heaped bodies. How much more could my demented mind withstand?

Back in the line NCOs were summoned and put in the picture. A creeping barrage would be laid down to help us take the final stretch of forest, after which we would be facing open fields and scattered farms. To cap it all our company was to be point company, with my section in the lead. I looked around at my friends; it was evident from their grim faces that they too viewed with alarm the prospect of our unit leading across those open fields.[4]

As the first shells fell on the enemy 'amidst solid walls of noise from the bombardment', Lieutenant Bernard deployed his platoon in the FUP 'among the trees into an arrowhead formation, with my [Whitehouse's] section out front and me the tip of the arrow':

Suddenly, with a mighty crash, the shells started landing among us, showering us with soil and twigs.

'Christ! What's happening?' someone yelled.

While the fighting was under way further forward, another road repair battle was under way to keep both tanks and infantry supplied. The Churchill is towing a Mk II Porpoise stores carrier.

'Bugger this, they're dropping short. Let's get out of it,' another voice cried. In unison the section turned and ran, doubled up, about twenty yards back, where our company commander stood with the artillery officer.

'What's going on?' demanded the officers.

'The xxxxing things fell among us. What are you xxxxing playing at you bastards?' In those few seconds we blasted off at the officers, not caring what we said. Had Field Marshal Montgomery himself been present we would have treated him with the same disrespect. Incredibly we had sustained no casualties from the misdirected shell fire.

'It's all right now,' soothed the artillery officer in a quieter tone, 'they'll be moving forward.' He talked into his phone to adjust the fall of shot. But our company commander was not so sympathetic or understanding.

Whitehouse noted that: 'We negotiated the rest of the Reichswald Forest without opposition.' The fixing effect of the Seaforths' attack helped, as did the barrage, which had been so heavy that the leading companies, keeping as close to the exploding shells as they could, overwhelmed the enemy positions before the stunned defenders had time to recover. German bunkers were grenaded as the attackers pressed on. Beyond the forest, heading for the hamlet of Nergena, however, was a different matter for 1 BW:

> We paused at the edge of the trees, weighing up a farmhouse in a field, about fifty yards ahead. A second lone farmstead was situated another hundred yards further on, a little to the left. Stepping out from the cover of the trees, we advanced in line towards the first building. Once in the open I braced myself for the inevitable Spandau fire, and it did not fail me, though it was obviously not coming from our immediate objective. The machine-gun's chilling, unmistakable sound – almost like cloth being ripped – always sent a shiver through me, even when it was not firing in my general direction.

As Whitehouse's 'platoon edged towards the farmhouse':

> spread out in line, the machine-gun's long burst caught several lads further up the line and I heard them cry out as they fell. The rest of us promptly bunched up behind the farm building, where we were pinned down as the bullets ricocheted off walls, zipped through windows and kicked up the soil on either side.
>
> Lieutenant Bernard disappeared into the farmhouse and came out with two Germans, who looked petrified. Several of our lads punched them in anger and the prisoners, with their hands held high, ran round to the front of the building and then hared off towards their own lines. It all happened so quickly we were caught napping. Though shots were fired at them, and one appeared to stumble, they made good their escape.

Overall, with the Germans shocked by the barrage, the attack was very successful. The 7th Black Watch reported they were at the edge of the Reichswald

Fallschirimjäger prisoner of war medics supervised by British soldiers treating German casualties near Hekkens.

and crossing the road at 1650 hours, and they had captured the Hekkens crossroads and hamlet of Nergena by 1800. By 1900 hours the brigade was digging in, having captured some 150 prisoners of war. Patrols sent out to the east by 1 BW during the course of the evening of 11 February confirmed, as expected, that the Kessel Bridge over the River Niers had been blown.

The *Sturmgeschütz* III

The *Sturmgeschütz* or *Stugs*, were very effective German assault guns of a pre-war design based on the chassis of the panzer III and later the Panzer IV. They were originally conceived as mobile weapon systems to provide the infantry with artillery fire support to supplement that of the towed infantry guns.

During the 1940 campaign they were used as intended but during Operation BARBAROSSA, on the exceptionally long Eastern Front they proved to be effective in the anti-tank role and finished the war as one of the most important German AFVs. Popular with military planners for its low-cost and similarly popular with its crews for its armour and low-profile, the *stug* became the workhorse of the Wehrmacht. As a tank-hunter it was to be found in all theatres; North Africa, the Mediterranean, NW Europe and the Eastern Front and accounted for more tank kills than the panzers put together. For instance, panzer ace *Hauptsturmführer* Michael Wittmann accrued most of his early kills commanding a Stug III rather than the Tiger.

In common with most German armoured vehicles the stug was subject to a constant series of upgrades of both armour and armaments. In the case of its gun originally it was fitted with a Krupp 75 L/24 Kanone, which was a short barrel gun designed to fire HE rounds at field fortifications and pillboxes at short and medium range. The Ausf F and G saw further changes that both simplified production and upgraded the armour but the biggest difference from late 1942 was the availability of the long 75mm gun that enabled the stug to defeat the sloped armour of the T34.

During the course of the war some 9,400 stugs were built matching the production of that other Wehrmacht stalwart the Panzer IV.

So successful and ubiquitous were the stugs, that over the course of the war they were no longer the preserve of the German artillery. They became the main equipment of some *panzerjäger* units and, as in the case of some panzer divisions, were also to be found in the *panzerwafer*. This was particularly marked as production difficulties increased along with a need to replace large amounts of equipment at short notice.

German armour also struggled with the ground conditions. This Stug became badly bogged after venturing off a road on the outskirts of the Reichswald.

Chapter Eight

The Niers Bridgehead, 12–13 February

As the situation in Gennep was far from clear during the evening of 11 February, Colonel Grant Peterkin, acting commander of 153 Highland Brigade, was only able to give his orders for the 12th around midnight. Consequently, there was again little sleep for the commanding officers and staff officers of either 1st or 5th/7th Gordons. Major Lindsay wrote:

> In the middle of the night I got orders to prepare to take the high ground north-east and east of Heyen, a mile south of Gennep, and 5th/7th Gordons were to attack at the same time on our left and secure the remaining features which overlooked the town. It was quite a complicated little operation, and I spent the five remaining hours of the night in my cellar Command Post planning it and the fire programme, and how to get the best inter-communication. 'Inter-com.' is the key to every battle for when it fails all control ceases, and it was particularly difficult since the companies' wireless sets were not good enough.[1]

The problem for the two Gordons battalions was that their FUP and start lines were overlooked by German positions around the station and in the housing estate, which were occupied by elements of III 20 and I and III 2 *fallschirmjäger* regiments (see map on following page). It was obvious that there would be a significant delay launching the advance south while enemy along the railway line were cleared by 5th Black Watch. H Hour for the attack, which was to be delivered by D and B companies, was 1130 hours; a time dictated by the opening of Lieutenant Cantley's bridge to traffic at 1030 hours. The war diary details Colonel Bradford's plan for 5 BW:

> After a recce the commanding officer ordered D Coy to attack the station and bridge and houses 784455 supported by tanks and [two troops of] Crocodiles which were due to cross the bridge first, B Coy were to then pass through D Coy to the Housing Estate.

The Black Watch's regimental history provides more detail:

> In the attack one platoon of infantry were to lead the Crocodiles towards the objective. But the track was hard to follow, and the tanks had to make their way between several houses to get back to the correct route. In the process they did no good at all to several gardens.

Lieutenant Colonel Bill Bradford DSO* commanded 5th Black Watch from July 1944 to the end of the war.

Operations in the area around Gennep Station on 12 February 1945.

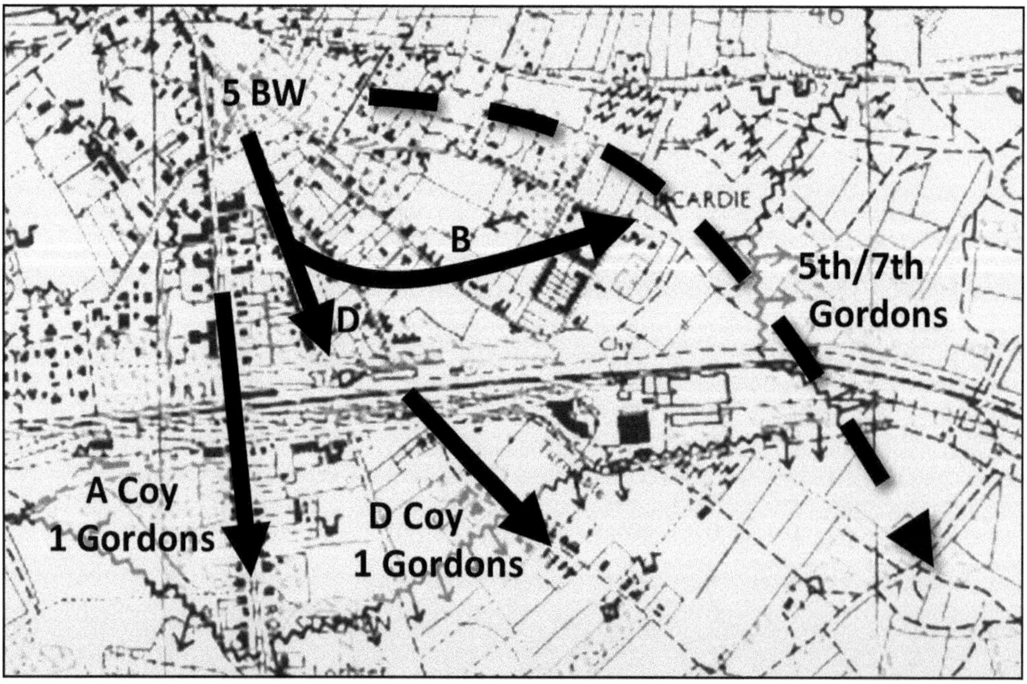

Lieutenants Crockett of 5 BW and Bowlby of A Squadron, 1st Fife and Forfar Yeomanry, together carried out a recce on foot and under fire to find a route through the streets and houses to a point where the station could be flamed. For this and their leadership in action they were both awarded the Military Cross. The Black Watch historian continued:

> Within range of the Station the Crocodiles functioned splendidly, heartily flamed the buildings, forcing the enemy garrison to retreat in disorder across the fields. The infantry had never worked with flame before and apparently did not realize it was safe to attack the instant the Troop Leader gave his signal to go ahead. The assault was held for a minute or two with the result that a number of the enemy, who by rights ought to have spent the rest of the war in a cage, got away. The Troop then advanced to the next objective, the rows of houses. These they flamed with such effect that twelve of them were completely gutted in a short time. The Black Watch then asked for still more flame for another house because of the persistent fire which came from it, and which was pinning the foot soldiers down. In spite of heavy mortaring from the enemy, Troop Three of 'A' Sqn were happy to oblige with a further little deed of kindness. They quickly made fireworks of the house, which was holding out, whereupon the infantry dashed forward and reached their objectives. Lieutenant Bowbly was wounded on the head by shrapnel during the attack and two trailers were knocked about but remained serviceable. On the whole a thoroughly successful action with all the objectives occupied and very light casualties.

Even though the casualties were 'light' the proportion of officers among them was, as always in this campaign, significant.

Gennep Station, a gutted ruin after the fighting.

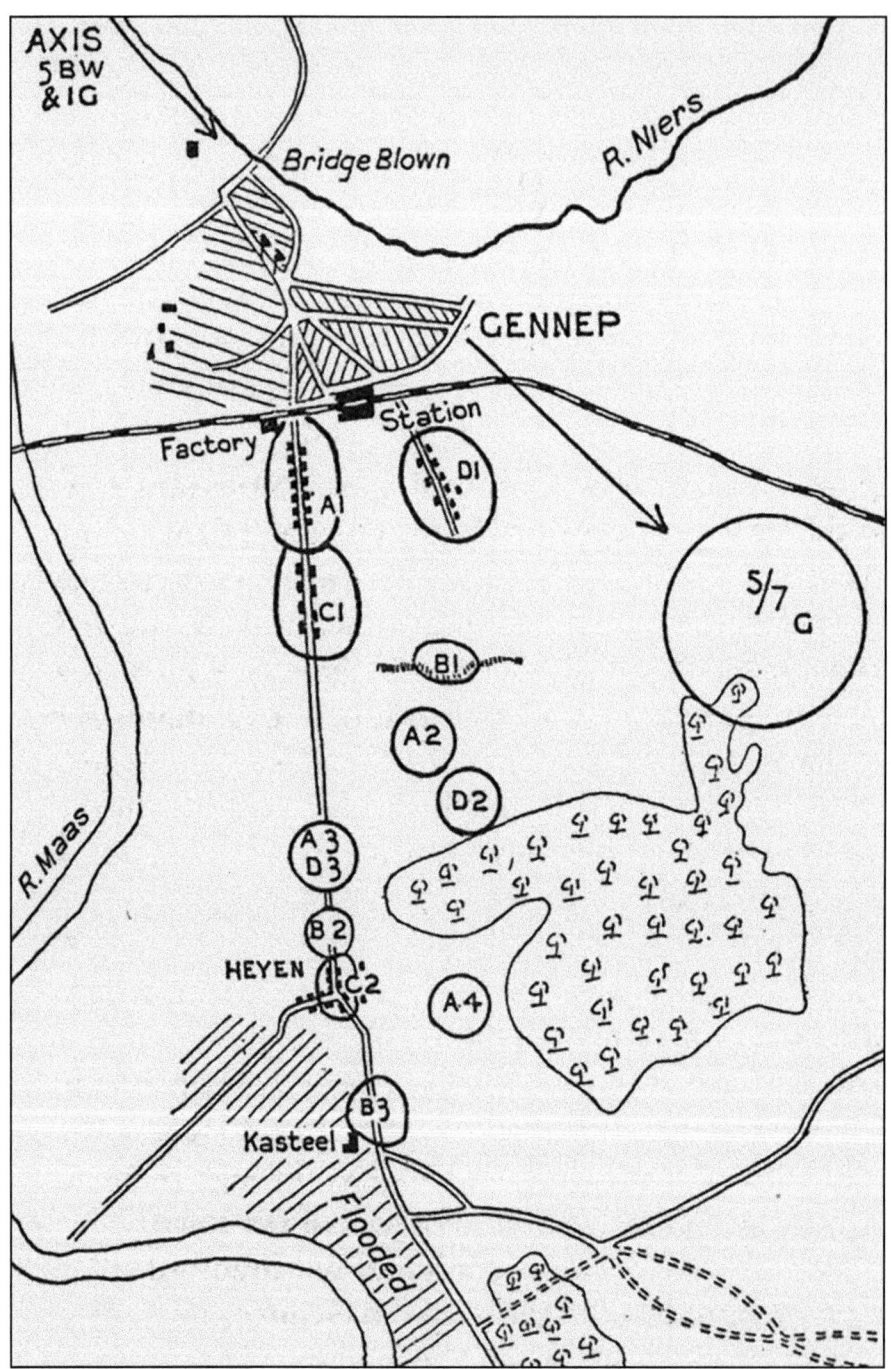

Major Lindsay's map of 1st Gordons' operations on 12 February, which he refers to below.

The Niers Bridgehead, 12–13 February 167

An extract of the 1:25,000 map covering the same area.

A crocodile flamethrower in action during a demonstration.

Major Lindsay's plan was for A and D companies, supported by armour and a complicated artillery fire plan that his battery commander had worked on during the night, to attack down the streets astride the station clearing the houses (A1 and D1 on Lindsay's map). H Hour for the advance south of the railway was at 1500 hours, once again giving only limited daylight for the battalions to complete the capture of their objectives:

> They had the benefit of a smoke-screen which shielded them from the high ground further south [which dominated Gennep], but also made it difficult to watch their progress, and to some extent hindered the troop of Churchill tanks supporting them. Neither company had any great difficulty ...
>
> Then C and B passed through them (to C1 and B1). B Company was directed on to a small sandy ridge covered with diggings, which they proceeded to charge in their now familiar style and for which they were well supported by the tanks. They claimed to have killed twenty Huns and that several more went away wounded and shrieking with pain. So far so easy, and I moved my headquarters up to C Company. I now had to send A, and then D, forward (to A2 and D2).

To prove the difficulties of radio communication, Major Lindsay could not get orders through to D company and had to resort to sending one of the Churchills across to them with a written message. A and D reached their objectives with little difficulty in the growing darkness, and it was once again raining hard.

C Company were halted by machine gun fire just short of the northern edge of the ruins of Heyen (C2). As it was too dark to locate the enemy, they were ordered 'not to get involved in a battle'. Consequently, the company went 'firm round a few houses at the roadside'. B Company were moved up just behind them (B2), along with mortars and guns of 61 Anti-Tank Regiment, which had crossed the bridge to join the brigade.

Daylight on 11 February found 5th/7th Gordons still in Ottersum awaiting the opening of the bridge and their turn to cross behind the armour into Gennep. After a long wait they eventually made their way to their FUP on the brigade's left flank at 1400 hours. Their task was 'to pass the battalion through 5 BW and clear the eastern portion of the town and consolidate on the open ground 800–900 yards beyond'.

As C and D companies were advancing through 5th Black Watch's positions, now at the bottom end of Picardie Weg, they were hit by enemy artillery and some of their own medium guns firing short. Casualties at this stage, even before they crossed the start line to begin the process of clearing the eastern part of Gennep, were serious and consequently they made little progress against 'stiff enemy resistance' among the housing. A combination of the supporting Churchills of 147 Regiment RAC and the Crocodiles of the Fife and Forfar Yeomanry, which were called up from the rear, enabled the infantry to assault and clear the area.

Lieutenant Cantley's bridge at Gennep, across which armour and both battalions of Gordons crossed the Niers.

As the 5th/7th reorganised amidst the houses they came under machine gun fire from the shell of an old factory but again a troop of Crocodiles came to their aid and the Germans withdrew across the railway line. The companies followed across the lines and dug in on their objectives just before nightfall.

A Second Niers Bridgehead, 12–13 February

While 153 Brigade fought to expand the Gennep bridgehead to the south during 12 February, with the blowing of the Niers bridge at Kessel and strong German defences south of the river, 154 Brigade spent the day regrouping, consolidating and preparing for an assault crossing. As Route HEART from Mook to Hekkens was now in British hands, the Highland Division's sappers could begin the process of clearing mines and repairing the shell holes and numerous craters that the enemy had blown in the road. It was, however, overlooked by artillery observers from the high ground in the bend in the river south of Hekkens and therefore work had to be done mainly at night or when it was possible to use smoke.

The significance of the German route denial effort was that the time taken to fill the blown culverts would inhibit movement and create delay, as the numerous drainage ditches and saturated ground meant vehicles could not drive across country. The Mook road was the only viable route for tanks into the Rhineland and the road junction town of Goch just 7 miles away. Therefore, committal of the Guards Armoured Division could not take place until the road was repaired and there was a second crossing of the Niers.

The war diary of 154 Brigade confirms that the 12th was 'Largely a day of reconnaissance':

> 7 A&SH were moved to area 8547. This meant that they were still in the Reichswald but could overlook the river. The forward platoon was in position by 0817 hours at 858473. An improvised enemy footbridge over the NIERS was reported to be intact here but owing to flooding around approaches it could not be used for vehicles. 'B' Coy 1/7 Mx [machine guns] was put in support of the Bn.
>
> At 1630 hours a platoon of 7 A & SH made contact with a company of 6 HLI of 53 Div at 870476. This was unexpected as they had been told to expect East Lancs. It transpired that the HLI Coy any had lost its bearings temporarily.
>
> A 7 Black Watch patrol went out at 1900 hours returning at 2200 hours to look at a possible crossing place of the R. NIERS at 8194. 274 Fd Coy were to clear the road for them. Search lights were used to assist them as a large crater had to be bulldozed. This party had to work all night and when it became light a smoke screen had to be laid for their protection.

In contrast to 12 February, the 13th was a day of preparation:

> Morning of the 13th was fairly quiet apart from spasmodic shelling of 7 Black Watch area. Sappers had cleared the GENNEP–HEKKENS road of mines

With fighting static on the edge of the forest, numerous trees were blown down by shell and mortar fire.

and filled in an anti-tank obstacle. 53 Div used this axis for supply. This passing as it did through the 7 Black Watch area [at the Hekkens crossroads] probably caused the shelling.

Of the enemy fire that also fell on 1 BW, Corporal Whitehouse wrote:

> We were shelled intermittently throughout the day and could only cower down and sweat it out ... and kept a sharp look-out for an enemy attack ... I popped my head over the edge of our 'slitter' and was perplexed to see arms stuck in the air from two of the four slitters – hoping to catch a Blighty wound.

The Welsh Division's axis forward from the western edge of the Reichswald had finally disintegrated and despite continuous efforts by the Highlanders' engineers and most of those not involved in the struggle to maintain the Kartenspielerweg MSR, it too became impassable and was closed to traffic at 1600 hours. This left the engineers and logisticians struggling to deliver combat supplies for that night's attack.

> At 0847 hours the Bde Comd held a planning conference for all COs to plan the operation involving the crossing of the River NIERS and the seizing of a bridgehead. No operation order was issued but co-ordinating conference notes were produced, after a further conference at 1400 hours.

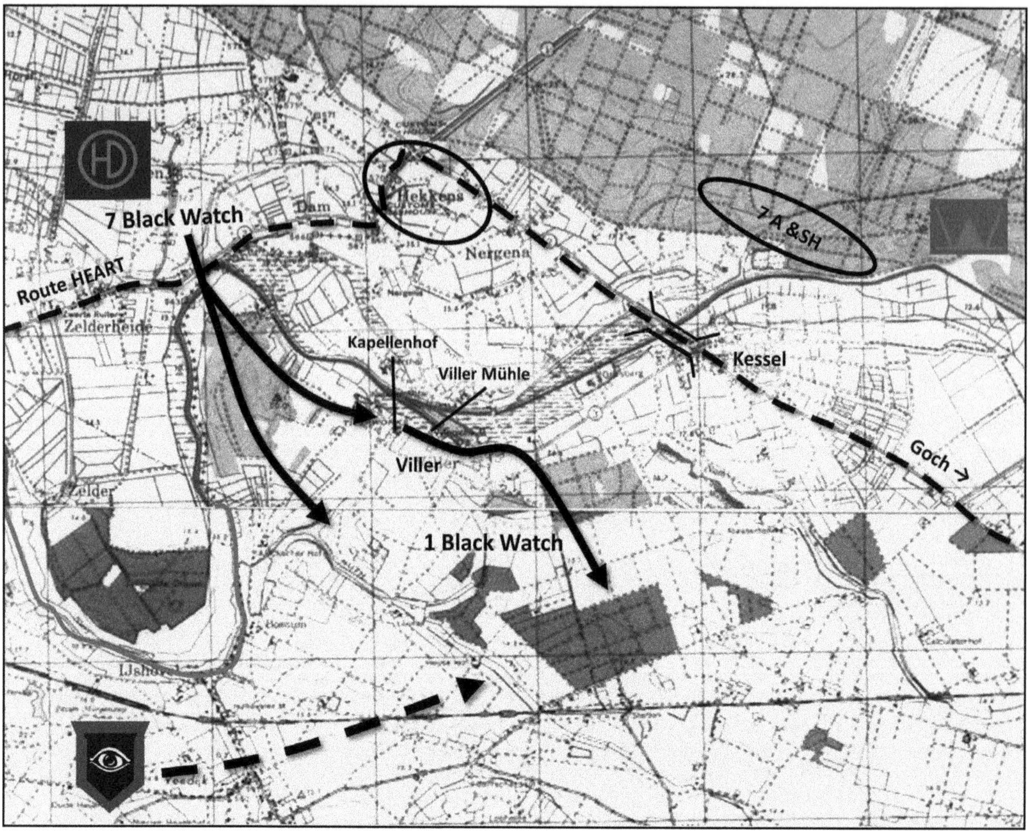

The assault crossing of the River Niers on the night of 13–14 February 1945.

The expansion of the Niers Bridgehead during 14 February 1945.

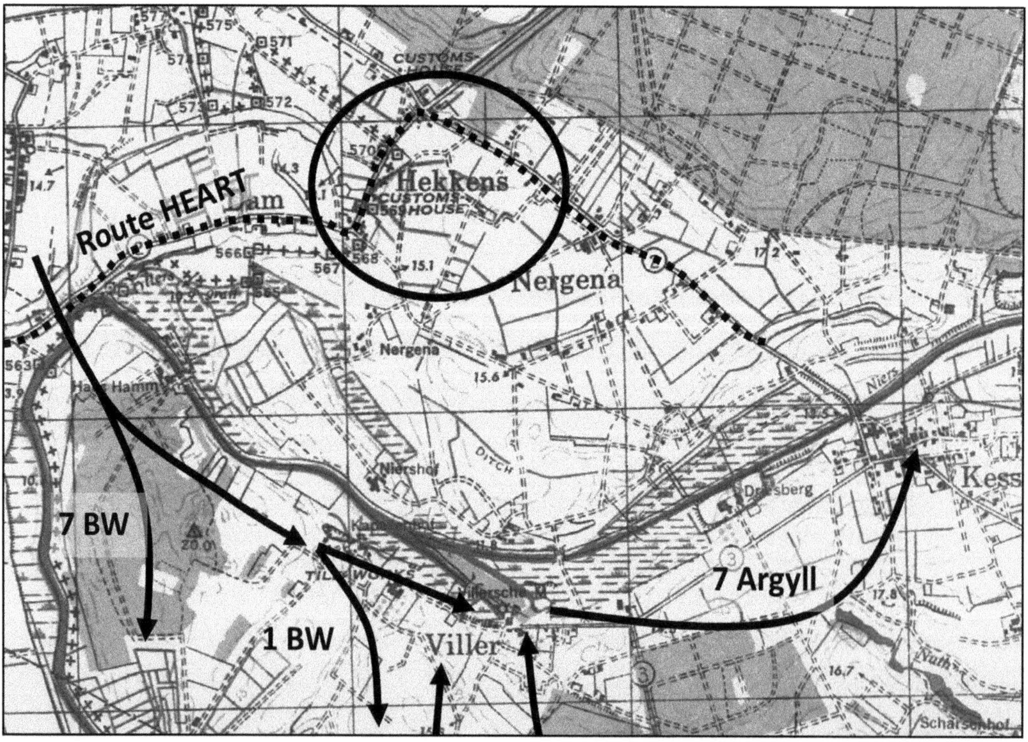

The plan was that following a heavy bombardment, including a participation in a PEPPERPOT by A Squadron, 107 RAC, 7 BW would conduct the assault crossing of the swollen river in a dozen Buffaloes at 2015 hours and seize the high ground in the river bend south of Viller. Then, in succession, 1 BW were to extend the bridgehead to the east and 7 A&SH strike north to secure Kessel and the bridging site. Once the site was in the hands of the Argylls, the sappers intended to start work immediately, as explained by Colonel Carr, the Highlanders' Commander Royal Engineers:

> As a result of our experience at Gennep, I thought it essential to use the confusion just after a night attack and the ensuing hours of darkness to launch a Bailey before first light so that the enemy artillery fire should not be in a position to prevent bridging operations. I realised that it would take some time for the Argylls to reach and clear Kessel village completely and report that bridging operations could start. I therefore decided to start dumping and building operations before the capture of the village was completed. Mine clearance and bridge reconnaissance parties could filter forward just as soon as the tactical situation permitted. Meanwhile in the shelter of a nearby farm, about 250 yards from the bridge, Bailey bridge lorries could deliver and turn round and preliminary building could proceed.[2]

In addition to the major bridge at Kessel, to reduce pressure on the valuable Buffaloes the sappers planned to build a Class 9 bridge at the assault crossing

A soldier of 1st Black Watch well dug-in with overhead cover of logs.

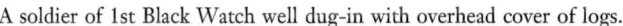

point using the Mark III Folding Boat Equipment (FBE). However, in the event, the flooded approaches to the bridging site, combined with the rate of flow and debris being washed downstream, washed away the first attempt and it was abandoned.

With Kartenspielerweg still restricted and Route HEART crammed with engineer bridging traffic, the trucks bringing forward 3in and 4.2in mortar ammunition were delayed and only just arrived in time for the bombs to be distributed to the mortar platoons. In the fire plan that started at 1600 hours, the Middlesexes' heavy 4.2-inch mortars were to neutralise Kessel.

With shells and mortar bombs having 'softened up' the defenders of 20 *Fallschirmjäger* Regiment, H Hour for the assault crossing was 2030 hours. At that time the Buffaloes carrying B Company 7 BW motored forward from the FUP to the Niers and took to the water between Zelderheide and Hekkens. The crossing itself was unopposed and B Company's advance on Kapellenhof faced only scattered opposition. The farm that was chosen for the battalion's tactical headquarters was, however, occupied by the enemy, who after an exchange of shots slipped away or surrendered. A dozen prisoners, mostly wounded, were taken.

Kapellenhof was secured by B Company after a short, sharp fight and, while they were reorganising, D Company took over the advance on Viller, the buildings of which clustered around a six-storey mill complex (Viller Mühle). Initially the attack went well but as the clearance progressed resistance in the village stiffened. The problem was a pillbox and the determined defence of a substantial house. D Company's assault failed but 2in mortar bombs fired through windows at close range smoked the defenders out as the house caught fire. The village was, however, not fully in 7 BW's hands, but they had taken eighty-six *fallschirmjäger* prisoners, at the cost of five ordinary ranks (ORs) killed and two officers and twenty-four ORs wounded.

As close to Route HEART as possible, the assault crossing site was at the crown of the bend in the Niers.

Up to this point the operation had gone well and 1 BW began to cross the Niers at 2200 hours. Corporal Whitehouse of B Company recalled:

> We moved down to the riverbank after dark and boarded the Buffaloes. I was always anxious about being on water with a full pack, since the prospects of survival would be slim if we sank, but my fears were groundless and apart from a few shells that created waterspouts nearby the journey was uneventful. Now that we were on the Fatherland's sacred soil, I expected the enemy to yield every inch of ground grudgingly, so it came as a tremendous surprise and bolstered morale when we saw about thirty Germans on the far bank with hands in the air, eager to board our Buffaloes for the return journey when we alighted.

Almost immediately 1 BW passed through D Company in Villers:

> ... reality soon returned. As the platoon moved forward down a road we were fired on from behind and Lieutenant Bernard and our company commander were among the casualties. Fortunately, our platoon commander was only nicked in the leg, but he had to go back for attention. The major, hit embarrassingly in the behind, continued to charge about like a mad bull,

Corporal Stan Whitehouse MM.

bellowing and insisting we eliminate the strongpoint before he would let the medics treat him. The firing was coming from the narrow window of a building we had just passed near a mill [Viller Mühle].

The company commander called for a PIAT. Corporal Whitehouse, having carried the weapon in Normandy, knew how to use it:

> 'Right, put a bugger through that little window,' said the major pointing out the enemy's strongpoint. The sergeant primed and slid the bomb into place and I took aim and fired. It was a very narrow ground-floor window that reminded me of a castle's mullion window, but the bomb found its mark and exploded on the sill.
> 'Good lad,' said the company commander ecstatically, for the moment forgetting his wound. 'That's fixed the bastards.' The major seemed on a high and wanted to continue, but his backside was now soaked with blood and the stretcher-bearers, helped by the sergeant, finally managed to get him to lie face down on the stretcher and, still shouting orders, he was carried to the nearby mill, now being used by our MO and the German MO to tend the wounded of both sides ...

Villers was reported as secure in 7 BW's hands at 0145 hours and 1 BW moved on to their objectives. Corporal Whitehouse continued:

> Up ahead were several clumps of woods which we all hoped would be cleared by someone else, but it was not to be. We were ordered to make a sweep in that area during the night and the prospect filled me with trepidation. Wood clearing during the day is unpleasant; at night it is terrifying.
> Luckily we cleared the woods without a hitch, though it was a miracle we never shot each other as we groped in the dark, flinching at ghostly shadows and the sharp snap of twigs underfoot. Moving from one wood to another we came across a huge ditch in a field and holed up there for the night. The ditch, which I could only assume to be an anti-tank ditch, was about ten feet wide and five feet deep and seemed ideal to me, but Shorty preferred our normal two-man 'slitters' and told his men to dig in about ten yards behind us. Later a company runner arrived with the order for us to stay in our present positions.

By dawn on 14 February, 154 Brigade had established a second Niers bridgehead and both Black Watch battalions were digging in under shell and mortar fire. The situation was, however, precarious as the number of serviceable Buffaloes had dwindled to three and without the class 9 bridge being finished, getting support weapons, reserves and a replenishment of ammunition across the river was slow. Armour support would, of course, have to await the building of the main bridge.

Meanwhile, in the Gennep bridgehead, soldiers of 1st/7th Middlesex were deployed with their Vickers machine guns to strengthen 153 Brigade's defences. Under cover of darkness, Private Haward, having dropped off gun, crew and ammunition, was turning his carrier to return to the rear when it threw a track. Replacing it would be a noisy business. As the crew:

> hit the shackle pin, an enemy *Spandau* zeroed in, firing tracers. Sparks were flying off the other side of the carrier, and then it stopped. It was fortunate that the broken track was on 'our side' of the carrier. Harry hit it again and the machinegun fired another burst. Harry said, 'Every time I hit it, that German opens up,' so this time he gave the pin two hits and the German responded with two bursts! Three taps were answered by three bursts. This enemy machine gunner obviously had a sense of humour. Eventually he lost interest and somehow the track stayed on long enough for the carrier to limp away a short distance for it to be put on properly.[3]

The Class 40 Bailey bridge at Kessel and a subsequently built Class 60 bridge alongside it to relieve congestion when it became XXX Corps' MSR.

The Land Mattress Rocket System

The Land Mattress originated as an anti-aircraft weapon system, which on an occasion in North Africa proved to be highly successful in stopping a dangerous German counter-attack. On his return to the UK in 1943 an officer pressed for the system to be developed for ground use but following a demonstration in 1943 the Royal Artillery were not enthusiastic. The Canadian liaison officer, however, reported on the system's effect and the idea was developed by the RCA, using RAF rockets and naval shells. The launcher for thirty two 60-pound rockets was also largely made up from redundant parts.

The British flirted with the Land Mattress during operations in the autumn of 1944 but remained unenthusiastic and the system was thus unique to the Canadians, eventually being in the hands of a light anti-aircraft battery, which became 1st Canadian Rocket Battery RCA. One of the problems was the supply of the rockets that needed special handling, with no less than seventy trucks required to collect VERITABLE's 2,000 rockets from the ports.

With a range of 8,000 yards, the 60-pound rocket's warhead was an adapted naval 5-inch shell, equivalent to a normal medium artillery shell of the AGRAs. The system was laid on target using normal field artillery equipment and procedures. The launcher fired rockets at quarter second intervals, firing all thirty two rockets in eight seconds. Loading was, however, slow but a well-practiced crew could manage a reload in an average of 10–12 minutes.

The devastating effect of 384 rockets landing on a target in such a short time made a battery salvo not only lethal, with blast and splinters, but also demoralising for those who were on the receiving end. The 'penetrating shriek' of the rockets added to the effect. This made the Land Mattress an ideal and important components of PEPPERPOT shoots, which were a key feature of VERITABLE's fire plan.

Chapter Nine

The Welsh Division – Attack and Counter-Attack

In the second phase of their operations to clear the bulk of the Reichswald, 53rd Welsh Division had, during 11 February, swung from the northern part of the forest in a south-easterly direction to secure the Kleve–Hekkens road. To their right was the 51st Highland and on the other flank, the 43rd Wessex began its push south-east from the Kleve area. The 53rd's opposition was three *fallschirmjäger* regiments that had either already been roughly handled or had been hurriedly redeployed to the Reichswald, into positions that were equally hurriedly prepared and inevitably poorly co-ordinated.[1]

During the morning, against mixed but generally lower levels of opposition, 158 Brigade with 147 Regiment RAC and 160 Brigade supported by 9 RTR, reached their objective along the Hekkens road. Lieutenant Beal of B Squadron recalled that:

> As we and 2 MON passed the start line at 0900 hours we came under heavy mortar fire and soon afterwards machine-guns and bazookas were encountered. There were several skirmishes during the advance and some prisoners of war were taken, but by 1000 hours the objective, just to the west of the farm Dammershof, had been captured. A Jagdpanther, which opened fire and advanced towards the positions, was engaged by M10 and forced to retire.

The *Jagdpanther* was just one element of the enemy action in the corner of the Reichswald. Fighting inside the north-eastern edge to the forest 'At 1100 hours C Squadron and 6 RWF crossed the Cleve—Hekkens road and destroyed some enemy machine-guns'. Despite encountering some stiff resistance that cost them forty casualties 'by 1350 hours the tanks and infantry were firmly established on their objective level with B Squadron'.

With five good hours of daylight remaining, this success, along with that of 158 Brigade, prompted General Ross to resume the advance to the Kleve–Asperden road, known as report line VIRGINIA, the third of the roads that bisected the forest. At 1330 hours, 4th Welch were ordered to resume the advance. Lieutenant Beal continued:

> At 1500 hours A Squadron and 4 WELCH passed between B and C Squadrons and occupied the farm at Dammershof by 1640 hours. A *Jagdpanther*

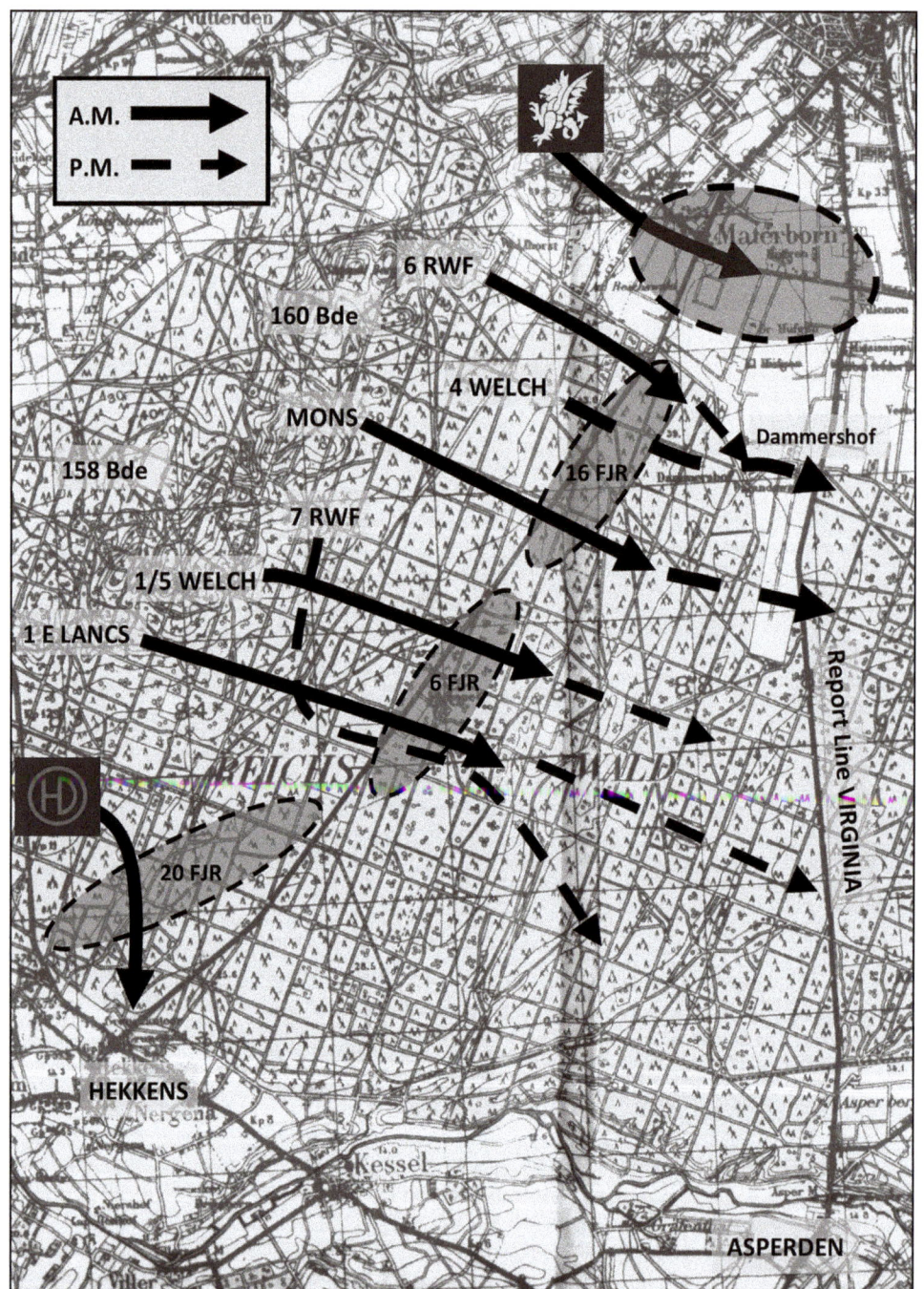

The 53rd Welsh Division's advance during 11 February 1945.

creeping about in the farmyard was KO'd by 75 mm AP from 3 Troop at a range of approximately 400 yards, two shots breaking the track and damaging the suspension. The crew baled out and sought refuge in the farm but were subsequently rounded up there by Lt. Tom Fawcett.

The infantry recorded that in approaching VIRGINIA they encountered 'generally slight opposition, capturing a few prisoners and one SP gun'. This, helpfully, positioned the battalion to the left rear of an enemy position in the Materborn area, which a battalion of the Wessex Division was attacking.

Sergeant Greenwood of 9 RTR wrote in his personal diary:

> Advanced in daylight this time: terrible journey thru extremely dense forest. Tanks performed miracles. Knocked out a Jack Panther [sic] – but we missed a second: no trace. Finally harboured about 7 p.m. in dark. Cold and wet. Infantry dug in by tanks. Pretty perilous position here.

Meanwhile, with 158 Brigade having made an advance in some cases of over 2 miles to reach VIRGINIA, they too broke through hastily occupied and thinly spread *fallschirmjäger* defences. Brigadier Wilsey was also ordered to continue the

Sergeant Greenwood of C Squadron 9 RTR.

advance and his brigade hastily reorganised for their next task, to continue towards the south-east corner of the Reichswald, a mile north of the bridge over the Niers at Asperden. The advance of 160 Brigade to Dammershof had been a mile but 158 Brigade had already covered almost twice that distance and were now expected to repeat that advance to reach VIRGINIA, which was also through some of the denser patches of plantation in the Reichswald.

With significantly further to advance and light fading, two of Brigadier Wilsey's battalions did well to cover almost 2 miles through the woods but were halted short of the Kleve–Asperden road. In doing so they lost two more of 147 RAC's supporting Churchills. The 1st East Lancs, however, had reached the road, where, having crossed a newly planted open part of the forest, D Company became isolated and pinned down. Their FOO of 330 Battery, however, broke up several enemy counter-attacks before C Company charged across the open ground, into the enemy flank and relieved the pressure on D Company.

The Welsh historian recorded that: 'At 8 pm the Divisional Commander ordered both Brigades to halt where they were, and plans were made for resuming the advance next day.' The East Lancs, having reached VIRGINIA, were forward on their own, with the enemy at close quarters. In this unenviable situation 'At about 8.30 pm the East Lancashires beat off an infantry counter-attack and throughout the night patrol activity, and minor encounters, continued along the whole front.'

Sergeant Greenwood in his 'perilous position' up with the infantry, recalled that at: 'About ten or eleven [he] saw flash accompanied by roar of bazooka.

A *Jagdpanther* of 655 *Schwere Panzerjäger* Battalion. Only a dozen or so were operational to the east of the Reichswald but those that ventured into the edge of the forest forfeited the vehicle's protection and the range of its 88mm gun.

Learned later that Sgt Mead killed by Jerry patrol. Entire crews on guard all night afterwards.'

The commanding officer, Lieutenant Colonel Veale, wrote in his post-operational report summarising the fighting from the armoured perspective:

> The ability of the Churchill tank to give close support to infantry through forests of the Reichswald type, both by day and night, was proven. It is believed that no other allied tank in service could have done as well, or even have reached the forest over the same country.

Corporal Parry-Jones of 2 Mons wrote of the day's infantry fighting:

> The German parachutists had a fearsome reputation that frankly worried us no end but unlike when we fought our first battles in Normandy against the SS by the time we got to the Reichswald, we knew what we were doing. They fought bloody hard but the big difference was they didn't want to die for Adolf and when it came to it they surrendered. By now we had quite a lot of young lads in our company but so many of the parachutists prisoners were mere boys and seemed happy enough that they were out of it.

Since the disasters of summer 1944, the Germans had been combing out men from the bloated ranks of the increasingly redundant Kriegsmarine and Luftwaffe. Many of these became reluctant infantrymen and in what was clearly the final stage of the war were often not prepared to make the ultimate sacrifice for the *Führer*. It would appear, however, from the patchy resistance by the *Fallschirmjäger* in the Reichswald, that leadership in particular made all the difference between a stiff fight and the sort of incident that Sergeant Williams of the 2nd Monmouthshires reported. He went forward to investigate a building at the edge of the forest, threw a grenade through a window and out came thirty Germans, who surrendered without a fight.

The advances into the south-east portion of the Reichswald meant that the Welsh Division had to move its fire support, logistic and communications forward, not least its seventy-two 25-pounders needed to keep within range of the advancing battalions. Captain Bolland, a staff officer in the division's Headquarters Royal Artillery, oversaw the business of dragging the guns from one position to another:

> The weather has been vile ever since the thaw set in so thoroughly. The mud is ten times worse than anything we have met before. In the last four nights I have been up all through the night without a moment's sleep trying to get the guns into action and to dump ammo along the roads and in fields which are nothing short of quagmires. The Hun has an unhappy habit of digging his funk holes underneath the roads so if a tank goes over them, they just give way.

The carriers that in normal circumstances would have brought forward the infantry's 3in and 4.2in mortars and their Vickers guns, in many cases became

A section of RWF soldiers advancing through the Reichswald.

bogged and the crews had to man-pack their heavy weapons forward. In addition, the large quantities of ammunition they habitually used required repeated trips back to bogged carriers and trucks. Typical of the comments was: 'Day after day, night after night, we laboured in the mud. By the end of it, I was exhausted to the point of being an automaton and I was skin and bone.'

A war correspondent writing in the *Yorkshire Post* reported an interview with Lieutenant Colonel Allen of 1st East Lancashires, who talked about the conditions in which his battalion fought:

> We had to shoulder forward what we could – our mortars and mortar bombs – and feel our way forward on a compass bearing. There were mines, there was always the mud. Often we were without food, often it came up late. We ate our breakfast at 4pm and our evening meal at 3am. We were cold.

We were wet. We were hungry and we kept on fighting. It was bloody. Observation was from one tree to the next. We were behind one tree and the Bosch was behind the next. A terribly wearing business for the men. Psychologically and mentally. It was nearly all bayonet, Sten and grenade fighting. The Bosch reserves fought very well, stubborn and had in many cases to be dug out with the bayonet.

Behind the advancing division, the engineers continued the road-making effort across the Groesbeek Heights into the Reichswald. Army engineer companies were extracting tons of hardcore from quarries and gravel pits and trucking it forward, only to see whole lorry loads disappear into the mud, but they persisted. Inside the forest acres of pine trees were cut down to make log or 'corduroy' roads. To preserve these roads for logistic traffic, as Lieutenant Beal wrote:

> Tanks were still forbidden the use of all roads so that the Stuarts of 9 RTR, endeavouring to get forward with the urgently required replenishments,

A 25-pounder in action. The picture belies the difficulties of getting the guns in and out of position.

Churchills harboured on a forest track preparing for action.

were halted in Groesbeek where they had to remain until we were withdrawn from the forest.

He also reported that his regiment was having considerable difficulty in maintaining radio communications and was in urgent need of their unit telecommunications technician:

> That it was necessary to obtain a written permit from Divisional HQ to get him forward in a jeep illustrates the stringency of the road discipline.
>
> Permission was obtained, however, to take essential supplies forward and at 2100 hours the DAA and QMG left Malden with a supply column with which he established a new ammunition point and petrol point on the main road Cleve–Hekkens. This time he had to go on 51st (H) Division's route south of the forest as the 15th (S) Division axis, hitherto used to replenish the ammunition point at Frasselt, had been flooded.

The Advance Resumed, 12 February

Having made a significant advance the previous day, 158 Brigade's battalions were to complete the advance to the Kleve–Asperden road, while 160 Brigade was to secure positions in the Reichswald's north-east corner.

Brigadier Barclay wrote:

> The Divisional plan for 12 February was for both leading battalions to press forward to the eastern edge of the Forest, with the 71st Brigade mopping up in the rear of the 158th. The latter brigade was to make every effort to capture the river bridge north of Asperden.

As dawn broke at VIRGINIA, where 1st East Lancs were still out on their own, and having not received a replenishment of combat supplies during the night, they remained under pressure. During the course of the morning the batteries of the battalion's radios, which had been man-packed forward, were failing and calls for artillery fire were not getting through. The 1st/5th Welch and 7 RWF were now 'bitterly opposed', and the Welch only closed up alongside the East Lancs on the Kleve–Asperden Road by 1200 hours with just four tanks of their supporting squadron still in action. By mid-afternoon they were approaching the eastern edge of the forest, where they started to dig in and were counter-attacked by XLVII Panzer Corps.

The diarist of 147 RAC recorded that at virtually every track junction they encountered enemy infantry dug in with numerous *panzerfausts* but by this stage fewer mines. 'The tactic employed was to advance with all guns blazing and drive through the bazooka boys as quickly as possible. This unnerved them and they were cleared up by the infantry.' The Welch, however, complained that the *fallschirmjäger*'s ample supply of *panzerfausts* were used as anti-personnel weapons, being fired at trees and tracks in front of the attacking infantry.

Further north, 2 Mons and B Squadron 9 RTR, began their advance at 0730 hours against stiff opposition and reached VIRGINIA at 1130 hours, taking thirty prisoners in the process. Along with other battalions across XXX Corps, 2 Mons record being bombed by jet aircraft, which is a measure of the seriousness the Germans were now regarding the situation in the Reichswald area.

XXX Corps' Fire Support

By 1945, in many respects the Germans were used to fighting at a material and physical disadvantage, but 'General Winter' was now denying XXX Corps the luxuries of superior firepower, numbers of troops and plentiful supply in comparison with those of the enemy. Up to this point those Allied officers reporting on the progress of the battle stressed that the main enemy had not been the Germans but the mud and floods. Now, however, with the arrival of serious German reinforcements the divisions of XXX Corps faced a major challenge.

The part played by the Allied air forces, particularly the RAF's Second Tactical Air Force, had up to this point already been constrained by the weather. With

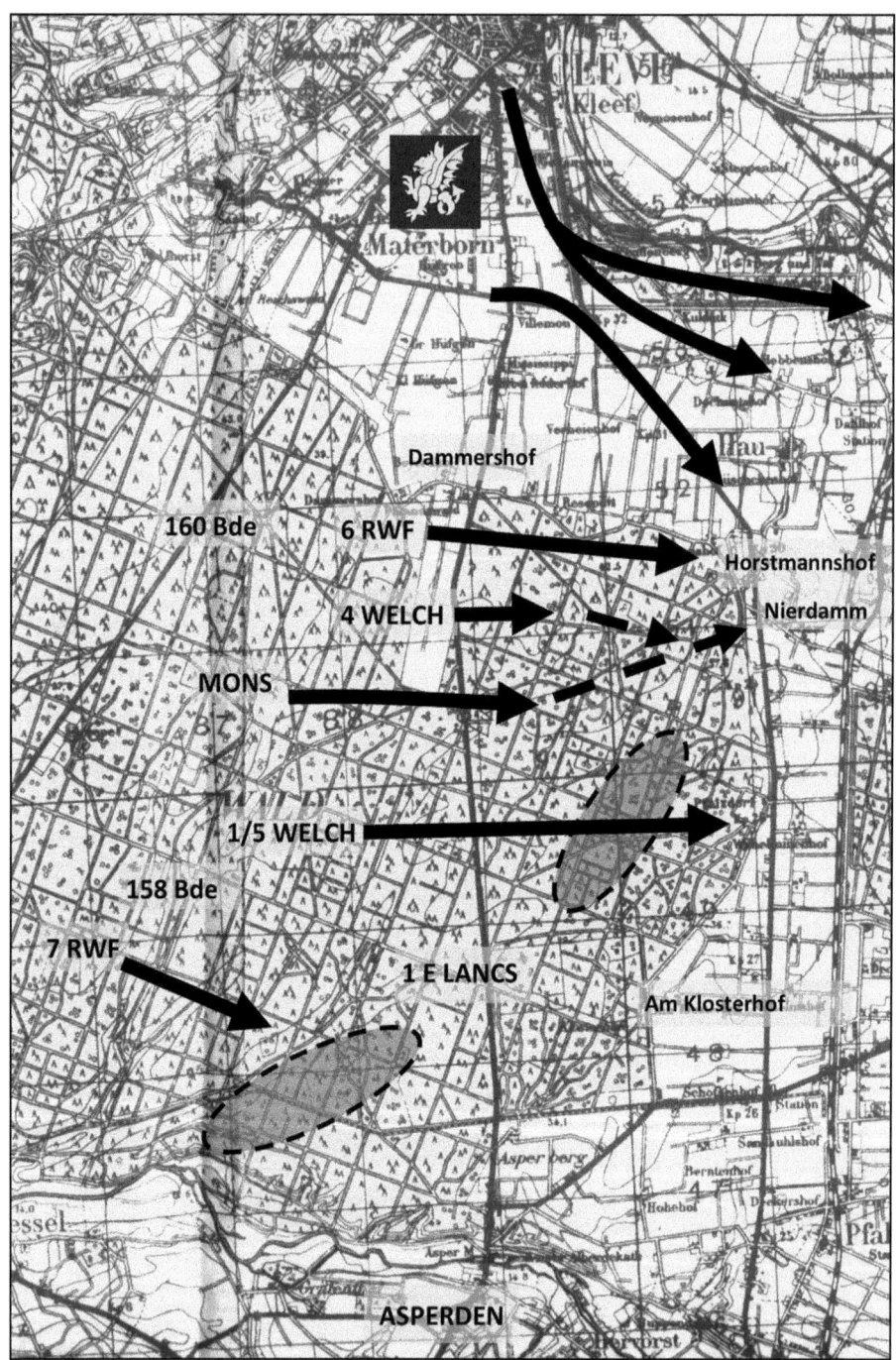

The 53rd Welsh Division's morning advance on 12 February 1945.

A Messerschmitt Me 262 jet aircraft.

observation, electronic warfare and ULTRA warning that German formations were on the move, it was an intensely frustrating time for the airmen. As a series of frontal systems swept in from the west there were two main problems. Firstly, being unable to identify targets thanks to low cloud, fog and heavy rain, and secondly, differing weather conditions that closed airfields up to 120 miles to the rear and kept aircraft on the ground.[2] Of these two factors, the former was more important part of the equation. Combined with the long hours of darkness, the overall weather conditions meant the result was intermittent interdiction of German reserves and a reliance on observed artillery fire in the close battle.

With limited air support, the four AGRAs under command of XXX Corps, plus 2nd Canadian AGRCA, which together with the seven divisional artillery groups fielded approximately 1,000 guns of all types as the battle developed, on their own theoretically provided a crushing weight of fire. Moving the medium guns and ammunition, however, from their initial positions west of Nijmegen and the Groesbeek Heights and then taking their turn on the two roads east was a slow process that often disrupted plans and reduced levels of support available. For instance: 'On 12 February, as 7th Medium Regiment, RCA moved forward, the single road available was flooded and only its 60-cwt trucks could get through.' Without its command vehicles and those of its FOOs there was a considerable delay in getting the regiment into action. Even having reached the new gun position through mud, flood and traffic, up on the Materborn feature their difficulties were not over. The regiment's war diarist recorded that it was nearly impossible for 12th Medium Battery RCA to get its guns into the designated

A cannon-armed Hawker Typhoon of 439 Squadron RCAF returning to its base on the borders of Holland and Belgium. The Squadron's motto was 'Fangs of Death'.

position due to the sodden terrain. The battery enlisted the assistance of an armoured bulldozer but still could only get one gun into position. The other guns were left on the road and a new area had to be found for the battery the next day.

Not only was it difficult to move the guns, but with rates of consumption of all nature of artillery ammunition totalling 80,000 to 100,000 rounds a day, delivering sufficient shells to the gun positions was an enormous challenge on the available roads. However, even with the combined effect of these difficulties, XXX Corps' artillery was more than a match for German firepower.

XLVII Panzer Corps Counter-Attacks

General Horrocks' concept of operations for XXX Corps had all along been for a speedy advance into the Rhineland, crucially before the Germans could react and the battle became another bitter dogfight. The thaw and the resulting ground conditions rather than effective resistance by General Fiebig's 84th Infantry Division had slowed the break-in battle and had bought time for First *Fallschirmjäger* Army's reserves to be committed. Elements of 6th *Fallschirmjäger* Division crossed the Rhine from Twenty-Fifth Army to fight in the battle for Kleve and initially a regiment of 7th *Fallschirmjäger* Division came north from the Geldern area to confront 51st Highland and 53rd Welsh Divisions. Slim though these reinforcements were, they were balanced by the problems XXX Corps had in developing momentum. The ground conditions continued to confine armour to roads and decent tracks, while behind the advance supply routes became virtually impassable, which together reduced the tempo of operations during the first four days of the battle to that of wading through mud.

Field Marshal von Rundstedt's headquarters had only belatedly released his reserve, XLVII Panzer Corps, on 10 February at 1745 hours with the code word '*Ziethen*'.[3] The corps was located further south refitting in hides in the Mönchengladbach, Kempen and Krefeld area. This was in accordance with the German estimate that the Second British and Ninth US Armies would attempt to break into the Rhineland, forcing crossings of the Maas in the Venlo area. It had taken some time for OB West to be convinced that the attack through the Reichswald by First Canadian Army was not a diversionary operation. Now confident in the knowledge that, thanks to the blowing of the valves in the Roer Dam, Ninth US Army could not attack across the river for some days, General von Lüttwitz's XLVII Panzer Corps could be safely sent north to reinforce General Schlemm. Despite the delay in identifying the presence of 'missing' British divisions, weather, ground and resistance around Kleve had bought time for most of von Rundstedt's reserves to be deployed.

Travelling the distance of between 50 and 75 miles to the Reichswald using dispersed hides, during which they were subject to some air interdiction, was not XLVII Panzer Corps' only deployment issue. The Russian capture of the oil fields in the east and Allied bombing of synthetic production plants and transport networks, plus depletion of reserves for the Battle of the Bulge, had produced a

Gerd von Rundstedt, the 69-year-old field marshal, was fighting his final battle in the Rhineland before being relieved of his command for the last time.

fuel crisis. The vehicles of 116th Panzer and 15th *Panzergrenadier* divisions consequently had to await the arrival of scarce fuel before they could march north to confront XXX Corps.

Meanwhile, with the front in First Canadian Army's area to the north of Nijmegen quiet, General Blastowitz started dispatching as many reinforcements as he dared from elsewhere in Army Group H, starting with several battalion-sized *kampfgruppen* from *fallschirmjäger* and 346th Infantry divisions.

German Plans

As 84th Infantry Division's strength east of the Reichswald diminished and the *Fallschirmjäger* in the forest itself lost their last positions, at Hitler's insistence XLVII Panzer Corps was ordered to recapture Kleve and the Materborn

Fallschirmjäger climbing aboard armoured cars of 115 Recce Battalion.

feature now held by XXX Corps. However, even though he passed these orders on to General Lüttwitz and XLVII Panzer Corps, General Schlemm's realistic intent was to shore up the First *Fallschirmjäger* Army's front by holding XXX Corps while a defensive line was established between Moyland and the Kleve Forest.

By the night of 11–12 February, 116th Panzer and 15th *Panzergrenadier* divisions were beginning to arrive east of the Reichswald. Both of these divisions were already severely reduced by the fighting in the Bulge and paucities of equipment of every kind and, hamstrung by the lack of fuel, they only dribbled forward from Geldern overnight. Initially at least General Wilck's 116th Panzer Division fielded a *kampfgruppe* based on a company of *Windhund* panzers, which were joined by the eight surviving *Jagdpanthers* and sundry *Jagdpanzer* IVs of 655th *Panzerjäger* Battalion and its own infantry under Major Brinkmann.

General Schlemm ordered von Lüttwitz to take over the south-western part of the Reichswald and the adjacent approaches to the Materborn feature. *Kampfgruppe* Brinkmann was to rebuff the Wessex Division's advance south towards Hau that was developing as the immediate threat overnight on 11–12. As more of the corps' units arrived, von Lüttwitz recast his plan: the panzers were to attack from the northern side of the Kleve Forest, while 15th *Panzergrenadiers*, commanded by *Oberst* Wolfgang Maucke, would be launched south of the forest and into the Reichswald, where the 53rd Welsh were still advancing that morning.

The badge of the 15th *Panzergrenadiers* was painted on all the division's vehicles.

The nature of the ground where these two attacks took place greatly influenced the differing outcomes of the fighting for the two divisions.

The northerly pincer of XLVII Panzer Corps' counter-attack was delivered by *Oberst* Maucke's 15th *Panzergrenadiers*. He was to attack into the Reichswald from the area south of the Kleve Forest with four much-reduced battalions supported by a company of *sturmgeschütz*.

The Counter-Attack

With ample warning of the approach of XLVII Panzer Corps, 43rd Wessex Division were able to halt astride the Goch Road at Hau and bring up their own and divisional anti-tank guns to form a strong defensive front. In addition, gunner FOOs of the field and medium regiment had the opportunity to co-ordinate the fire plan and plot defensive fire tasks. Consequently, as the attack developed, the Wessex were able to beat off first the probing attacks by reinforced recce, and then in the afternoon attacks by a *kampfgruppe* based on 60 *Panzergrenadier* Regiment. In open terrain German losses in both infantry and tanks were heavy.

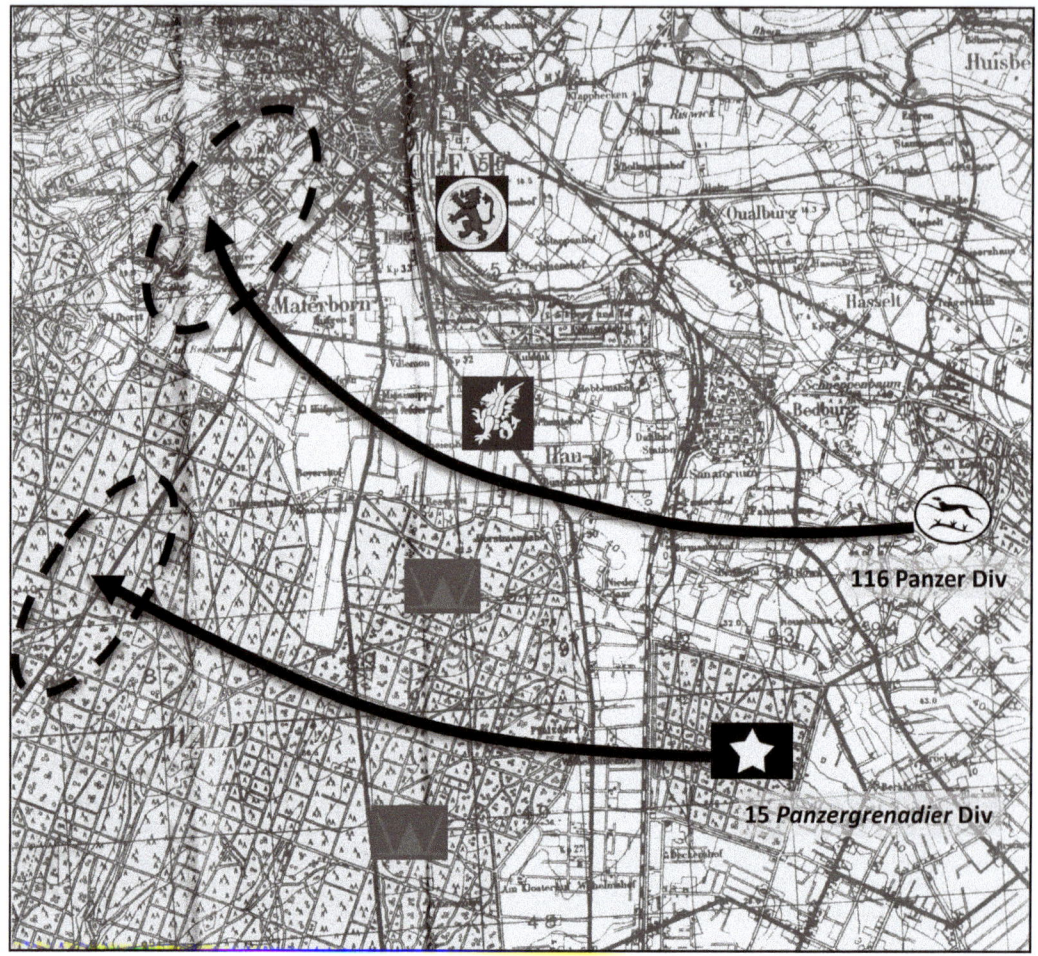

General von Lüttwiz's outline plan for XLVII Panzer Corps' counter-attack.

At the same time as the attacks fell on the Wessex at Hau, another *kampfgruppe* based on I/156 PzGrs was being launched towards the north-east tip of the Reichswald and the hamlet of Horstmannshof. From there it was intended to continue the advance along the edge of the forest towards the Materborn feature, but it ran into the leading company of 4th Welch, which had just approached the edge of the Reichswald.

Having reached a track junction near the extreme north-east edge of the forest, the 4th Battalion's leading company was violently counter-attacked, driven back and its commander killed. The commanding officer (Lieutenant Colonel Frisby) rallied the company and with it, and another, cleared the area, restoring the situation.

Having reached the north-west tip of the great forest and encountered 160 Brigade, 156 PzGr's attack faltered and was halted, having also been broken up by massed artillery brought down by 160 Brigade's observers. Defeat of the German counter-attack in this quarter was also aided by anti-tank fire, along with that of machine guns from the Wessex Division in the area of Hau.

The fact that this arm of the German counter-attack did not fully come into contact with the Welsh Division is illustrated by Lieutenant Beal's observation:

> Later 8 Troop were sent to the eastern edge of the forest just south of Hau, clearing up some machineguns and taking seven prisoners of war en route. On reaching the objective a fierce action was fought in complete darkness and pouring rain, ending in the capture of another forty prisoners. This was only a raid, and after remaining on the edge of the forest for an hour 8 Troop returned to the squadron laager at 2100 hours.

Oberst Maucke's attack was carried out by four battalions with 115 PzGrs on the right and 104th PzGrs on the left, supported by artillery, mortar fire and a number of *sturmgeschütz*. It fell astride the brigade boundary of 6th RWF (160 Brigade) and on the right 1st/5th Welch (158 Brigade):

> The attack was beaten off, partly by well-directed artillery and partly by small arms fire which the defending Infantry withheld until the attackers were within about 300 yards. This caused serious losses to the enemy, who withdrew in disorder.

Sergeant Machin of 1st/5th Welch described the attack at 1615 hours:

> The enemy made a real blunder in deciding to counter-attack B Company. It was a gunner's dream as they came on in extended order and exposed their left flank to D Coy some 300 yds to the south. Both companies opened up with their Brens, Vickers and Besas. It was too much for the Boche who broke ranks, leaving some thirty casualties behind. During the night the gunners went to work on the Bosch with a vengeance ...

The divisional historian continued his account:

> About the same time small parties of the enemy operating further South attempted to infiltrate into the East Lancashires' positions, but they were mopped up by a platoon from the reserve company and a troop of tanks. Just before dusk some 200 Germans were seen opposite the positions of the same battalion, and it looked as if a counter-attack was about to develop. The enemy were, however, dispersed by artillery fire and by the unit carriers which were brought up to a position from which fire could be opened 'mounted'.
>
> During the afternoon 1st Highland Light Infantry had been sent forward from mopping up with 71 Brigade to reinforce 158 Brigade but in the event, they were not needed and returned to the parent formation. Also going back to leaguer were the Churchills, with squadrons now reduced to four operational tanks, the rest having been knocked-out, damaged, broken down or badly bogged.
>
> That evening on the 160th Brigade front the Monmouths were ordered forward to the edge of the Forest to the left of the 4th Welch. They met with

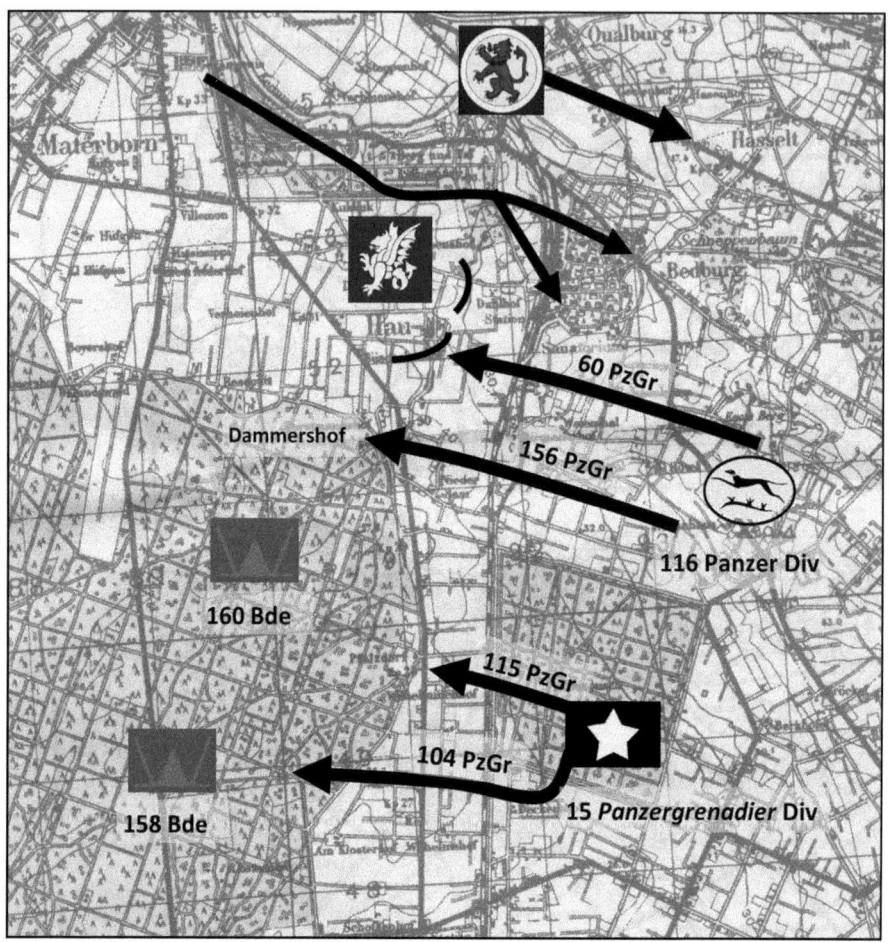

The counter-attack of XLVII Panzer Corps on 12 February 1945.

slight opposition and by 2000 hours the battalion was digging-in beyond the edge of the forest astride the Goch road facing the village of Niederdamm.

After five days in action, that evening, as a result of boggings, breakdowns and battle damage, out of 100 Churchills on the two regiments establishment, 34 Armoured Brigade reported the following operational tank state:

9 R Tanks: 14 battleworthy with a further 8 capable of support to the infantry in the forest.
147 RAC: 24 battleworthy – of which several were capable of support to infantry in the forest only.

With the Guards Armoured Division coming up for the breakout through the 51st Highland Division and the fight through the Reichswald complete,

34th Armoured Brigade was withdrawn to refit. No so, of course, the infantry divisions.

The attacks of XLVII Panzer Corps had, as General Schlemm expected, failed to get anywhere near recapturing the Materborn feature or Kleve. Allied intelligence was forewarned of the approach of von Lüttwitz's command, and the Wessex Division was able to rush forward supporting arms and weapons to produce a sound defence by the time of the counter-attack. General Wilck complained that his division had been rushed into battle incomplete and directly off the line of march with precious little time for battle procedure. By the time the *Windhund* attacked the already deployed Wessex Division, the result was almost a foregone conclusion. For 15th *Panzergrenadiers* it was a different matter as their encounter with the 53rd Welsh Division had all the uncertainties of meeting engagement; but they had also been rushed into battle, and were outnumbered, outgunned and, consequently, lost heavily in a hard fight at close quarters.

XLVII Panzer Corps' attacks had, however, achieved General Schlemm's realistic aims. They had brought the advance of the Wessex Division on Goch to a halt and curtailed the Welsh Division's aims to form a second pincer on Goch. At a considerable cost in men, and equipment, particularly to 15th *Panzergrenadier* Division, they had bought time for all available German reinforcements to concentrate against First Canadian Army.

The British intelligence staffs, however, were not impressed by the scale of the attacks during the 12th, one noting somewhat pessimistically in his evening INTSUM that: 'The Corps [XLVII Panzer] probably has more ambitious plans

A Churchill of 147 Regiment RAC driving through the trees of the Reichswald.

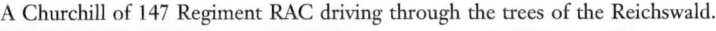

for tomorrow and it must be reckoned with that the recapture of the Materborn feature is amongst them.' A German officer during questioning later asserted that the Germans had a very different view of the day's fighting: 'There was no more talk of major counter-attacks, but a defensive stalemate had been temporarily achieved.'

With those words it can be said that the battle for the Reichswald was over, and the fighting morphed into VERITABLE's next phase. Now clearing the 'Reichswald Plug' into more open country, this would see the deployment of General Simonds' II Canadian Corps and the capture by First Canadian Army of the nodal Rhineland towns of Goch, Kalkar and Uedem. The battle, however, ground on in the same very difficult circumstances for a further month. The thaw in late January and early February had condemned the soldiers of XXX Corps and II Canadian Corps to fighting in appalling ground and weather conditions, with all that they implied. Matters were made infinitely worse due to the Ninth US Army's Operation GRENADE being stalled at the River Roer, consequent on Bradley's failure to capture the dams in a timely manner. Thus, British and Canadian soldiers faced all that the Germans could throw at them to halt operations that opened the way to final victory.

The first Phase of Operation VERITABLE was over. Instead of the hoped for dash into the Rhineland across frozen ground, the First Canadian Army now faced not only sodden ground but fortified towns and defensive lines. It would be another three weeks of bitter fighting before the Rhineland was clear and the Rhine Crossing could be prepared.

An infantry platoon advances from Holland into the Rhineland during VERITABLE.

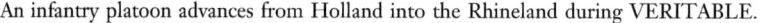

Appendix I

Order of Battle: Phase 1 Grouping

51st Highland Division – Major General Rennie, CB, DSO, MBE

152nd (Highland) Brigade – Brigadier Cassels CBE, DSO
   2nd Seaforth Highlanders
   5th Seaforth Highlanders
   5th Cameron Highlanders

153 (Highland) Brigade – Lieutenant Colonel Grant Peterkin
   5th Black Watch
   1st Gordon Highlanders
   5th/7th Gordons Highlanders

154 (Highland) Brigade – Brigadier Oliver CBE, DSO, TD
   1st Black Watch
   7th Black Watch
   7th Argyll & Sutherland Highlanders

2 Derbyshire Yeomanry (Recce)
1/7 Middlesex (Machine gun)

Royal Artillery – Brigadier Shiel CBE DSO MC
   126th Field Regiment
   127th Field Regiment
   128th Field Regiment
   61st Anti-Tank Regiment
   40th Light Anti-Aircraft Regiment

Royal Engineers
   274 Field Company
   275 Field Company
   276 Field Company
   239 Field Park Company

Under Command
   107th Regiment RAC
   A & B Squadrons, 1st Fyfe and Forfar Yeomanry – Crocodiles
   D Squadron, 1st Lothian Yeomanry – flails

79th Medium Regiment RA
6th Field Regiment RA
146 Anti-Tank Battery (SP), 63rd Anti-Tank Regiment RA
Det 4th Survey Regiment
C Flight, 652 Air Observation Post Squadron
Detachment 100 Radar Battery
Troop 356 Search Light Battery
2 × troops, 82 Assault Squadron RE – AVRE

53rd Welsh Division – Major General Ross, CB, DSO, MC

71st Infantry Brigade – Brigadier Elrington DSO, OBE
    4th Royal Welsh Fusiliers
    1st Oxfordshire and Buckinghamshire
    1st Highland Light Infantry

158th Infantry Brigade – Brigadier Wilsey DSO
    7th Royal Welsh Fusiliers
    1st East Lancashire Regiment
    1st/5th Welch Regiment

160 Infantry Brigade – Brigadier Coleman DSO, OBE
    6th Royal Welsh Fusiliers
    4th Welch Regiment
    2nd Monmouthshire Regiment

53rd (Welsh) Recce Regiment
1st Manchester Regiment (Machine gun)

Royal Artillery – Brigadier Friedberger DSO
    81st Field Regiment
    83rd Field Regiment
    133 Field Regiment
    71st Anti-Tank Regiment
    25th Light Anti-Aircraft Regiment

Royal Engineers
    224 Field Company
    282 Field Company
    555 Field Company
    285 Field Park Company

Under Command
    9th Royal Tank Regiment
    147th Regiment RAC
    Westminster Dragoons (1 × Sqn) – Flails
    A Squadron, 141 Regiment RAC – Crocodile

Buffalo Landing Vehicle Tracked (LVT) was used by 51st Highland Division during operations on the The Niers.

72nd Medium Regiment RA
19th Canadian Field Regiment (SP)
56 Canadian Anti-Tank Battery (SP)
Detachment 100 Radar Battery
Troop 356 Search Light Battery
A Flight, 662 Air Observation Post Squadron
2 × troops, 82 Assault Squadron RE – AVRE

A British infantryman dressed and equipped in fighting order.

Appendix II

German, Canadian and British Ranks

German	British
Oberschutze	Private First Class
Gefrieter	Lance Corporal
Obergefrieter	Corporal
Obergefrieter	Senior Corporal
Stabsgefrieter	HQ Corporal (Admin)
Unteroffizier	
Unterfelwebel	Lance Sergeant
Felwebel	Sergeant
Oberfelwebel	Colour/Staff Sergeant
Stabsfelwebel	Sergeant Major
Leutnant	Second Lieutenant
Oberleutnant	Lieutenant

Despite increasing numbers of German soldiers who sought opportunities to surrender, the majority who stood and fought exacted a heavy price for the allied victory in the Rhineland.

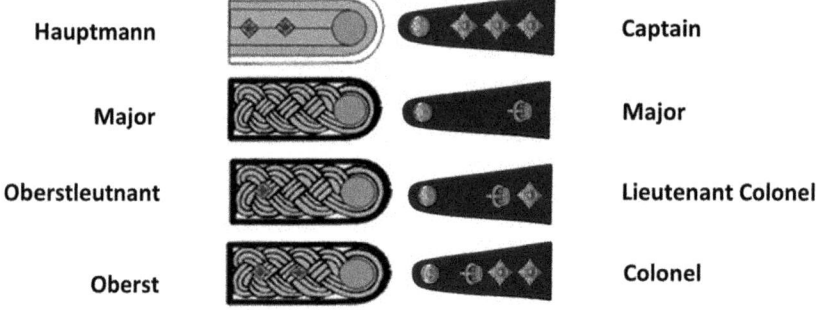

Hauptmann		Captain
Major		Major
Oberstleutnant		Lieutenant Colonel
Oberst		Colonel

Notes

Introduction
1. Borthwick, Alistair, *Sans Peur, A British Infantry Unit's actions 1942–1945* (Eneas Mackay, Stirling, 1964).

Chapter 1: Winter 1944–45
1. Operation WYVERN was a XXX Corps plan made during October. The new Canadian plan made in November was named VALEDICTION.
2. The first shipping only reached Antwerp on 28 November following the clearance of the Scheldt. Reliance on road convoys from distant Normandy continued for some weeks.
3. Stacey, Colonel C.P., *The Victory Campaign* (Queen's Printer, Ottawa, 1960).
4. Ibid.
5. Fitting ice stripper.
6. This was probably snow that had drifted into the anti-tank ditch and had yet to melt.
7. Eisenhower, Dwight D., *Crusade in Europe* (Hutchinson, 1948).

Chapter 2: The Defenders of the Reich
1. The defences of urban areas would also serve as strongpoints if the British attacked across the Maas on the direct route to the Rhine.
2. Post-war analysts visiting the Reichswald counted about seventy concrete structures in the forest, mostly small. Even the seven larger ones were too small to accommodate the larger anti-tank guns of 1944–45. Most of these mounted machine guns.
3. Map extract from, BAOR, *Battlefield Tour Operation VERITABLE* (BAOR, 1947).
4. Defence Overprint Sheet B (Rhine) Edition of 15 Oct 44 – 1:25,000. Defence Overprint, Groesbeek North Edition of 2 Feb 45 – 1:25,000.
5. This is a myth. The stoutly built German houses tended to have half cellars, the small windows of which, being just above ground level, coincidentally served as loopholes. The cellars were mainly used for shelter from shelling.
6. A proportion of the soldiers were from 1st *Wahn* Battalion. This was a psychiatric unit for men recovering from battle exhaustion. Subsequently, soldiers from the 2nd and 3rd *Wahn* Battalions also joined the division when it was reconstituted in the autumn and winter of 1944.
7. There is some dispute over the issue of *Jagdpanzer* IVs to the 655th. One authority states that these vehicles were only issued after the battle of the Rhineland, while others theorise that these issues were in fact replacements. It is likely that one of the *Panzerjäager* IV companies was detached to a panzer division fighting in the east.

Chapter 3: The Opening Fires
1. G (Training) HQ BAOR, *Battlefield Tour – Operation Veritable* (BAOR, Germany, 1947).
2. 4th (Durham) Survey Regiment was a pre-war Territorial unit from Gateshead. They were XXX Corps troops for most of the North West European Campaign. The other regiment was 2nd Canadian Survey Regiment, also corps troops, in their case, II Canadian Corps.
3. Blackburn, George, *The Guns of Victory* (McClelland & Stewart Inc. 1997).
4. Historical Section, *Report 155, Operation Veritable: Maas and the Rhine, The Winter Offensive between the 8–25 Feb 45 (Preliminary Report)*, Canadian Military Headquarters.
5. BAOR, *Battlefield Tour – Operation VERITABLE* (HQ BAOR, Germany, 1947).

Chapter 4: Attack on the Forward Position

1. The problem was that the ground had been churned up by the advance of the gun tanks and when the heavily laden AVREs followed they were more likely to become bogged. The lighter Shermans and most Kangaroos had track extensions or 'grousers' fitted that aided cross-country movement, but at the cost of speed and increased engine damage.
2. With concrete bunkers, the pyramid feature, just inside the German border, is regarded by many as an outlier of the Siegfried Line.
3. In common with the other divisions, casualties over winter had not been fully replaced due to the British manpower crisis, and in the case of 1 BW they had no D Company. 7 BW, also of three rifle companies, had no C Company.
4. Nonchalance under fire was a trademark of the officers of the veteran 51st Highland Division and was deemed necessary to lead the mercurial Jocks.
5. Major Lowe was one of those who had a premonition of his death in the coming battle. With his radio operator alongside him, he made an obvious target for German riflemen.
6. Lieutenant General 'Boy' Browning, landing by glider near Grafwegen at the opening of MARKET GARDEN on 17 September, claimed to be: 'The first British soldier to piss on Germany in this war.'
7. Brigadier Sinclair was sick in hospital at the beginning of VERITABLE. Consequently, the brigade was commanded by Lieutenant Colonel Grant-Peterkin and the 1st Gordons by Major Lindsay.
8. Major Martin Lindsay had been the commanding officer of 9 Para but was sacked over a minor breach of BIGOT security in the run-up to D Day. The officer who reported him, Major (later Lieutenant Colonel) Otway, took over as CO 9 Para.
9. John McGregor, *The Spirit of Angus: The War History of the County's Battalion of the Black Watch* (Phillimore & Co. Ltd, 1 January 1988).

Chapter 5: Advance through the Reichswald, 9 February

1. Special Interrogation Report: General Alfred Schlemm. Quoted in Historical Section *Report 155, Operation Veritable: Maas and the Rhine, The Winter Offensive between the 8–25 Feb 45 (Preliminary Report)*, Canadian Military Headquarters.
2. The Mk V Churchill was designed to provide tank regiments with organic close support. Each troop had one tank with a 95mm howitzer and forty-seven HE rounds. There were 241 built in 1943.
3. Carter and Kann, *Maintenance in the Field, Vol II 1943–1945* (The War Office, 1961).
4. The military had long used boxes stuffed with hay to keep food warm but by the middle of the twentieth century they were now heavy metal containers, with the hay having been replaced by hot water. This could keep food warm for several hours.
5. Swabb, Jack, *Field of Fire, Diary of a Gunner Officer* (Sutton Publishing, 2005).
6. In the sixth year of war the British manpower pool had dwindled badly and along with it the pool of potential officers. Up to this point, having been a volunteer force, the Canadian Army had no shortage of officer material coming forward and a system of loan service was established – CANLOAN. Canadian officers were found in infantry units where the paucity of junior officers was most keenly felt. It was judged to be a very effective scheme.
7. Renouf, Tom, *Black Watch – Liberating Europe* (Little Brown, London, 2021).

Chapter 6: The Reichswald and the Maas Plain, 10 February

1. BAOR, *Battlefield Tour Operation VERITABLE – DS Edition* (G Training HQ BAOR, 1947).
2. Barkley, Brigadier CN, *History of the 53rd (Welsh) Division in the Second World War* (MLRS reprint).
3. T. Jones, interview with the author 2009.
4. Borthwick, Alastair, *Sans Peur* (Eneas Mackay, Stirling, 1946).

Chapter 7: The Gennep Bridgehead and the Hekkens Crossroads, 11 February

1. The guns firing the creeping barrage back on the Groesbeek Heights were at an oblique angle to the advance, therefore the Highlanders would not be able to get under or 'lean on the barrage' as closely as they would like to have done.
2. A group of officers, typically company commanders, those from support platoons and attached arms gathered to receive orders having viewed the ground from an OP.
3. Conventional wisdom is that commanders, as orders descend the chain of command, take one third of the time available, allowing the remaining two thirds for their subordinates down to section level to carry out their own recces, orders and rehearsals.
4. Whitehouse and Bennet, *Fear is the Foe: A Footslogger from Normandy to the Rhine* (Robert Hale, London, 1995).

Chapter 8: The Niers Bridgehead, 12–13 February

1. Sensitive valve technology and the low-power VHF available from batteries of map pack radios were the problem. Communications invariably broke down when on the move and when direct line of sight was screened by trees, building or the ground.
2. Carr, Lieutenant Colonel, *A Sapper's Life*, quoted in www.ww2talk.
3. Haward and Barber, *Fighting Hitler from Dunkirk to D-Day: The Story of Die Hard* (Pen & Sword, Barnsley, 2021).

Chapter 9: The Welsh Division – Attack and Counter-Attack

1. As was the case with SS formations by 1945, the *fallschirmjäger* were no longer the quality of opponents of earlier battles. They, however, retained a hardcore of able and committed officers and NCOs, which made them a more difficult enemy to come up against than the average Wehrmacht formation.
2. Doctrine was for fighter and fighter-bomber airfields to be established 50–70 miles from the front and those for the bombers of the Second Tactical Air Force 100–120 miles.
3. Zithen was a renowned Prussian military family name and regimental title. Lieutenant General Graf von *Zieten* commanded a corps in the Prussian Army during the Waterloo Campaign.

Despite increasing numbers of German soldiers who sought opportunities to surrender, the majority that stood and fought, exacted a heavy price for the allied victory in the Rhineland.

Index

Air Support 54–6
Antwerp 2, 7, 17, 45, 205
Armoured Recovery Vehicle (ARV) 91–2, 102
Armoured Vehicle Royal Engineer (AVRE) 16, 20, 56, 57, 61, 62, 67, 69, 77, 91, 200, 206
Artillery 16, 18, 20, 22, 38, 40, 42, 45–53, 58, 102, 103, 105, 108, 110, 115, 121, 124, 136, 140, 153, 158, 160, 161, 162, 168, 169, 173, 183, 185, 187, 189, 190, 194, 195, 199, 207
Artillery Ammunition 18
Assembly Area 10–20, 53, 56, 57, 61, 64, 69, 71, 83, 93, 100–1

Bailey Bridge 17, 85, 145, 151–4, 173, 177
Barrage 52, 53, 56, 57, 58, 61, 62, 63, 69, 74, 77, 82, 98, 115, 116, 145, 154, 158, 159
Blackburn, Lieutenant 20, 46, 49, 205
Blaskowitz, General 27, 29, 31, 42
Bombing offensive, Strategic 6, 19, 54, 191
Borthwick, Captain 123, 124, 138, 154, 158, 205
Brandenburg Feature 63, 98
British Army:
  21st Army Group 2, 3, 92
  Second Army 2, 3
  XXX Corps vi, vii, 7, 10–15, 18, 19, 22, 32, 36, 40, 53, 54, 55, 92, 93, 97, 109, 130, 147, 151, 158, 177, 187, 189, 190, 192, 193, 198, 205
  Guards Armoured Division 14, 36, 151, 170, 196
  15th Scottish Division vii, 13, 14, 19, 32, 47, 59, 61, 73, 97, 101, 102, 103, 129, 131, 147
  43rd Wessex Division vi, 14, 34, 129, 147, 179, 181, 193–4, 197
  51st Highland Division vii, 13, 14, 15, 36, 43, 48, 51, 66–90, 97, 103–27, 129, 131, 136–45, 179, 186, 196, 199

53rd Welsh Division vii, 13, 14, 15–16, 22, 47, 59, 61–6, 67, 78, 97–103, 129, 130–4, 171, 179, 186 188, 190, 193, 197, 200, 206, 207
79th Armoured Division 14, 16, 20, 61, 62
6 Guards Armoured Brigade 14, 64
34 Armoured Brigade 12, 16, 21, 22, 61, 65, 99, 133, 196
Army Groups RA (AGRA) 14, 16, 49
44 Lowland Brigade 97, 100, 129, 199
71 Brigade 15, 61, 63, 97, 195, 200
152 Brigade 104, 105, 118–27, 129, 134, 135, 138–43, 154, 158
153 Brigade 67, 82, 85–90, 103, 106, 108, 115, 118, 129, 134–8, 143, 146, 147–54, 163, 170, 176, 199
154 Brigade 66, 68, 70, 72, 81, 85, 86, 103, 105, 108, 115, 119, 123, 124, 158, 170, 176, 199
158 Brigade 61, 97, 98, 99, 100–1, 102, 158, 179, 181, 195, 200
160 Brigade 61, 65, 97, 98, 100, 102, 131, 179, 182, 187, 194, 195, 200
9 RTR 65, 99, 100, 131, 134, 179, 181, 185, 187, 196
107 Regiment RAC 21, 22, 67, 60, 70, 78, 80, 81, 85, 103, 110, 118, 120, 136, 140, 150, 156, 173, 199
147 Regiment RAC 61, 62, 69, 102, 169, 179, 182, 187, 196, 197
Lothian and Border Horse *see* Sherman flail
Fife and Forfar Yeomanry 16, 140, 165, 169, 199
1st Black Watch 60, 70–1, 73, 82, 86, 105, 108, 158, 173, 176, 199
5th Black Watch 86, 89–90, 113, 115, 144, 146, 147, 148, 150, 151, 163, 165, 169, 199
7th Black Watch 67, 69–70, 73, 75, 77, 82, 158, 160, 170, 171, 176, 199
1st Gordons Highlanders 85, 86, 88, 103, 105, 106, 108, 110, 111, 112, 115, 118, 143, 150, 151, 152, 163, 169, 199

5th/7th Gordon Highlanders 67, 81, 82, 83, 86, 89, 105, 108, 119, 134, 136, 143, 145, 163, 169, 199
5th Queen's Own Cameron Highlanders 111, 115, 119, 123, 124, 126, 140 142, 143, 158, 169, 199
7th Argyll & Sutherland Highlanders 67, 84, 86, 108, 124, 154, 158
2nd Seaforth Highlanders 119, 126, 138, 139, 140, 142, 143, 199
5th Seaforth Highlanders vii, 119, 123–6, 138, 139, 154, 199
1st/7th Middlesex (MG) 48, 115, 118, 140, 174, 176, 199
1st East Lancashire 97, 99, 100, 101, 170, 182, 184, 187, 194, 200
4th Welch 98, 100, 101, 131, 179, 194, 195, 200
1st/5th Welch 101, 102, 187, 195, 200
6th Royal Welsh Fusiliers 98, 99, 100, 101, 200
7th Royal Welsh Fusiliers 101, 103, 187, 195, 200
1st Ox and Bucks LI 61, 63, 65, 66
1st Highland Light Infantry 63, 65
6th Highland Light Infantry 170
2nd Monmouthshire 65, 100, 101, 131, 132, 179, 200
Bulge, Battle of 7, 17, 23, 24, 27, 36, 40, 42 191, 193

Cab-rank 55
Canadian Army:
    First Canadian Army vi, vii, 1, 2, 3, 4, 7, 11, 17, 18, 22, 26, 53, 97, 103, 191, 192, 197, 198, 206
    II Canadian Corps viii, 10, 11, 18, 198, 205
    2nd Canadian Division viii, 10, 13, 20 52, 56, 86
    3rd Canadian Division 10, 13, 42, 97, 147
CANLOAN 120, 206
Churchill Crocodile 16, 56, 61, 62, 67, 140, 141, 142, 143, 163, 165, 169, 170, 199
Churchill Tank 8, 13, 16, 21, 23, 56, 61, 64–5, 69, 70 76, 78, 79, 80, 85, 91, 99, 101, 108, 133, 140, 141, 143, 151, 168, 183, 197, 206
CLUB BLACK 8, 13, 66, 84
CLUB RED 8, 13
Composite (Compo) Ration 103, 104, 105
Concentration Area 19
Counter battery fire 49, 53

Crerar, General vi, viii, 2, 3, 4, 9, 10, 11, 12, 23, 53, 130

Deception Plan 11–12
Dempsey, General 2, 3
Dyson, Corporal 69, 70, 73, 74, 75, 77, 80, 82, 136, 151

Eisenhower/Supreme Commander 1, 2, 3, 4, 6, 23, 24, 26, 29, 205

Fiebig, Major General 36, 37, 40, 53, 90, 93, 190
Fighter bomber 55, 56, 130, 207
Fire Plan 48, 49, 52, 158, 168, 174, 193
Foley, Lieutenant 21, 45, 51, 52, 71, 73, 78, 80, 140
Forward Line 32, 34, 50, 84, 108, 206
Frasselt 97, 98, 99, 100, 138, 139, 141, 154, 186
Freundenburg Feature 66, 83, 108, 118, 119, 124

Gennep 10, 53, 66, 93, 105, 108, 113, 115, 118, 129, 134, 135, 136–7, 143, 154, 163, 170, 173, 176, 207
German Army:
    Army Group H 27, 29, 53, 192
    First Fallschirmjäger Army 27, 32, 33, 53, 190, 193
    Twenty Fifth Army 42, 129, 190
    XLVII Panzer Corps vii, 53, 129, 147, 187, 190–7
    LXXXVI Corps 27, 30, 40, 42, 92
    15th *Panzergrenadier* Division 193, 194, 197
    116th *Windhund* Panzer Division 192, 193
    84th Infantry Division 36, 37, 38, 53, 61, 77, 90, 95, 190, 192
    2nd *Fallschirmjäger* Division 146
    6th *Fallschirmjäger* Division 190
    7th *Fallschirmjäger* Division 29, 53, 93, 95, 190
German strategic recovery 1944 1, 5, 100
Goch 9, 13, 14, 54, 95, 135, 136, 170, 193, 196, 197, 198
Grafenwegen 67, 86, 105, 206
GRENADE, Operation 4, 5, 10, 23, 96, 127, 147, 198,
Groesbeek Heights 10, 13, 19, 20, 21, 22, 28, 29, 46, 49, 51, 59, 61, 66, 90 124, 133, 143, 185, 189, 205, 207

Hekkens 32, 97, 98, 99, 100, 102, 118, 119, 123, 124, 125, 126, 129, 131, 133, 135, 138, 139, 140, 141, 143, 154–61, 170, 171, 174, 179, 186, 207
Hitler 2, 5, 6, 7, 27, 36, 95, 96, 192, 207
Hochwald Layback 10, 32, 35
Horrocks, General vi, viii, 10, 11, 12, 13, 16, 19, 20, 22, 32, 45, 54, 59, 60, 96, 97, 130, 131, 154, 190

Jagdpanther 40, 41, 179, 182, 193
Jagdpanzer IV 40, 41, 193, 205, 206

Kartenspielerweg 66, 118, 119, 127, 133, 139, 141, 142, 171, 174
Kessel 13, 105, 118, 129, 134, 143, 158, 161, 170, 173, 174, 177
Kiekeberg Woods 66, 67, 86, 87, 103, 105, 106, 113, 118, 129
Kleve (Cleve) vii, 8, 9, 10, 13, 14, 32, 37, 53, 54, 90, 95, 97, 118, 129, 131, 133, 147, 158, 179, 182, 186, 187, 190, 101, 102, 193, 197
Kranenberg 14, 59, 97, 103, 123, 158

Land Mattress rocket system 16, 17, 87, 178
Leigraaf Anti-tank ditch 32, 69, 71
Lindsay, Major 85, 88, 106, 108, 111, 112, 113, 115, 150, 151, 163, 166, 206
Logistics 17–19, 45, 103
Luftwaffe 5, 6, 37, 42, 55, 183

Maas, River 1, 3, 4, 7, 912, 14, 17, 22, 24, 27, 28, 29, 32, 36, 55, 66, 67, 77, 85, 95, 97, 104, 108, 115, 118, 129, 134, 138, 144, 191, 205
MARKET GARDEN, Operation 1, 2, 3, 20, 74, 206
Materborn Feature 8, 9, 14, 32, 55, 56, 97, 102, 129, 131, 181, 189, 193, 193, 194, 197, 198
Messerschmitt Me 262 6, 13, 187, 189
Montgomery, Field Marchal vii, 1, 2, 3, 4, 6, 10, 13, 15, 19, 23 24, 160
Mook 22, 105, 108, 112, 113, 118, 125, 136, 137

Niers, River 9, 13, 14, 32, 36, 105, 115, 118, 129, 134, 135, 136, 137, 138, 139, 143–4, 146, 147, 151–4, 161, 163 169, 170, 171, 172, 174, 175, 176, 182, 207

Nijmegen 2, 9, 13, 14, 19, 22, 29, 30, 36, 129, 189, 192
Nutterden 55, 56, 97

Pak 40 75mm Anti-tank gun 39, 63, 88
Panzerfaust 8, 30, 142, 151
Panzerjäger 39, 162
Panzershreck (Raketen panzerbuhse) 39–40
PEARL BLACK 8, 13, 14, 129
PEPPERPOT shoots 48, 52, 69, 173
Pyramid Feature 66, 86, 87, 115, 206

Recovery, armoured 91–2
Reichswald Plaug vii, 3, 4, 7–9, 13, 42, 56, 148
Rennie, General 15, 66, 67, 118, 134, 158, 199
Rhineland vii, viii, 3, 4, 5, 6,7, 10, 11, 14, 27, 30, 32, 33, 65, 95, 127, 129, 158, 170, 190, 191, 198, 205
Roer and dams 26, 28, 96, 127, 191
Road repair 22
Ross, Major General 61, 62, 131, 179, 200
Ruhr 1, 3, 23, 27, 29
Rundstedt, Field Marshal von 27, 29, 95, 191

Schlemm, General vii, 27, 24, 30, 32, 42, 53, 93, 95, 96, 129, 191, 193, 197, 206
Sherman Flail (CRAB) 16, 22, 56, 61, 62, 67, 69, 78, 80, 120, 199
Sherman Tank 56
Siegfried Line vii, 1, 14, 27, 31, 37, 54, 61, 97, 98, 100, 101, 126, 129, 138, 141, 143, 206
Simonds Lieutenant General viii, 10, 198
Simpson, General 3, 4, 26, 97
Stoppelburg feature 97, 99, 100, 101, 102, 131
Straube, General 27, 30, 31
Sturmgeschütz 120, 161–2, 193, 185
Sturmgewhr 44 38

Territorial Army 15, 22

Uedem 9, 35, 55, 198
ULTRA 130, 189
US Army:
   First US Army 6, 24, 96
   Nineth US Army 3, 4, 10, 32, 53, 96, 191

Venlo 3, 27, 29, 53, 191
VERITABLE, Operation 9–14
Weasel 22, 66, 90, 103

Notes 211